CONTENTS

HARRAP'S

a sound approach to
French
Grammar

by David Foster and Bernard Sweeney

To log onto the website please visit
www.satfg.harrap.co.uk and register using this code

CDF3-SEYU-YZQ2-HKG3

First published by Chambers Harrap Publishers Ltd 2007
7 Hopetoun Crescent
Edinburgh EH7 4AY

ISBN 978 0245 60787 5

Text Editors
Stuart Fortey
Kate Nicholson

Publishing Manager
Anna Stevenson

Prepress
Heather Macpherson
Becky Pickard

Voices
Pauline Gaberel
Georges Pilard

Designed and typeset by Chambers Harrap Publishers Ltd, Edinburgh
Printed and bound by Legoprint, Italy

INTRODUCTION

If you are an advanced student of French, either in the sixth form at school or studying for a degree at university, then *A Sound Approach to French Grammar* is aimed at you. In this book our aim is to improve your knowledge of French in a new and attractive way.

How?

First, through straightforward explanations of points our students tell us they have found difficult or for which they may need some revision. We will guide you through the technical terms associated with language learning, then we will offer numerous examples and allow you to listen to them as you read them. Repeating what you hear as you look at the text will help you to retain the information. Short exercises with answers, all of which you will be able to listen to, follow each section to reinforce your understanding.

Read and listen, repeat and finally test – this is our guiding principle.

Of course you will be able to use our book as a reference grammar which you can carry with you; indeed we have provided a complete index to help you find the point you need quickly. However, our aim has not been to cover every possible item of grammar but to enable you to demonstrate a firm grasp of the essential points in your written and spoken work.

We recognise that you wish to be as accurate as you can. It may help you to write down your answers to the exercises before seeing, listening to and repeating our suggested version.

The accompanying website contains all the text of the book as well as the recordings of every item of French; register your book at **www.satfg.harrap.co.uk** and enter the unique 16-digit registration code on page i to gain free access to the online version. Buttons on the pages will lead you through the book in any way you choose. You can read it page by page, use the indexes to find quickly the specific point you require or follow our 'trail'. This is our recommended path through the book and the online version, leading you painlessly from point to point. When you have completed the trail, you will have covered the essentials of French grammar.

The printed version of the text is followed by two indexes, one mainly English, one French. For the university student, using an index in French is to be encouraged. With this in mind, we have used both English and French grammatical terms throughout and therefore you may look up either **demonstrative adjective** or **adjectif démonstratif** and can be sure you will be guided to the correct section.

We hope that our approach meets your needs and wish you every success.

David Foster

Bernard Sweeney

ACKNOWLEDGEMENTS

We should like to acknowledge the help and encouragement of Naaman Kessous of Lancaster University who generously agreed to read and comment upon portions of the text.

Our thanks are also due to Jean-François Stienne, formerly of St Bede's College, Manchester, who undertook to read the whole book and offered numerous valuable suggestions.

TRAIL STARTS
HERE → 1

We'll start with the verb, the one and only element that can be found in **any** sentence.

TECHNICAL TERMS

Verb – a word which describes an action or a state: *We **live** here, we **are** happy, we often **sleep** in class, you **have stolen**, he **had left**, she **will speak**, they **would listen**, I **coughed**.*

Tense – the time when the action occurs, will occur or occurred. It may interest you to note that the word for **time** in French (**le temps**) also means **tense**.

Subject – the person(s) or thing(s) performing the action of the verb: ***We** live here. **The dog** is sad. **Money** cannot buy happiness.*

Infinitive – the part of the verb you will find in dictionaries and vocabularies and which means **to ... (do)**: **chanter** *to sing*, **finir** *to finish*, **vendre** *to sell*. A verb like **chanter**, whose infinitive ends in **-er**, will often be referred to as **an -er verb** as it follows a pattern common to many verbs.

Clause – a part of a sentence containing a verb and its subject. In the sentence *She buys clothes when she goes into town* there are two clauses: the **main** clause (*she buys clothes*) and a **subordinate** or **dependent** clause (*when she goes into town*) which cannot stand on its own. All sentences contain at least one main clause.

There are ten **tenses** of verbs in French, five one-word tenses (**temps simples**) and five **compound** or two-word tenses (**temps composés**). There are links between these which help both to explain them and to make learning them easier, and we'll be pointing these out as we go.

TEMPS SIMPLES	TEMPS COMPOSÉS
present **Le présent**	perfect **Le passé composé**
imperfect **L'imparfait**	pluperfect **Le plus-que-parfait**
future **Le futur**	future perfect **Le futur antérieur**
conditional **Le conditionnel**	conditional perfect **Le conditionnel passé**
past historic **Le passé simple**	past anterior **Le passé antérieur**

French, like its precursor Latin, is an **inflected** language. This means that its verbs are made up of two parts, a **stem** and an **ending**. We will use colour to pick out the endings and any irregularities and we strongly advise you to listen to the recordings of the verbs as you study them. Very often, the sound of the words will be especially helpful in remembering their spelling.

There are many reference books which offer complete verb lists and we are not attempting to compete with these. However we will give examples of the **regular** verbs and list their variants (those with a small change to the stem) together with some of the most common **irregular** verbs and those we know cause difficulties.

There are three major groups of **regular** verbs; three other, smaller sets which we can best treat as **regular**; and many **irregular** verbs, among which – unfortunately for the learner – are some of the most commonly used.

The first group of regular verbs, the **-er** verbs, is by far the most common and is sometimes referred to as the first **conjugation**. Two smaller groups form the second and third conjugations, those **-ir** verbs formed like **finir** and the **-re** verbs such as **vendre**. The three other sets which we will treat as regular (ie following a pattern) are those like **venir**, **sortir** and **prendre**.

PRESENT TENSE – LE PRÉSENT

English has two forms of present tense, one simple, one compound – *he **goes**, he is going*; *we **sleep**, we are **sleeping***; *they **read**, they are **reading***. The second of these is commonly referred to as the **continuous present**. French uses **one simple present tense** to translate both of these while, as we will see later, there is a way of stressing the continuous present tense if this is required.

REGULAR VERBS

Group I: -er verbs

EXAMPLE: **donner** – to give

je donne	*I give / am giving*
tu donnes	*you give / are giving*
il / elle / on donne	*he / she / one gives / is giving*
nous donnons	*we give / are giving*
vous donnez	*you give / are giving*
ils / elles donnent	*they give / are giving*

[For convenience, we have translated **on donne** here as *one gives*. In English, this use of the pronoun *one* is rare these days, whereas in French **on** is commonplace. See our section on the passive.]

You will have noticed from the recording that the spoken language has fewer distinct endings than the written language. All the singular endings, **-e** and **-es**, together with the third person plural, **-ent**, are silent (or **mute**). Try listening again.

[For ease of reference, **je, tu, il / elle** are known as the **first, second** and **third persons singular** while **nous, vous, ils / elles** are the **first, second** and **third persons plural**.]

All **-er** verbs have these endings (we will treat **aller** as an almost total exception). However, there are a considerable number of verbs in the group which, purely because of the way they have to be pronounced, make changes to the spelling of the stem thus **altering the vowel sound** which precedes the ending.

1. Verbs ending in -cer

[Pronunciation note: In English, a letter **c** followed by an **a**, an **o** or a **u** is pronounced **hard** as a **k** (**c**at, **c**ot, **c**ut) while a **c** followed by an **e** or an **i** is pronounced **soft** as an **s** (**ce**ase, **ci**nder). The same applies in French.]

In these verbs, the **c** must be pronounced as an **s** throughout, so we find **ç** (c cedilla) before **-ons**.

EXAMPLE: **lancer** – *to throw, to launch*

je lance	*I throw / am throwing*
tu lances	
il lance	
nous lançons	
vous lancez	
ils lancent	

As a simple rule of thumb, we never put a **ç** before an **e** or an **i**, but always before any other vowel where the **c** is pronounced **s**.

2. Verbs ending in -ger

[Pronunciation note: In English, a letter **g** followed by an **a**, an **o** or a **u** is pronounced **hard** as the **g** in **ga**te, **go**t or **gu**t, while a **g** followed by an **e** or an **i** is usually pronounced **soft** as in the words **ge**sture and **gi**nger. Again, the same applies in French, the soft **g** being pronounced like the **j** in the word **je**.]

In these verbs, the **g** must be pronounced like **j** in **je** throughout, so we find an extra **e** before **-ons**.

EXAMPLE: **manger** – *to eat*

je mange	*I eat / am eating*
tu manges	
il mange	
nous mangeons	
vous mangez	
ils mangent	

3. Verbs ending in -e (or -é) + consonant + er

[Pronunciation note: The problems which students find with these verbs are in our experience best solved by **listening to their sound while studying the spelling**. You will notice that, where the ending is **mute**, care must be taken with the written forms which involves adding (or changing) an accent or doubling a consonant.]

a. Verbs ending in -eler and -eter

Most, but unfortunately not all, such verbs **double** the **l** or the **t**, thus altering the sound of the preceding **e**.

EXAMPLE: **appeler** – *to call*

j'appelle	*I call / am calling*
tu appelles	
il appelle	
nous appelons	
vous appelez	
ils appellent	

EXAMPLE: **jeter** – *to throw*

je jette	*I throw / am throwing*
tu jettes	
il jette	
nous jetons	
vous jetez	
ils jettent	

b. Other verbs ending in -e + consonant + -er and verbs ending -é + consonant + -er alter the final -e (or -é) of the stem by changing it where necessary to è.

EXAMPLE: **mener** – *to lead*

je mène	*I lead / am leading*
tu mènes	
il mène	
nous menons	
vous menez	
ils mènent	

Like **mener**, and therefore **not** like **appeler** or **jeter**, we have **acheter** *to buy* (**il achète**), **lever** *to lift* (**il lève**), **geler** *to freeze* (**il gèle**), **modeler** *to model* (**il modèle**), **peler** *to peel* (**il pèle**).

EXAMPLE: **répéter** – *to repeat*

je répète	*I repeat / am repeating*
tu répètes	
il répète	
nous répétons	
vous répétez	
ils répètent	

4. Verbs ending in -oyer and -uyer

These verbs retain the **y** only in the **nous** and **vous** forms – the first and second persons plural. All other persons have an **i**:

EXAMPLE: **employer** – *to use*

j'emploie	*I use / am using*
tu emploies	
il emploie	
nous employons	
vous employez	
ils emploient	

EXAMPLE: **ennuyer** – *to annoy*

j'ennuie	*I annoy / am annoying*
tu ennuies	
il ennuie	
nous ennuyons	
vous ennuyez	
ils ennuient	

5. Verbs ending in -ayer

With these verbs the change from **y** to **i** is optional.

EXAMPLE: **payer** – *to pay*

je paie (je paye)	*I pay / am paying*
tu paies (tu payes)	
il paie (il paye)	
nous payons	
vous payez	
ils paient (ils payent)	

Group II: -ir verbs

EXAMPLE: **finir** – *to finish*

je finis	*I finish / am finishing*
tu finis	*you finish / are finishing*
il finit	*he finishes / is finishing*
nous finissons	*we finish / are finishing*
vous finissez	*you finish / are finishing*
ils finissent	*they finish / are finishing*

Once again it is useful to note that the three singular forms are identically pronounced. The **-iss-** addition will be found again in the imperfect tense and in the present subjunctive.

Not all verbs whose infinitives end in **-ir** follow this pattern; however some which do are: **punir** *to punish*, **démolir** *to demolish*, **abolir** *to abolish*, **chérir** *to cherish*, **établir** *to establish*, **fournir** *to provide* (*furnish*), **polir** *to polish* (note the **-ish** ending which will indicate that the verb is of this type) and **choisir** *to choose*, **grandir** *to grow up*, **bâtir** *to build*.

Group III: -re verbs

EXAMPLE: **attendre** – *to wait*

j'attends	*I wait / am waiting*
tu attends	*you wait / are waiting*
il attend	*he waits / is waiting*
nous attendons	*we wait / are waiting*
vous attendez	*you wait / are waiting*
ils attendent	*they wait / are waiting*

Listen once again to this verb and note how the three singular persons are identically pronounced. The **-ent** ending causes the final consonant of the stem to be heard – the **d** in the case of attendre.

Two verbs which follow this pattern in almost every part are **battre** *to beat, to shuffle* (*cards*), *to break* (*a record*), which has **je bats, tu bats, il bat, nous battons, vous battez, ils battent** and **rompre** (*to break*) which has **je romps, tu romps, il rompt, nous rompons, vous rompez, ils rompent**. Like **rompre** is **interrompre** *to interrupt*.

By no means all verbs whose infinitives end in **-re** follow this pattern, as we will see from examples in the tables of irregular verbs which follow. However, a significant number are of this type and others bear close similarities to this pattern. When we come to list them we will show when they follow the rule and when they don't.

Group IV: Venir, tenir and their compounds (verbs ending in -venir and -tenir)

EXAMPLE: **venir** – *to come*

je viens	*I come / am coming*
tu viens	
il vient	
nous venons	
vous venez	
ils viennent	

Once again careful attention should be paid to the pronunciation of this verb.

Compounds of **venir** include **revenir** *to come back* (*to return*), **se souvenir de** *to remember*, **parvenir** *to reach*, **devenir** *to become*. Compounds of **tenir** *to hold*, include **retenir** *to hold back* (*to retain*), **contenir** *to contain*, **maintenir** *to maintain*, **soutenir** *to uphold* (*to sustain*).

Group V: Sortir, partir, dormir, servir, mentir, sentir

These verbs are identically formed. However, they are all in very common use and we feel it is sensible to set each of them out individually. Note how the last letter of the stem in the infinitive shows itself once again in the plural.

- **sortir**
  je sors   *I go out / am going out / I come out / am coming out*
  tu sors
  il sort
  nous sortons
  vous sortez
  ils sortent

- **partir**
  je pars   *I set out / am setting out / I leave / am leaving*
  tu pars
  il part
  nous partons
  vous partez
  ils partent

- **dormir**
  je dors   *I sleep / am sleeping*
  tu dors
  il dort
  nous dormons
  vous dormez
  ils dorment

  Also: **s'endormir** *to fall asleep / go to sleep*

- **servir**
  je sers   *I serve / am serving*
  tu sers
  il sert
  nous servons
  vous servez
  ils servent

  Also: **se servir de** *to use*

- **mentir**
  je mens   *I tell lies / am lying*
  tu mens
  il ment
  nous mentons
  vous mentez
  ils mentent

  Also: **se repentir** *to repent*

- **sentir**

je sens	*I feel / am feeling*
tu sens	
il sent	
nous sentons	
vous sentez	
ils sentent	

Group VI: Prendre and its compounds

EXAMPLE: **prendre** – *to take*

je prends	*I take / am taking*
tu prends	
il prend	
nous prenons	
vous prenez	
ils prennent	

Once again, listening to the sound of the words should help you with the spelling, especially of the plural forms (without the **d**) and of the **nn** in the third person (remember **ils jettent, ils appellent, ils viennent**).

Some compounds are: **apprendre** *to learn / to teach*, **comprendre** *to understand*, **surprendre** *to surprise*, **reprendre** *to take (up) again*.

IRREGULAR VERBS

Now for the irregular verbs. You will remember that we said that ours is not a comprehensive list, but a selection of the most commonly used verbs which we know cause problems. We said that even here some of their parts follow the above rules. Where they vary, we will point this out by the use of colour. Using the recordings as you study them will help.

We will begin with the two most important verbs, **être** and **avoir**, and put the remaining ones in alphabetical order.

- **être** – *to be*

je suis	*I am*
tu es	*you are*
il est	*he is*
nous sommes	*we are*
vous êtes	*you are*
ils sont	*they are*

- **avoir** – *to have*

  j'ai   *I have*

  tu as

  il a

  nous avons

  vous avez

  ils ont

  Also: **il y a** *there is / are*

We would advise you to listen most carefully to the difference in sound between **ils sont** and **ils ont**. This is a distinction it is most important both to detect and to make in your own speech.

- **aller** – *to go*

  je vais   *I go / am going*

  tu vas

  il va

  nous allons

  vous allez

  ils vont

  Note: **il va y avoir** *there is / are going to be*

- **boire** – *to drink*

  je bois   *I drink / am drinking*

  tu bois

  il boit

  nous buvons

  vous buvez

  ils boivent

- **connaître** – *to know (people and places)*

  je connais   *I know*

  tu connais

  il conn<u>aî</u>t

  nous connaissons

  vous connaissez

  ils connaissent

  Like **connaître** are: **paraître** *to seem, to appear;* **apparaître** *to appear, to come into view.*

- **craindre** – *to fear*
  je crains   *I fear / am afraid (of)*
  tu crains
  il craint
  nous craignons
  vous craignez
  ils craignent

We are including **craindre** because it will serve as an example of verbs ending in **vowel + indre**, such as **plaindre** *to pity* (**se plaindre** *to complain*), **éteindre** *to extinguish*, **joindre** *to join*.

- **devoir** – *to have to (must)*
  je dois   *I have to / I must*
  tu dois
  il doit
  nous devons
  vous devez
  ils doivent
  Note: **il doit y avoir** *there must be*

- **dire** – *to say / to tell*
  je dis   *I say / am telling*
  tu dis
  il dit
  nous disons
  vous dites
  ils disent

- **écrire** – *to write*
  j'écris   *I write / am writing*
  tu écris
  il écrit
  nous écrivons
  vous écrivez
  ils écrivent

- **faire** – *to do / to make*
  je fais   *I do / am doing / I make / am making*
  tu fais
  il fait
  nous faisons
  vous faites – often misspelt
  ils font

- **mettre** – *to put / to place*
  je mets   *I put / am putting*
  tu mets
  il met
  nous mettons
  vous mettez
  ils mettent

- **ouvrir** – *to open*
  j'ouvre   *I open / am opening*
  tu ouvres
  il ouvre
  nous ouvrons
  vous ouvrez
  ils ouvrent

You will find these endings familiar. Although the infinitive ends in **-ir**, it takes the same endings as **-er** verbs in the present tense. Other verbs which follow this pattern are **couvrir** *to cover*; **offrir** *to offer, to give as a present*; **souffrir** *to suffer*.

- **pouvoir** – *to be able to (can)*
  je peux / je puis   *I am able to / I can*
  tu peux
  il peut
  nous pouvons
  vous pouvez
  ils peuvent

Je puis is very formal, whereas its question form, **puis-je**, is in common use. The sound of **ils peuvent** will remind you of its written form.

Note: **il peut y avoir** *there may be*

- **recevoir** – *to receive*
  je reçois   *I receive / am receiving*
  tu reçois
  il reçoit
  nous recevons
  vous recevez
  ils reçoivent

You will remember our note regarding the use of **ç**!

- **savoir** – *to know (how to)*

  je sais   *I know (how to)*

  tu sais

  il sait

  nous savons

  vous savez

  ils savent

Note: **savoir** means *to know* (*facts*). For *to know / to be acquainted with* (*people and places*), **connaître** is used.

- **suivre** – *to follow*

  je suis   *I follow / am following*

  tu suis

  il suit

  nous suivons

  vous suivez

  ils suivent

Note the **je** form. **Je suis le chien** almost certainly will not mean what at first sight you might think!

- **voir** – *to see*

  je vois   *I see / am seeing*

  tu vois

  il voit

  nous voyons

  vous voyez

  ils voient

- **vouloir** *to wish / to want*

  je veux   *I wish / want*

  tu veux

  il veut

  nous voulons

  vous voulez

  ils veulent

IMPERSONAL VERBS

Certain verbs, as is obvious from their meaning, only exist in the third person singular (**it**):

falloir	*to be necessary*	**il faut**
neiger	*to snow*	**il neige**
pleuvoir	*to rain*	**il pleut**

It is also worth noting that the verb **rester** (*to stay / to remain*) may be used impersonally:

Il reste dix euros.
There are ten euros left. (Literally: *There remain ten euros.*)

Il me reste dix euros.
I have ten euros left.

We said earlier that, although French does not have an equivalent for the English **continuous present** (eg *she is working*), it is possible where necessary to emphasise the continuous nature of an action. To do this we use **être en train de + infinitive** (*to be in the process of doing, to be busy doing*):

Elle est en train de lire le journal.
She is (busy) reading the newspaper.

Il est en train d'écrire sa lettre.
He is (busy) writing his letter.

Nous sommes en train de faire le ménage.
We are (busy) doing the housework.

TRAIL → 2
page 195

→ TRAIL 5

ASKING QUESTIONS

In French, there are four ways to ask a question:

a. By the **sound of the voice (intonation)**:

Tu as assez d'argent ?
Do you have (Have you) enough money?

Nous allons au cinéma ?
Are we going to the cinema?

Ils sont prêts à partir ?
Are they ready to leave?

[Intonation can also be used in English – *They are ready to leave?*]

b. By placing **est-ce que (qu')** before the statement:

Est-ce que tu as assez d'argent ?

Est-ce que nous allons au cinéma ?

Est-ce qu'ils sont prêts à partir ?

c. While the above are by far the forms most used in conversation, there is a third, more formal, method known as **inversion**, which involves turning round the verb and its subject:

As-tu assez d'argent ? (NB the hyphen)

Allons-nous au cinéma ?

Sont-ils prêts à partir ?

When forming a question using inversion, you will need to separate two vowels by inserting a **-t-**. This happens only in the **third person singular** of **avoir** and the **-er verbs** together with the very rare forms **vainc-t-il/elle ?** and **convainc-t-il/elle ?** from **vaincre** (*to conquer*) and **convaincre** (*to convince*) where the final **-c** is not pronounced:

A-t-elle de l'argent ? (NB the hyphens)
Does she have (Has she) any money?

Y a-t-il de l'eau dans le puits ?
Is there (any) water in the well?

Habite-t-il ici ?
Does he live here?

Ouvre-t-elle toutes les fenêtres à minuit ?
Does she open all the windows at midnight?

Travaille-t-on tous les samedis ?
Do they (we / you) work every Saturday?

Now let us consider this question:

Is the dog in the garden?

We can say in French:

i. Le chien est dans le jardin ?

ii. Est-ce que le chien est dans le jardin ?

iii. Le chien est-il dans le jardin ?

In this last example we are asking a question in inverted form about a **noun**, and here we cannot translate word for word the English question form *Is the dog in the garden?* Rather, we must begin by highlighting the **noun**, followed by an **inversion**. The following examples illustrate the same point:

Votre mère travaille-t-elle chez Renault ?
Does your mother work for Renault?

Le maire et sa femme dînent-ils au restaurant tous les soirs ?
Do the mayor and his wife dine out every night?

[Notice that in English questions we often use the words **do** or **does**. Don't be tempted to translate this word for word, as this would simply not be French. *Is he eating?* is the question form of *he is eating; does he eat?* is the question form of *he eats.*

Il mange chez son ami.
He eats at his friend's (house).

Mange-t-il chez son ami ?
Does he eat at his friend's?

Il mange chez son ami ce soir.
He is eating at his friend's this evening.

Mange-t-il chez son ami ce soir ?
Is he eating at his friend's this evening?

The French **mange-t-il** is the only possible inverted form.]

You will, however, find inversion with a noun in French when there is a question word or words at the head of the sentence:

Comment va ton père **?**
How is your father? (Of course we could say: **Ton père, comment va-t-il ?**)

À quelle heure commence le film **?**
What time does the film start?

Combien de temps dure cette symphonie **?**
How long does this symphony last?

However this does not apply when the question word is **pourquoi**:

Pourquoi le chien aboie-t-il **?**
Why is the dog barking?

When the question has **je** as the subject, except in a few instances which we give below, the inverted form of the question is no longer used (it would in any case not sound very pleasant), the question being formed with the use of **est-ce que**: **Est-ce que je vais rester à la maison ?** *Am I going to (Will I) stay at home?*

Exceptions to this are:

avoir: **ai-je ?**

être: **suis-je ?**

pouvoir: **puis-je ?**

savoir: **sais-je ?**

dire: **dis-je ?**

devoir: **dois-je ?**

This need not be a problem as you can always use **est-ce que** to form the question.

[With **pouvoir**, inversion is not possible with **je peux** – **Est-ce que je peux avoir l'addition, s'il vous plaît ?** *May I have the bill, please?*]

d. By adding **n'est-ce pas** to a statement to seek confirmation. **N'est-ce pas** will be translated in many different ways, depending on the context:

Elle va bien, n'est-ce pas ?
*She is well, **isn't she**?*

Vous êtes prêt, n'est-ce pas ?
*You are ready, **aren't you**?*

Il n'est pas content, n'est-ce pas ?
*He isn't happy, **is he**?*

N'est-ce pas is thus the **only French equivalent** of a whole variety of English expressions – *shall we?, shouldn't they?, couldn't you?, had I?, didn't she?, wouldn't he?* etc.

USING NEGATIVES

In this section, we deal only with **ne … pas**. Other negatives can be found in section B.

Let us take a look at some examples:

Elle ne va pas à la piscine.
She isn't going (doesn't go) to the swimming pool.

Ne va-t-elle pas à l'église ?
Isn't she going (Doesn't she go) to church?

You will see that the negative **surrounds the verb**. Notice that in the second example, the word **pas** is placed as soon as possible after the verb, but **cannot separate words linked by hyphens**.

Here are some further examples:

Ne viennent-elles pas ce soir ?
Aren't they coming this evening?

Le docteur ne travaille-t-il pas aujourd'hui ?
Isn't the doctor working today?

Jean et Marie ne sont-ils pas d'accord ?
Don't Jean and Marie agree?

N'y a-t-il pas de vin ?
Isn't there any wine?

GIVING COMMANDS (IMPERATIVES)

There is a **tu** form of the command, giving an order to **one** friend, **one** relative, **one** child or **one** animal. Note the emphasis on the singular – one. Simply use the **tu** form of the verb without the **tu**:

Finis tes devoirs !
Finish your homework!

Dis la vérité !
Tell the truth!

Bois beaucoup d'eau !
Drink lots of water!

However the final **-s** in **all -er verbs** (including the verb **aller**) is dropped in commands:

Donne les bonbons à ta sœur !
Give the sweets to your sister!

Va chercher du pain !
Go and fetch some bread! (NB no *and* in French.)

[The **-s** is retained **only** when the command is immediately followed by **-y** or **-en**. For example, **Vas-y** ! *Go there! / Get stuck in! / Go on! / Get on with it!* etc, **manges-en** ! *eat some!* In this way the pronunciation is made easier.]

Similarly, to give a command to **more than one person or animal** or to **one person** we address as **vous** rather than **tu**, we use the **vous** form of the verb without the **vous**:

Allez au marché !
Go to the market!

Revenez aussitôt que possible !
Come back as soon as possible!

Faites vos devoirs !
Do your homework!

Dites la vérité !
Tell the truth!

Venez voir !
Come and see! (NB no *and* in French.)

There is a third form, usually included with commands. This uses the **nous** form of the verb without the **nous** and translates into English as *let's (go)* or *let us (go)*:

Allons au cinéma !
Let's go to the cinema!

Chantons ensemble !
Let's sing together!

Faisons de notre mieux !
Let's do our best!

The command forms of **être**, **avoir**, **savoir** and **vouloir** are the only ones not to follow this pattern.

• **être**

Sois sage, mon fils !
Be good (Behave yourself), son!

Soyez prudents, messieurs !
Be careful, gentlemen!

Soyons prêts à partir à neuf heures !
Let's be ready to leave at nine!

• **avoir**

Aie confiance en cet homme-là !
Put your trust in that man!

Ayez pitié de moi !
Have pity on me!

Ayons soin d'arriver à l'heure !
Let's be careful to arrive on time! (Let's make sure we arrive on time!)

• **savoir**

Sache bien que je ne suis pas content !
Be quite clear that I'm not happy!

Sachez que mon père ne le fera pas !
Be aware that my father will not do it!

Sachons la vérité !
Let's know the truth!

- **vouloir**

  Veuillez vous asseoir, madame !
  Please take a seat, madam!

[This is a very polite request. You would be unlikely to meet any other command form of this verb and you would be more likely to hear: **Voulez-vous vous asseoir, madame ?**]

Forming **negative commands** is easy:

Ne dis pas la vérité !
Don't tell the truth!

Ne bois pas trop d'eau !
Don't drink too much water!

Ne donne pas les bonbons à ta sœur !
Don't give the sweets to your sister!

N'aie pas peur !
Don't be afraid!

N'allez pas au marché !
Don't go to the market!

Ne soyons pas méchants !
Let's not be nasty (naughty)!

Ne faites pas de bêtises !
Don't do anything silly!

TRAIL → 6
page 196

◆ ◆ ◆

→ TRAIL 7

PRONOMINAL VERBS

We have now covered the various aspects of the present tense which we have found to cause difficulties. To complete this section, we will look at the **pronominal verb**, often referred to as the **reflexive verb**.

These are verbs you will find in dictionaries introduced by the word **se – se cacher, se lever, se laver, s'arrêter** etc.

Such verbs contain a **noun** and a **pronoun** or two **pronouns** which refer to the same person or persons:

Ma copine se promène dans le jardin.
My friend is walking in the garden.

Ses amis se battent tout le temps.
His/Her friends are always fighting.

Le bus ne s'arrête pas ici.
The bus doesn't stop here.

Je me lave.
I wash / am washing (myself). (I'm having a wash.)

Both **je** and **me** clearly refer to the same person.

Tu te caches derrière l'arbre.
You are hiding behind the tree.

Nous nous levons de bonne heure.
We get up early.

[Without wishing to be too technical, we must here define the word **pronoun**. Pronouns are simply words which stand in place of nouns – **je**, **tu**, **il**, **elle**, **on**, **nous**, **vous**, **ils**, **elles** we have already used. In English, other pronouns include *me*, *him*, *her*, *it*, *us*, *them*, *myself*, *yourself* etc.]

The verb **se laver** means *to wash (oneself)*. Here we give its present tense in full:

je me lave	*I wash / am washing (myself)*
tu te laves	
il se lave	
elle se lave	
on se lave	
nous nous lavons	
vous vous lavez	
ils se lavent	
elles se lavent	

The words in coloured type above are referred to as the **reflexive pronouns**.

Naturally, if the action of washing is not being applied to myself, yourself etc, **laver** alone is used:

Il lave l'auto le dimanche.
He washes the car on Sundays.

As you can see, there is nothing unusual about the forms of the verb. You will, though, need to learn the verb **s'asseoir** *to sit (oneself) (down)*:

je m'assieds

tu t'assieds

il s'assied

nous nous asseyons

vous vous asseyez

ils s'asseyent

[There is another form of this verb which is sometimes used in conversation: **je m'assois**, **tu t'assois**, **il s'assoit**, **nous nous assoyons**, **vous vous assoyez**, **ils s'assoient**.]

The reflexive pronoun is also used where the English has **each other**, **one another**.

*They know **one another**.*
Ils se connaissent.

*The girls speak **to each other** every day.*
Les jeunes filles se parlent tous les jours.

When you use the continuous present, with **être en train de + infinitive**, remember to change the reflexive pronoun:

Je suis en train de m'habiller.
I am getting dressed.

Tu es en train de te laver.
You are having a wash.

Elle est en train de se maquiller.
She's (busy) putting on her make-up.

Nous sommes en train de nous déshabiller.
We're getting undressed.

Vous êtes en train de vous peigner les cheveux.
You're combing your hair.

Ils sont en train de se battre.
They're fighting.

Asking questions

We can, of course, use **tone of voice** or **est-ce que ...** or add **n'est-ce pas** to ask questions with pronominal verbs as with any others. Here we set out examples of their inverted forms. You will notice that the reflexive pronoun still stands **before the verb**:

Te lèves-tu tous les jours à midi ?
Do you get up every day at twelve?

Se promènent-elles dans le parc le week-end ?
Do they walk in the park at weekends?

Se lave-t-elle les cheveux ?
Is she washing her hair?

Nous levons-nous de bonne heure demain matin ?
Are we getting up early tomorrow morning?

Vos parents s'arrêtent-ils de fumer ?
Are your parents stopping smoking?

Vous ennuyez-vous au bureau ?
Do you get bored at the office?

Using negatives

Ne and **pas** surround the pronominal verbs as they do all others. As always, the **reflexive pronoun** must stand **before the verb**:

Elle ne se lève pas avant onze heures.
She doesn't get up before eleven o'clock.

Nous ne nous promenons pas quand il pleut.
We don't go for a walk when it's raining.

Where a question is negative, this rule about the position of the reflexive pronoun still applies:

Ne te souviens-tu pas de cette soirée ?
Don't you remember that evening?

Ne se téléphonent-elles pas toutes les deux heures ?
Don't they ring each other (one another) every two hours?

Cet enfant-là ne se couche-t-il pas avant minuit ?
Doesn't that child go to bed before midnight?

Giving commands

Our best advice is that you learn the forms of the command for one pronominal verb. You can then apply this to all the others. We will use **se cacher** as our example:

Cache-toi !
Hide (yourself)!

Ne te cache pas !
Don't hide (yourself)!

Cachez-vous !
Hide (yourself / yourselves)!

Ne vous cachez pas !
Don't hide (yourself / yourselves)!

Cachons-nous !
Let's hide (ourselves)!

Ne nous cachons pas !
Let's not hide (ourselves)!

Applying this to other verbs we can say:

Assieds-toi !
Sit down!

Ne t'assieds pas !

Lève-toi !
Stand (Get) up!

Ne te lève pas !

Asseyez-vous !
Sit down!

Ne vous asseyez pas !

Levez-vous !
Stand (Get) up!

Ne vous levez pas !

Asseyons-nous !
Let's sit down!

Ne nous asseyons pas !

Levons-nous !
Let's stand (get) up!

Ne nous levons pas !

When the reflexive pronoun follows the verb, it must be **linked to it by a hyphen**.

You will remember that the **tu** form command of an **-er** verb drops the **-s**.

TRAIL → 8
page 197

→ TRAIL 9

DEPUIS, VENIR DE ...

We will conclude our section on the present tense with a mention of two cases where the French **present** is used to translate the English **perfect** tense. In both cases, this is because in the two languages events are seen **from a different perspective**.

Depuis

Consider the sentence: *He has been a gardener for two years.* In English we consider his activity as a gardener from **the time when he started working** (in the past) and so use a verb in the **perfect** tense. The French, from the point of view that **he is still working**, use the **present** tense and the word **depuis** (which means *since*):

Il est jardinier depuis deux ans.

Here are some further examples:

Nous parlons français depuis sept ans.
We've been speaking French for seven years.

Mon père travaille chez Citroën depuis vingt ans.
My father has been working for Citroën for twenty years.

To ask a question, we follow the same rule:

Depuis quand sont-ils en Espagne ?
How long have they been in Spain? (since when ...)

Depuis combien de temps boivent-elles du vin ?
How long have they been drinking wine? (since how long ...)

There are other ways of expressing the same idea. Thus the following four sentences are identical in meaning:

a) **Il neige depuis deux jours.**
   It's been snowing for two days.

b) **Ça fait deux jours qu'il neige.**

c) **Voilà deux jours qu'il neige.**

d) **Il y a deux jours qu'il neige.**

The use of **depuis** may be regarded as formal while example **b)** is frequently used in conversation.

Here are some further examples:

a) Elle étudie le français depuis sept ans.
She's been studying French for seven years.

b) Ça fait sept ans qu'elle étudie le français.

c) Voilà sept ans qu'elle étudie le français.

d) Il y a sept ans qu'elle étudie le français.

Venir de ...

In the sentence *They have **just arrived** in London*, the **perfect** tense is used in English as the action has clearly happened in the past. The French emphasise the **immediate** past time of the action by employing a construction using the **present** tense of the verb **venir**, followed by **de** and an **infinitive**: **Ils viennent d'arriver à Londres**. [It is worth pointing out here that when **any verb** follows **de** it will be in the **infinitive**.]

Below are some further examples:

Henry vient de marquer un but.
Henry has just scored a goal.

Le petit Jacques vient de dire son premier mot.
Little Jacques has just said his first word.

Elles viennent de manger.
They've just eaten.

We will revisit **depuis** and **venir de** ... as part of our section on the **imperfect** tense.

TRAIL → 10
page 198

◆ ◆ ◆

→ TRAIL 11

PERFECT TENSE – LE PASSÉ COMPOSÉ

TEMPS SIMPLES	TEMPS COMPOSÉS
present **Le temps présent**	perfect **Le passé composé**

This is the first of our **compound** tenses and is used to express **single** or **completed** actions in the **past**. In fact its English name 'perfect' comes from the Latin *perficio* – I finish or I make completely – and has nothing to do with our normal interpretation of the word as representing perfection or an ideal.

▶ TECHNICAL TERMS

Past participle – the form of a verb that follows *has, have, had, will have, would have* to form compound tenses – such as *broken, forgotten* or *brought*. It may also be used as an adjective – the *broken* vase, a *forgotten* promise.

Auxiliary verb – in English, this is a part of the verb *to have – has, have, had, will have, would have* – while in French it will be a part of **avoir** or **être**. English also uses the word *did*, especially in questions and negatives, to form a past tense with the infinitive as in **Did** *they speak? – He* **did** *(speak) but she* **didn't** *(speak)*. In the perfect tense in French, this can *only* be rendered by using **avoir** or **être** with the **past participle**.

Direct object – the person or thing which directly receives the action of a verb – *I see* **you**, *he hits* **the ball**, *they heard* **the applause**.

Indirect object – the person or thing normally linked to the verb by the word *to* – *he spoke* **to you**, *they gave the presents* **to us**, *they returned the goods* **to the shopkeeper**. Often in English, the word *to* is left out – *he showed* **her** *the letter, I gave* **the children** *the cake, they sent* **my parents** *the bill*. In French, we have to say the equivalent of *to* **her**, *to* **the children**, *to* **my parents**. In the above examples, *the presents, the goods, the letter, the cake* and *the bill* are **direct** objects.

The English **perfect** tense is made up of the **present** tense of the verb *to have* and the **past participle** – *I have been, she has written, they have drunk*.

For the most part, the French **passé composé** is similarly formed, using the **present** tense of **avoir** and the **past participle (participe passé)** – **j'ai été, elle a écrit, ils ont bu**.

We must also point out that this tense is much more often used in French than in English as it **also translates the English simple past tense** – *I was, she wrote, they drank* – **always** in speech and nowadays (with the exception of novels set in the past) most commonly in writing.

So, all we need to know for the moment is the present tense of **avoir** and **how to form the past participle**. The first of these we'll take as read, the second is as follows:

All **-er** verbs: remove **-er** from the infinitive and add **-é** – **donné, lancé, mangé, appelé, jeté, mené, répété, employé, ennuyé, payé, allé ***.

Regular **-ir** verbs like **finir** and those like **sortir**: remove **-ir** from the infinitive and add **-i** – **fini, sorti *, parti *, dormi, servi, menti, senti**.

Regular **-re** verbs like **attendre**: remove **-re** from the infinitive and add **-u** – **attendu**.

Venir, **tenir** and their compounds: remove **-ir** from the infinitive and add **-u** – **venu** *, **tenu**.

* **être** verbs, see below

The past participle of **prendre** is **pris**, so that of **apprendre** is **appris** and the other compounds of **prendre** follow the same pattern.

There are, of course, a good number of **irregular** past participles (as indeed there are in English) and all students of French simply have to learn them. The first list below includes only the remaining verbs from the ones we detailed under the present tense:

être		**j'ai** été
		I have been / was
avoir		**tu as** eu
		you (have) had
boire		**il a** bu
		he has drunk / drank
connaître		**elle a** connu
		she has known / knew
craindre		**on a** craint
		we (have) feared
devoir		**vous avez** dû
		you (have) had to / must have
dire		**nous avons** dit
		we (have) said
écrire		**ils ont** écrit
		they have written / wrote
faire		**elles ont** fait
		they have done / did
mettre		**j'ai** mis
		I (have) put
ouvrir		**tu as** ouvert
		you (have) opened
		and also:
	couvrir	**il a** couvert
		he (has) covered
	offrir	**elle a** offert
		she (has) offered
		she has given / gave
	souffrir	**on a** souffert
		we (have) suffered
pouvoir		**nous avons** pu
		we have been able / were able / may have / could
recevoir		**vous avez** reçu
		you (have) received

savoir	**ils ont** su	
	they have known / knew	
suivre	**elles ont** suivi	
	they (have) followed	
voir	**j'ai** vu	
	I have seen / saw	
vouloir	**tu as** voulu	
	you (have) wanted	

Other verbs with irregular past participles include:

courir	*to run*	couru
lire	*to read*	lu
mourir *	*to die*	mort
naître *	*to be born*	né
rire	*to laugh*	ri
sourire	*to smile*	souri
vivre	*to live*	vécu
s'asseoir *	*to sit down*	assis

* être verbs, see below

Impersonal Verbs:

falloir	*to be necessary*	**il a** fallu
neiger	*to snow*	**il a** neigé
pleuvoir	*to rain*	**il a** plu

◆ ◆ ◆

THE PERFECT TENSE WITH ÊTRE

We feel that the rules regarding the agreement of the past participle are best approached through those verbs which require the auxiliary **être** to form their perfect tense. This is also the case for **all pronominal verbs**, but we will deal with these in a later section.

We give below the essential 16 verbs which are commonly known as **être** verbs. There are various ways of learning these, but one thing is certain – **knowing them is essential**. We can set most of these out in pairs of opposite meanings.

aller		*to go*
venir *		*to come*
	revenir	*to return (to come back)*
	devenir	*to become*
arriver		*to arrive*
partir		*to leave*

sortir	*to go out*	
entrer	*to enter*	
rentrer	*to return (to go / to come back)*	
monter	*to go (come) up*	
descendre	*to go (come) down*	
naître	*to be born*	
mourir	*to die*	
rester	*to stay*	
retourner	*to return (to go back)*	
tomber	*to fall*	

* Not all compounds of **venir** are **être** verbs. **Convenir** (to agree) and **prévenir** (to warn), for example, form their compound tenses with **avoir**.

One way of memorising them is to use a mnemonic such as 'Mr (&) Mrs D Vandertrap' (you could usefully think up your own):

Monter

Revenir

Mourir

Rentrer

Sortir

Devenir

Venir

Aller

Naître

Descendre

Entrer

Rester

Tomber

Retourner

Arriver

Partir

Past participle agreement

Let us consider these sentences:

Il est <u>allé</u> au cinéma.
He went to the cinema.

Elle est <u>allée</u> à l'église.
She went to church.

Ils sont <u>allés</u> aux magasins.
They went to the shops.

Elles sont <u>allées</u> à la piscine.
They went to the swimming pool.

Vous êtes <u>allé</u> au marché.
You went to (the) market.

Vous êtes <u>allée</u> au café.
You went to the café.

Vous êtes <u>allés</u> en France.
You went to France.

Vous êtes <u>allées</u> à Paris.
You went to Paris.

Nous sommes <u>allés</u> au Portugal.
We went to Portugal.

Nous sommes <u>allées</u> en Irlande.
We went to Ireland.

As you can hear, the past participle is pronounced **in the same way** throughout despite the variety of spellings. This can be a major stumbling block to students of French when asked to show their knowledge of written forms.

The past participle in each case is **matched** to the subject of the verb. Where the subject is **feminine** we add an **-e**, where it is **plural** an **-s**. Thus **-es** is added when the subject is **feminine and plural**. This is called **agreement of the past participle**.

Looking at the four examples using **vous**, we are reminded in the spelling of the past participle that **vous** can be used to **one** person (of either sex) or to **more than one** person – the agreement depends on the person or people addressed.

Similarly, in the second example using **nous**, we can be **certain** that **all** the people concerned are female. The French language, it has to be admitted, is sexist and **Nous sommes allés au Portugal** could be referring to a group of 400 women accompanied by just one man. The **presence of a single male** is enough to dictate a masculine plural agreement!

[We ought here to give a special note about the use of the subject pronoun **on** and the agreement of past participles of **être** verbs.

On est allé(e)s au café.
We / You / They went to the café.

You will notice that **on**, while it always has a singular auxiliary verb, will nevertheless show plural past participle agreement as the subject of an **être** verb with the people to whom it refers.]

Of our 16 **être** verbs only the past participle of **mourir** changes its pronunciation when there is a feminine subject. Compare:

Il est mort. Elle est morte.
He / She has died.

Ils sont morts. Elles sont mortes.
They have died.

Remember: **the past participle of the 16 être verbs always agrees with the subject.**

[We must point out here that some **être** verbs, when they have a direct object, will form their perfect tense with **avoir**:

Elle a descendu la rue.
She went down the street.

Ils ont monté les bagages au premier étage.
They took the luggage up to the first floor.

Maman a sorti son mouchoir.
Mum took out her handkerchief.

You can see that here there is now no agreement of the past participle with the subject.]

THE PERFECT TENSE WITH AVOIR

The past participle of an **avoir** verb **never agrees with the subject**. Here are some examples:

Elle a mangé avant de partir.
She ate before leaving.

Nous avons acheté des journaux.
We bought (some) newspapers.

Ils ont envoyé une lettre.
They sent a letter.

However, past participles of **avoir** verbs are sometimes made to agree and we set out below the rule which governs this.

No doubt you will have heard this rule: **The past participle of avoir verbs agrees with a preceding direct object**. Your teachers will have spoken of this and may even have used the term **PDO**.

We'll begin with some examples. As you listen you will appreciate how often the agreement is **not sounded** – it **must** be there in the written form:

a. **Où sont les livres que j'ai achetés ?**
Where are the books (which / that) I bought?

b. **Quelles nouvelles avez-vous reçues ?**
What news did you receive?

c. **Vos amis ? Je les ai vus au cinéma hier soir.**
Your friends? I saw them at the cinema last night.

d. **Vos amies ? Je les ai vues au cinéma hier soir.**
Your friends? I saw them at the cinema last night.

e. **Tu as perdu ta montre ? Oui, je l'ai perdue à l'école.**
Have you lost your watch? Yes, I lost it at school.

Here are some further examples, but this time the agreement causes a change in pronunciation:

f. **Les fenêtres ? Je les ai ouvertes ce matin.**
The windows? I opened them this morning.

g. **Quelles mesures a-t-il prises ?**
What measures did he take?

h. **La lettre que tu as écrite est sur la table.**
The letter (which / that) you wrote is on the table.

i. **Je n'aime pas la jupe qu'il lui a offerte.**
I don't like the skirt (which / that) he gave her.

We have underlined in each case the word which triggers the agreement. You will note that it comes before (precedes) the past participle. Also in every sentence, it is the **direct object** of the verb.

L', where it means **la**, and **les** ALWAYS cause agreement of the past participle as they stand before (they precede) the auxiliary verb and when used in this way are always direct objects.

    a. What did I buy? – books (to which **que** refers)

    b. What did you receive? – news

    c. and d. Who did I see? – them (your friends – first males or a group containing at least one male, then all females)

    e. What did you lose? – it (your watch)

    f. What did I open? – them (the windows)

    g. What did he take? – measures

    h. What did you write? – the letter (to which **que** refers)

    i. What did he give to her? – the skirt (to which **qu'** refers)

By asking questions like these we will always be able to pick out the **direct object**.

Once an agreement is needed, we simply add **-e** to agree with a **feminine** preceding direct object, **-s** with a **plural** preceding direct object and therefore **-es** with a **feminine plural** preceding direct object.

[However we do not add an **-s** to a word ending in **s**:

Voici le livre qu'il a mis sur la table.
Here is the book (which / that) he put on the table.

Voici les livres qu'il a mis sur la table.
Here are the books (which / that) he put on the table.]

Now let's look at the following three sentences:

    a. **J'ai acheté <u>les livres</u> à Paris.**
       I bought the books in Paris.

    b. **Vous avez reçu <u>les nouvelles</u>.**
       You received the news.

    c. **J'ai vu <u>tes amis</u> au cinéma.**
       I saw your friends at the cinema.

Let's ask the same questions as before:

    a. What did I buy? – the books

    b. What did you receive? – the news

    c. What did I see? – your friends

In each sentence we have a plural direct object, yet the past participle shows no agreement. This is because the **direct object comes** AFTER **the verb** – it does not precede it.

THE PERFECT TENSE OF PRONOMINAL VERBS

These are always **être** verbs. Students are often told to make their past participles agree in the same way as the 16 **être** verbs. This advice is given with the intention of avoiding complications but it is not entirely true. Let's study the following examples:

a. Elles se sont parlé.
They spoke to one another.

b. Ils se sont dit au revoir.
They said goodbye to each other.

c. Elle s'est lavé les cheveux.
She washed her hair.

d. Nous nous sommes rendu compte de notre erreur.
We realised our mistake.

e. Elle s'est demandé pourquoi il n'était pas venu.
She wondered why he hadn't come.

You will have noticed that we have made no agreement to the past participles.

We'll try to make the rule as simple as possible. To do so, we are avoiding certain complications you are unlikely to meet.

1. If the verb is **always** a pronominal verb, make the past participle agreement as you would for any of the 16 **être** verbs:

    Elle s'est souvenue de cette soirée magnifique.
    She remembered that magnificent party.

    Ils se sont emparés de la liasse de billets.
    They grabbed hold of the bundle of notes.

    Elles se sont repenties de leurs péchés.
    They repented of their sins.

These verbs **do not exist** in a non-pronominal form but always as **se souvenir de, s'emparer de, se repentir de**.

2. For the many verbs that have both a pronominal and a non-pronominal form – **(se) parler, (se) cacher, (se) demander, (se) laver** etc – the rule of agreement depends on whether the reflexive pronoun is a **direct** or an **indirect** object. We **never** make agreements with indirect objects.

Compare:

Elles se sont parlé.
Elles se sont cachées.

Clearly, **parler** and **cacher** exist as non-pronominal verbs. We therefore look at the reflexive pronoun (**se**) in each case. With **parler**, **se** means *to one another* or *to each other* and is therefore an **indirect object** (see our definitions of technical terms) and therefore we make no agreement.

With **cacher** we can ask the question: What did they hide? Answer: themselves – a **direct object** requiring an agreement.

We can now see why, in the sentence **Ils se sont dit au revoir**, there is no agreement of the past participle. We have identified the reflexive pronoun as an indirect object. **Se** is translated as *to one another*.

However, can we do the same with the sentence: **Elle s'est lavé les cheveux**? Now we cannot translate **s'** as *to herself* as this would make no sense in English. Yet it **is** an

indirect object. We ask ourselves the question: What did she wash? Answer: her hair – the **direct object**. You may remember the sentence in our technical terms – *He showed her the letter* – where we pointed out that in French we need to say *he showed the letter* (direct object) *to her* (indirect object). So, as **les cheveux** is the direct object, the **s'** has to be an **indirect object** even though we cannot translate it into English using the word **to**.

[A verb can have two or more direct objects only if these are linked by *and* or *or*.]

In the same way there is no agreement of the past participle in the sentence **Nous nous sommes rendu compte de notre erreur**. The direct object is **compte**. While we would translate the sentence as *We realised our mistake*, it is similar in form and meaning to the English *We took account of our mistake*. Here *account* (the thing we took) is the direct object.

The use of **se demander** (**Elle s'est demandé pourquoi il n'était pas venu**) needs some further explanation. The French equivalent of *she wondered* is *she asked herself*. The verb **demander** requires that the person addressed be an indirect object – we ask *to* someone:

Il a demandé à son père de ne pas ronfler.
He asked his father not to snore.

So when she *wondered* why he hadn't come, she actually *asked to herself*. And we remember **never** to make agreements with **indirect** objects.

Nevertheless, the reflexive pronoun is most commonly the **direct object** of the verb and in such cases we **do** make the agreement.

Ils se sont cachés.
They hid.

Elles se sont levées.
They stood up.

L'étudiante s'est assise.
The student sat down.

◆ ◆ ◆

ASKING QUESTIONS

As with the present tense, there are four ways of asking questions in the perfect tense:

a. By **tone of voice – intonation**:

Elle est arrivée hier soir ?
Did she arrive last night?

Il a déjà vu le film ?
Has he already seen the film?

Elles se sont levées trop tard ?
Did they get up too late?

Les professeurs sont arrivés de bonne heure ?
Did the teachers arrive early?

b. By placing **est-ce que (qu')** before the statement:

Est-ce qu'elle est arrivée hier soir ?

Est-ce qu'il a déjà vu le film ?

Est-ce qu'elles se sont levées trop tard ?

Est-ce que les professeurs sont arrivés de bonne heure ?

c. By using **inversion**:

Est-elle arrivée hier soir ?

A-t-il déjà vu le film ?

Se sont-elles levées trop tard ?

Les professeurs sont-ils arrivés de bonne heure ?

Note the use of the **hyphens** linking the **auxiliary** verb with the **subject** and the insertion of the **-t-** in the third person singular of avoir.

d. By adding **n'est-ce pas**:

Ils sont arrivés, n'est-ce pas ?

They've arrived, haven't they? (They arrived, didn't they?)

USING NEGATIVES

(Only **ne ... pas** for the moment.)

The following examples will make the word order clear:

Le train n'est pas encore parti.
The train hasn't left yet.

Je n'ai pas voulu faire ce travail.
I didn't want to do this work.

Nous ne nous sommes pas lavés ce matin.
We didn't have a wash this morning.

Est-ce que vous n'avez pas fini de laver la vaisselle ?
Haven't you finished doing the washing-up?

Ne s'est-elle pas promenée dans la forêt ?
Didn't she have a walk in the forest?

Le marchand n'a-t-il pas répondu à ta lettre ?
Didn't the dealer answer your letter?

While we can say that **ne ... pas** will always surround the **auxiliary** verb, we must note that:

a. any **reflexive pronoun** must be placed **before** the part of **être**

b. as we saw with the present tense, **words joined by hyphens cannot be separated**.

The best way to familiarise yourself with the order of words is to **listen to the recording as you read the sentences** and to **repeat aloud** what you hear.

What we have said above about the **rules of agreement of the past participle** and **word order in questions and negatives** applies to **all the compound tenses**.

TRAIL → 12
page 198

◆ ◆ ◆

→ TRAIL 13

IMPERFECT TENSE – L'IMPARFAIT

If we have a tense called the 'perfect', we ought not to be surprised to find one called the 'imperfect'. Nor should we be surprised that where the **perfect** tense expresses **single** or **completed** actions in the past, the **imperfect** expresses **incomplete** actions and **repeated** actions as well as **continuous states**. It is also used in **descriptions**.

We will set out in ten points what we feel should be known about the imperfect.

1. It is a one-word **past** tense, formed from the **nous** form of the **present tense** with **-ons** removed and the following endings added (common to **all** verbs). We'll use **dire** as our example:

   je disais   *I was saying / used to say / said (regularly)*

   tu disais

   il / elle / on disait

   nous disions

   vous disiez

   ils / elles disaient

As you listen to this you will note that the endings **-ais**, **-ait** and **-aient** are pronounced identically.

2. There is just one exception to this: **être**, whose present tense **nous** form doesn't end in **-ons**. Here the stem for the imperfect is **ét-** (note the acute accent).

   j'étais   *I was*

   tu étais   *you were*

   il / elle / on était

   nous étions

   vous étiez

   ils / elles étaient

Other exceptions are impersonal verbs (these verbs, by definition, have no **nous** form).

falloir	to be necessary	**il fallait**
neiger	to snow	**il neigeait**
pleuvoir	to rain	**il pleuvait**

3. Careful attention should be paid to those verbs whose **nous** form in the present ends in **-ions**. Here the **nous** and **vous** forms of the imperfect will have the rather strange looking **-ii-**:

nous oubliions
we were forgetting

vous étudiiez
you were studying

nous riions
we were laughing

As you will hear from the recording, there are two ways of pronouncing these, one of which sounds exactly like the present.

So far, so good. The formation of the imperfect is straightforward. Its usage is more complicated.

4. Put simply, the imperfect corresponds to the English *was* or *were* with the form of the verb ending in *-ing*:

Je faisais des courses quand je l'ai vu.
*I **was shopping** when I saw him.*

Quand je suis arrivé elle mangeait son dîner.
*When I arrived she **was having** dinner.*

[NB **nous mangions, vous mangiez** – no **-e-**. Also with other verbs ending in **-ger**.

Similarly, with verbs ending in **-cer**, we have **je lançais, tu lançais, il lançait, ils lançaient**, but **nous lancions, vous lanciez**.]

Ils ronflaient déjà quand je suis allé me coucher.
*They **were** already **snoring** when I went to bed.*

The verbs in the imperfect express continuous or continuing actions, which **were going on** at the time of the main action.

5. The imperfect is used for **habitual** or **repeated** actions in the past:

Il se levait tous les jours à sept heures et demie.

In English, we have a variety of ways of expressing this idea:

*He **got up** every day at half past seven.*
*He **used to get up** …*
*He **would get up** …*

Tu oubliais souvent de faire tes devoirs.
*You often **forgot** to do your homework.*
*You often **used to forget** …*
*You **would** often **forget** …*

There are two distinct problems here. First, in English we normally use the **simple past tense** when referring to **habitual** or **repeated** actions. The French will **always** make the distinction between **tu oubliais** and **tu as oublié**. Secondly, in the third example using the word *would*, students often confuse the *would* of the **repeated action** and the *would* of the **conditional**. This we will deal with later.

6. The imperfect is also used to **describe** how things, people or places were, looked or seemed.

Le médecin était malade.
The doctor was ill.

Elle était grande et mince.
She was tall and slim.

Elle portait une robe bleue.
She wore (was wearing) a blue dress.

Il avait l'air content.
He seemed happy.

Nous étions un peu déçus.
We were a bit disappointed.

Son père mesurait un mètre quatre-vingts.
His father was six feet tall.

7. In our section on the present tense, we said we would return to the use of **depuis** in the imperfect tense.

Ils étaient à l'hôpital depuis trois semaines.
*They **had been** in hospital for three weeks.*

Elle habitait à Londres depuis deux ans.
*She **had been living** in London for two years.*

Je vous attendais devant le cinéma depuis une demi-heure.
*I **had been waiting** for you outside the cinema **for** half an hour.*

In these cases English uses *had been ... for* (a period of time). The French see it as something that **was still happening**. This may be clearer if we add another action to our examples:

Ils étaient à l'hôpital depuis trois semaines quand la nouvelle est arrivée.
... when the news came.

Elle habitait à Londres depuis deux ans quand son mari a perdu son poste.
... when her husband lost his job.

Je vous attendais devant le cinéma depuis une demi-heure quand j'ai vu un accident dans la rue.
... when I saw an accident in the street.

In each example, the first action was going on (*was ... -ing* and so imperfect) when the second one happened.

8. The other point we said we would return to is **venir de**...:

Il venait de s'installer à Paris.
*He **had just settled** in Paris.*

Nous venions de déménager.
*We **had just moved house**.*

Les chiens venaient de mordre le facteur.
*The dogs **had just bitten** the postman.*

Where the English has *had just (done)*, French has the verb **venir** in the **imperfect** followed by **de** (or **d'**) and the **infinitive**.

36

9. As we said in point 5, the imperfect is used to describe repeated actions in the past, eg:

Quand j'étais jeune, je jouais souvent au foot.
When I was young, I often played football.

However, if the time limit is **clearly specified**, the imperfect is **not** the correct tense to use. The **perfect** (we said it was for **completed** actions) is used instead.

L'été dernier, j'ai souvent joué au foot.
Last summer, I often played football.

You will see that in our first example the time limit is vague, whereas the second sets the clear limit of last summer.

Similarly:

Louis XIV a régné soixante-douze ans.
Louis XIV reigned for 72 years.

We consider his reign a historic event, a **completed** action, so we use the **perfect**. This will become clearer with some more examples:

Pendant les vacances il pleuvait tous les jours.
During the holidays it rained every day.

La semaine dernière il a plu tous les jours.
Last week it rained every day.

Pendant une heure il n'a pas arrêté de parler.
For an hour he didn't stop talking.

À l'école il n'arrêtait pas de parler.
At school he didn't stop talking.

Admittedly, the difference between the tenses can seem confusing. Indeed, it is often **subjective**, depending on the way the speaker or writer sees the action:

À l'école il n'a pas arrêté de parler.
At school he didn't stop talking.

Here the writer is referring to the person's **whole career** at school: a completed action within a definite time scale.

Our previous example, using the imperfect, stresses the **habitual** talking and ignores time limits – it could be all term or simply describing how different he was at school as opposed to at home.

If we were to say:

Aujourd'hui à l'école il n'a pas arrêté de parler.
Today at school ...

it is clear that we are giving **specific time limits**.

You can be certain that the use of the **perfect** is correct if there is a **clear statement of the duration of the action**, what the French may call 'une **précision temporelle**'.

10. Following on from the previous point, we consider differences between the imperfect and perfect when describing how people looked, seemed or felt. You would not be surprised to see:

Il avait peur.
He was afraid.

Il voulait partir.
He wanted to leave.

Il savait ce qu'il fallait faire.
He knew what had to be done.

But you will also find:

Il a eu peur. Il a voulu partir. Il a su ce qu'il fallait faire.

Here we are talking about the **specific moment** when he **became** afraid, **realised** that he wished to leave, when what had to be done **came to him**. This is even clearer if you were to put **soudain** (*suddenly*) at the start of each sentence. This usage of the perfect tense with these verbs is less common than the imperfect, but can be quite dramatic.

Again we would advise you to try the exercises and listen to the answers, not forgetting to repeat them aloud.

PLUPERFECT TENSE – LE PLUS-QUE-PARFAIT

TEMPS SIMPLES	TEMPS COMPOSÉS
present **Le présent**	perfect **Le passé composé**
imperfect **L'imparfait**	pluperfect **Le plus-que-parfait**

The pluperfect tense is the one which, in English, uses the word **had** and the **past participle**. It is perhaps best described if we consider its name in French – the 'more than complete'. It is used for events in the past which were over before the main action, also in the past, took place:

Ils avaient quitté la maison avant mon arrivée.
*They **had left** the house before I arrived.*

In French, the **formation of the pluperfect** is quite straightforward – we use the **imperfect** of **avoir** or **être** and the **past participle**.

Below, we give a listing of verbs in the pluperfect – **avoir** verbs, **être** verbs and **pronominal** verbs. Our examples will demonstrate that the rules regarding the order of words in questions and negatives and those for past participle agreements are **exactly the same as in the perfect** (and the other compound tenses). Again we would advise you to listen and say them out loud.

j'avais parlé
I had spoken

tu ne les avais pas mangés
you hadn't eaten them

avait-il plu ?
had it rained?

est-ce qu'elle en avait pris ?
had she taken any?

on avait souffert
we had suffered

nous n'avions pas dormi
we hadn't slept

en aviez-vous voulu ?
had you wanted any?

est-ce qu'ils avaient ri ?
had they laughed?

n'avaient-elles pas attendu ?
hadn't they waited?

j'étais arrivé(e)
I had arrived

est-ce que tu étais parti(e) ?
had you left?

était-il mort ?
had he died?

elle n'était pas morte
she hadn't died

on était allé(e)s *
we had gone

nous étions monté(e)s
we had gone up / upstairs

étiez-vous descendu(e)(s) ?
had you come down / downstairs?

ils y étaient venus
they had come there

n'étaient-elles pas revenues ?
hadn't they come back?

* You will remember that the past participle of an **être** verb with **on** as its subject will show plural agreement with the people to whom it refers.

je m'étais assis(e)
I had sat down

tu ne t'étais pas levé(e)
you hadn't got up

s'était-il lavé ?
had he had a wash?

est-ce qu'elle s'était déshabillée ?
had she got undressed?

on s'était promené(e)s
we had had a walk

nous étions-nous réveillé(e)s trop tard ?
had we woken up too late?

vous ne vous étiez pas bien amusé(e)(s)
you hadn't had a good time

s'étaient-ils battus ?
had they had a fight?

ne s'étaient-elles pas parlé ?
hadn't they spoken to one another? (no agreement here!)

It is not always necessary to use the pluperfect to express how one past action had occurred before another:

Après avoir mangé**, elle est sortie.**

There are various ways of translating this sentence, including the use of a pluperfect:

*After **eating** she went out.*

*After **having eaten** she went out.*

***When she had eaten** she went out.*

This construction is known as the **perfect infinitive**. As you can see (and hear) the auxiliary verb is in the infinitive.

Après être rentrée **à la maison, elle a téléphoné à son ami.**
After returning home, she rang her friend.

Après nous être levés**, nous avons aidé nos parents à faire le ménage.**
After we had got up, we helped our parents with the housework.

Once again, rules regarding word order and agreement of the past participle are the same as for all the compound tenses.

In our examples you will have noted that *she* ate and *she* went out, *she* returned home and *she* rang her friend, *we* got up and *we* helped our parents. This construction is only possible when the **same person performs both actions**.

We have now covered the first two single word tenses and the corresponding compound tenses that they help to form. We saw that the **present** tense of **avoir** and **être** is used in the formation of the **perfect** and now we have seen that the **imperfect** of these auxiliary verbs is used to form the **pluperfect**.

TRAIL → 14
page 202

◆ ◆ ◆

→ TRAIL 17

FUTURE TENSE – LE FUTUR

The English future tense is a compound one, using the word *shall* or *will* with the part of the verb which forms the **infinitive**. For example:

I shall write (or more commonly, *I'll write*)

you will see (*you'll see*)

he will read (*he'll read*)

we shall speak (*we'll speak*)

they will hear (*they'll hear*)

Exchanging *shall* for *will* and vice versa is often used to add extra stress – '*Cinderella, you **shall** go to the ball!*' In this case it may be necessary in French to add an adverb such as **vraiment** (*really, truly*) to give the same sense.

◆

We must be aware of the pitfalls of our own language. Before we go any further, we ought to point out that *shall* and *will* are often used in English with meanings other than future time:

The sentence *You **shall** write to your parents* could imply duty or obligation. It could well be translated **Tu dois écrire à tes parents.** *You **ought to write / must write** to your parents.*

If we say *I **will** not **give** you the money*, we could be expressing reluctance or determination. We would then translate it as **Je ne veux pas te donner l'argent.** This is often the sense of **will** in questions such as **Veux-tu te laver les dents ?** *Will you **brush** your teeth?*

◆

The French **future** is a **simple**, one-word tense, but before we introduce it, we'll show you an easier way of expressing future action, one which is **very commonly used in speech**. This is the **exact equivalent** of the English *we are going to* (go / examine / buy/ etc) and uses the **present tense** of **aller** and the **infinitive**:

Je vais aller en ville.

This construction, known as the **immediate future** (in French **le futur proche**), here translates *I **am going to go** to town*, *I'll go to town*, *I **shall go** to town* and even *I'll be going to town*. It will only be used for actions in the **near** future.

Il va examiner la carte.
He is going to look at the map.

Elles vont acheter des chaussures.
They are going to buy (some) shoes.

◆

Something you will be delighted to discover is that there is very little new to learn in order to construct the future tense. Indeed, as with the imperfect, **the endings for ALL verbs are the same** – not only that, you know them already; they are the **present tense** of the verb **avoir** (if we take off the **av-** in the first and second persons plural):

present of avoir	future tense endings
j'ai	-ai
tu as	-as
il a	-a
nous avons	-ons
vous avez	-ez
ils ont	-ont

Now all we need is a **stem**. For most verbs, this is the **infinitive** (in the case of infinitives ending in **-re** the final **-e** is removed):

je donner**ai**	*I shall give*
tu finir**as**	*you will finish*
il vendr**a**	*he will sell*
nous prendr**ons**	*we shall take*
vous suivr**ez**	*you will follow*
ils ouvrir**ont**	*they will open*

There are quite a number of verbs which have **irregular stems** in the future tense. We will list here only the verbs we covered under the present and perfect tenses. We'll put in green the ones with irregular future stems:

donner	je donnerai	
lancer	tu lanceras	no **ç** throughout
manger	il mangera	no extra **e** throughout
appeler	elle appellera	**ll** throughout
jeter	on jettera	**tt** throughout
mener	nous mènerons	**è** throughout
acheter	vous achèterez	**è** throughout
répéter	ils répèteront	**è** throughout
	also: **préférer** – **elles préfèreront**	
	espérer – **j'espèrerai** *	
employer	tu emploieras	**i** throughout

(The otherwise identically formed verb **envoyer** – *to send* – has **tu enverras** here and **-err-** throughout.)

ennuyer	il ennuiera	**i** throughout
payer	elle payera / paiera	
finir	on finira	examples for regular **-ir**
attendre	nous attendrons	and **-re** verbs
venir	vous viendrez	
sortir	ils sortiront	
partir	elles partiront	
dormir	je dormirai	
servir	tu serviras	

mentir	il mentira
sentir	elle sentira
prendre	on prendra
être	nous serons
avoir	vous aurez
aller	ils iront
boire	elles boiront
connaître	je connaîtrai
courir	tu courras
craindre	il craindra
devoir	elle devra
dire	on dira
écrire	nous écrirons
faire	vous ferez
mettre	ils mettront
mourir	elles mourront
ouvrir	j'ouvrirai
pouvoir	tu pourras
recevoir	il recevra
savoir	elle saura
suivre	on suivra
voir	nous verrons
vouloir	vous voudrez
s'asseoir	ils s'assiéront

* Most books continue to use the old spelling – **répéteront**, **préféreront**, **espérerai**. The new spelling reflects the way in which these verb forms are pronounced and is recommended by the Académie française.

Impersonal verbs:

falloir	*to be necessary*	**il faudra**
neiger	*to snow*	**il neigera**
pleuvoir	*to rain*	**il pleuvra**

Generally speaking, you will find that an English future tense is translated by a French future tense. However, French will frequently require the future when **future time is meant** but where English uses a present tense:

Quand j'irai en ville, j'achèterai des vêtements.

We, of course, would say:

*When I **go** to town I'll buy some clothes.*

Quand je serai de retour, je vous passerai un coup de fil.
When I am (get) back, I'll give you a ring.

Clearly **lorsque** (which also means *when*) will be followed in similar fashion by the future as will **dès que** and **aussitôt que** which both mean *as soon as*.

Dès que j'aurai la lettre, je viendrai vous voir.
As soon as I have the letter I will come and see you.

[It is worth mentioning here that where **si** means *if*, it will **not** be followed by a future tense:

S'il fait beau, je me promènerai à la campagne.
If it is fine, I'll go for a walk in the country.

Here French follows the same pattern as English – *If it is fine …*]

FUTURE PERFECT TENSE – LE FUTUR ANTÉRIEUR

The future perfect tense in English uses *will* (or *shall*) *have* with the **past participle**:

*I **shall have arrived** before you. Before she cuts the cake he **will have toasted** the bride.*

In other words, it is used to express a future action which **will have taken place** before the main action.

TEMPS SIMPLES	TEMPS COMPOSÉS
present **Le présent**	perfect **Le passé composé**
imperfect **L'imparfait**	pluperfect **Le plus-que-parfait**
future **Le futur**	future perfect **Le futur antérieur**

There are no real difficulties here – we use the **future** tense of **avoir** or **être** and the **past participle**:

Il aura accepté le cadeau avant son anniversaire.
He will have accepted the present before his birthday.

Ils seront morts avant de devenir riches.
They will have died before they become rich.

Nous nous serons levés à neuf heures ; il arrivera dix minutes plus tard.
We'll have got up at nine; he'll arrive ten minutes later.

It should by now go without saying that the rules for the agreement of the past participle and the positioning of words in negatives and questions are exactly the same in the future perfect as in the perfect and the pluperfect.

j'aurai acheté
I'll have bought

tu ne les auras pas vus
you'll not have seen them (you won't have seen them)

aura-t-il plu ?
will it have rained?

est-ce qu'elle aura dormi ?
will she have slept?

on aura souffert
we'll have suffered

nous n'aurons pas écrit
we'll not have written (we won't have written)

en aurez-vous voulu ?
will you have wanted any (some)?

est-ce qu'ils auront souri ?
will they have smiled?

n'auront-elles pas réfléchi ?
won't they (will they not) have considered (reflected)?

je serai sorti(e)
I'll have gone out

est-ce que tu seras devenu(e) riche ?
will you have become rich?

sera-t-il mort ?
will he have died?

elle ne sera pas morte
she will not have died

on sera tombé(e)s
we'll have fallen

nous serons arrivé(e)s
we'll have arrived

serez-vous parti(e)(s) ?
will you have left?

ils y seront allés
they'll have gone there

ne seront-elles pas rentrées ?
won't they (will they not) have returned?

je me serai assis(e)
I'll have sat down

tu ne te seras pas levé(e)
you'll not have got up

se sera-t-il lavé ?
will he have had a wash?

est-ce qu'elle se sera habillée ?
will she have got dressed?

on se sera promené(e)s
we'll have had a walk

nous serons-nous réveillé(e)s ?
will we have woken up?

vous ne vous serez pas bien amusé(e)(s)
you'll not (you won't) have had a good time

se seront-ils battus ?
will they have had a fight?

ne se seront-elles pas posé la question ?
won't they (will they not) have asked themselves the question ? (no agreement here!)

◆

Note that this tense is used following **quand, lorsque, dès que** and **aussitôt que** where English would not have a future perfect. Consider this sentence:

He says that he will come down **when he has** (**as soon as he has**) **finished** his essay.

We will find no future perfect in our English here but French puts it differently:

Il dit qu'il descendra quand il aura fini **son essai.**

(**Il dit qu'il descendra** lorsqu'il aura fini **son essai.**

Il dit qu'il descendra dès qu'il aura fini **son essai.**

Il dit qu'il descendra aussitôt qu'il aura fini **son essai.**)

French is stressing here that he will not come down until **he will have completed the work** at some future point in time. [The same tenses are required following **après que** after.]

We will give another example, this time using the future perfect of an **être** verb:

He says he will get back to work when (as soon as) she has arrived.

Il dit qu'il se remettra au travail quand elle sera arrivée.

Il dit qu'il se remettra au travail lorsqu'elle sera arrivée.

Il dit qu'il se remettra au travail dès qu'elle sera arrivée.

Il dit qu'il se remettra au travail aussitôt qu'elle sera arrivée.

◆ ◆ ◆

THE CONDITIONAL – LE CONDITIONNEL

The conditional, often known as the future conditional, is the equivalent of the English compound form *would* (*do*).

To form the conditional we simply take the **future stem** and add the **imperfect endings**:

je répèterais

tu choisirais

il vendrait

elle serait

on aurait

nous ferions

vous pourriez

ils voudraient

elles s'assiéraient

So, there is nothing complicated in the formation of this tense, nor is there in its meaning and use. As we are fond of saying, it will help you if you listen to (and repeat) the recorded examples:

Elle a dit qu'elle irait au marché.
*She said she **would go** to the market.*

Tu voudrais aller avec elle ?
***Would** you **like** to go with her?*

On n'aurait pas de mal à le trouver.
*We **would have** no difficulty in finding him.*

Il est évident que nous ferions de notre mieux.
*It is obvious that we **would do** our best.*

Pourriez-vous venir me chercher à la gare mardi prochain ?

Although we can clearly translate this as :

***Would** you **be able** to pick me up at the station next Tuesday?*

more frequently we would say:

***Could** you …?*

[You will remember that we used *would* to translate a **habitual** action in the past where French uses the imperfect:

Elle se levait tous les jours à sept heures.
She would get up every day at seven.

This should not be confused with the *would* of the conditional where a habitual action is not involved.

Si elle voulait arriver à l'école de bonne heure demain matin, elle se lèverait à sept heures.
If she wanted to get to school early tomorrow morning, she would get up at seven.]

◆

You will remember that we indicated at the beginning of our section on the future that *I / we **shall** (do)* is the formally correct usage to which, in the conditional, *I / we **should** (do)* corresponds. In other words, *should* will not always imply obligation:

Our first examples imply **no obligation**:

Je serais content d'avoir des renseignements supplémentaires.
*I **should be** happy to have further information.*

Nous serions prêts à vous recevoir la semaine prochaine.
*We **should be** ready to receive you next week.*

On the other hand, the next examples demonstrate *should* implying **obligation** and requiring the use of **devoir** or **falloir** (**il faut**):

Tu devrais aller la voir.

Il te faudrait aller la voir.

*You **should** (**ought to**) go and see her.*

Sa mère lui a dit qu'il devrait se laver les dents deux fois par jour (qu'il lui faudrait se laver les dents ...
*His mother told him he **should** (**ought to**) brush his teeth twice a day.*

TRAIL → 18
page 203

◆ ◆ ◆

→ TRAIL 21

THE CONDITIONAL PERFECT – LE CONDITIONNEL PASSÉ

The conditional perfect, following on logically from the future conditional, is used to express what I *would have done*, what they *would have expected* etc.

TEMPS SIMPLES	TEMPS COMPOSÉS
present **Le présent**	perfect **Le passé composé**
imperfect **L'imparfait**	pluperfect **Le plus-que-parfait**
future **Le futur**	future perfect **Le futur antérieur**
conditional **Le conditionnel**	conditional perfect **Le conditionnel passé**

The move from conditional to conditional perfect is quite straightforward – we use the **conditional** of **avoir** or **être** and the **past participle** with the now familiar **agreements** and **word order** for the compound tenses.

j'aurais dit
I would have said

tu ne les aurais pas reçus
you wouldn't have received them

aurait-il voulu rester ?
would he have wanted to stay?

est-ce qu'elle aurait dormi ?
would she have slept?

on aurait ouvert **la porte**
we would have opened the door

nous ne l'aurions pas **lu**
we wouldn't have read it

en auriez**-vous** acheté ?
would you have bought some?

est-ce qu'ils auraient couru ?
would they have run?

n'auraient**-elles pas** écrit ?
wouldn't they have written?

je serais descendu(e)
I would have come down

est-ce que tu serais revenu(e) ?
would you have come back?

serait**-il venu** ?
would he have come?

elle ne serait **pas** rentrée
she wouldn't have returned

on serait monté(e)s
we would have gone up

nous serions sorti(e)s
we would have gone out

seriez**-vous** entré(e)(s) ?
would you have gone in?

ils seraient morts
they would have died

ne seraient**-elles pas** mortes ?
wouldn't they have died?

je me serais caché(e)
I would have hidden

tu ne te serais **pas** habillé(e)
you wouldn't have got dressed

se serait**-il ennuyé** ?
would he have got bored?

est-ce qu'elle se serait endormie ?
would she have gone to sleep?

on se serait promené(e)s
we would have gone for a walk

nous serions**-nous dit bonjour** ?
would we have said hello to one another? (no agreement here!)

vous ne vous seriez **pas bien** amusé(e)(s)
you wouldn't have had a good time

se seraient**-ils battus** ?
would they have had a fight?

ne se seraient-**elles pas** couchées **?**
wouldn't they have gone to bed?

As you can see, the meaning in each of our examples must include the words *would have*.

TRAIL → 22
page 204

→ TRAIL 51

Our table of tenses is now almost complete. The two tenses which remain are **not used in the spoken language**. This does not mean, however, that you need not know them! The one-word tense, the past historic, is linked to its corresponding two-word tense, the past anterior. We thus continue to stress the link between simple and compound tenses.

THE PAST HISTORIC – LE PASSÉ SIMPLE

The past historic is the exact equivalent of our simple past tense, translating *he arrived*, *they spoke* etc, and describing **single, non-repeated actions**. In question form, it also translates *did he arrive?, did they speak?* etc.

Unlike its English counterpart, however, it is not used in modern speech and nowadays is most commonly found in works of literature when a past tense is used. For the student of today, it is necessary to recognise this tense and its use may be required in prose translation.

There are only four sets of endings for the past historic tense and once we know the first person singular, we can be sure that the other persons will follow the pattern. As you will see, **all** the **nous** and **vous** forms have circumflex accents.

a. All **-er** verbs. Here we can even use **aller** as an example:

j'allai	**je donnai**
tu allas	**tu lanças**
il alla	**il mangea**
nous allâmes	**nous employâmes**

vous all**â**tes	vous ennuy**â**tes
ils all**è**rent	ils pay**è**rent

b. All regular **-ir** and **-re** verbs and many irregular ones:

je fin**is**	j'attend**is**
tu fin**is**	tu attend**is**
il fin**it**	il attend**it**
nous fin**î**mes	nous attend**î**mes
vous fin**î**tes	vous attend**î**tes
ils fin**irent**	ils attend**irent**

c. **Venir**, **tenir** and their compound forms:

je v**ins**	je ret**ins**
tu v**ins**	tu ret**ins**
il v**int**	il ret**int**
nous v**î**nmes	nous ret**î**nmes
vous v**î**ntes	vous ret**î**ntes
ils v**inrent**	ils ret**inrent**

d. All other irregular verbs:

Examples:

être	**avoir**
je f**us**	j'**eus**
tu f**us**	tu **eus**
il f**ut**	il **eut**
nous f**û**mes	nous e**û**mes
vous f**û**tes	vous e**û**tes
ils f**urent**	ils **eurent**

We will now list the remaining verbs from our selected list, in each case giving simply the first person singular. Where the rather cut-off nature of the stem may make identification of the verb difficult, or when the stem is very irregular, we will use underlining to stress this:

lancer	je lan<u>ç</u>ai	ç throughout except **ils lancèrent**
manger	je mang<u>e</u>ai	extra **e** throughout except **ils mangèrent**
appeler	j'appel**ai**	single **l** throughout
jeter	je jet**ai**	single **t** throughout
mener	je men**ai**	no grave accent on first **e** throughout
répéter	je répét**ai**	é throughout
employer	j'employ**ai**	y throughout
ennuyer	j'ennuy**ai**	y throughout
payer	je pay**ai**	no form with **i**

sortir	je sortis
partir	je partis
dormir	je dormis
servir	je servis
mentir	je mentis
sentir	je sentis
prendre	je pris
boire	je <u>b</u>us
connaître	je connus
courir	je cour<u>u</u>s
craindre	je craignis
devoir	je <u>d</u>us
dire	je <u>d</u>is
écrire	j'écrivis
faire	je <u>f</u>is
lire	je <u>l</u>us
mettre	je <u>m</u>is
mourir	il mourut
naître	je <u>naqu</u>is
ouvrir	j'ouvris
pouvoir	je <u>p</u>us
recevoir	je reçus
rire	je <u>r</u>is
savoir	je <u>s</u>us
sourire	je souris
suivre	je suivis
vivre	je <u>véc</u>us
voir	je <u>v</u>is
vouloir	je voulus
s'asseoir	je m'ass<u>is</u>
falloir	il fallut
neiger	il neig<u>ea</u>
pleuvoir	il plut

◆

While the translation into English of the past historic is quite straightforward, it is important to note that **elle alla** and **elle est allée** can both be translated as *she went*, but only **elle est allée** can also be translated as *she has gone*.

If we think about *she has gone* in English, it is clear that this would only be used in **conversation** or in a **letter**. In neither of these cases would the past historic be used by a French speaker.

Consider the following scene:

M. Dubois rentra chez lui vers six heures du soir. Il ne vit pas sa fille Jacqueline qui faisait d'habitude ses devoirs dans la cuisine. Il demanda donc à sa femme :

« Jacqueline n'est pas là ?

– Ah non ! Elle est allée au cinéma avec ses amies, répondit-elle. »

In English we could write:

*M. Dubois **returned** home* (p. hist) *about six o'clock in the evening. He **did** not **see*** (p. hist) *his daughter Jacqueline who usually **did*** (imperfect for habitual action in the past) *her homework in the kitchen. So he **asked*** (p. hist) *his wife:*

'Isn't Jacqueline here?'

*'No! She **has gone*** (perfect) *to the cinema with her friends,' she **replied*** (p. hist).

Even if his wife had replied,

*'No! She **went** to the cinema with her friends at five o'clock.'*

the French would still have required the perfect tense in direct speech.

Your instinct would probably have been to write the scene as follows:

M. Dubois est rentré chez lui vers six heures du soir. Il n'a pas vu sa fille Jacqueline qui faisait d'habitude ses devoirs dans la cuisine. Il a donc demandé à sa femme :

« Jacqueline n'est pas là ?

– Ah non ! Elle est allée au cinéma avec ses amies, a-t-elle répondu. »

This version is, of course, entirely acceptable. However, you may have to read novels in the past which usually have their main verbs in the past historic – hence your need to be able to recognise the tense.

THE PAST ANTERIOR – LE PASSÉ ANTÉRIEUR

The past anterior, the last of our ten tenses, is linked in our table with the past historic and is almost always found in conjunction with it.

TEMPS SIMPLES	TEMPS COMPOSÉS
present **Le présent**	perfect **Le passé composé**
imperfect **L'imparfait**	pluperfect **Le plus-que-parfait**
future **Le futur**	future perfect **Le futur antérieur**
conditional **Le conditionnel**	conditional perfect **Le conditionnel passé**
past historic **Le passé simple**	past anterior **Le passé antérieur**

The formation of the past anterior does not pose any problem. Following all the rules for compound tenses (order of words with questions and negatives, agreement of past participle, position of pronouns) we take the **past historic** of **être** or **avoir** and the **past participle**:

Quand elle eut mangé, son père alla au bureau.

Dès qu'elles furent arrivées, on les invita à prendre un verre.

Une fois qu'il se fut assis, elle se leva pour répondre à la question.

The meaning in English of this tense is equally uncomplicated. It is always translated by *had (done)*:

*When she **had eaten**, her father went to the office.*

*As soon as they **had arrived**, they were invited to have a drink.*

*Once he **had sat down**, she rose to answer the question.*

You will find the past anterior used after:

a. quand / lorsque (*when*)

b. dès que / aussitôt que (*as soon as*)

c. après que (*after*)

d. une fois que (*once*)

e. à peine ... que (*scarcely / hardly*)

to stress that **one action took place before another action given in the past historic**. Thus:

Après qu'elle eut téléphoné à la police, la famille sortit en courant de la maison.
*After she **had rung** the police, the family **ran** out of the house.*

À peine fut-il descendu de l'autobus, qu'il commença à pleuvoir.
*Hardly **had** he **got off** the bus, when it **began** to rain.*

You should note here the **inversion** when the sentence begins with **à peine** and the fact that in this construction **que** translates the English *when*. **Il fut** à peine **descendu** ... is also possible.

[Occasionally, you may find a past anterior used simply to stress how quickly an action was completed:

En vingt minutes il eut terminé son essai.
*In twenty minutes he **had finished** his essay.*

The story here will have the past historic as its main tense.]

This concludes our treatment of the ten tenses. We hope you will enjoy doing the exercises and find them useful. We feel that listening to the spoken version of the correct answers will be of considerable help to you.

We appreciate that verb forms in French can seem difficult, but knowing them is the key to expressing yourself in the language.

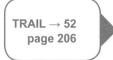

TRAIL → 52
page 206

◆ ◆ ◆

→ TRAIL 45

THE SUBJUNCTIVE – LE SUBJONCTIF

The subjunctive has often created problems for the student in the sixth form and at university. The verb forms themselves can be difficult to learn as can the instances when the subjunctive is required.

Let us begin by saying that the subjunctive is not a tense. It is a **mood** of the verb which exists in four tenses.

You will now be wondering what we mean by the word **mood**. The mood tells us how or in what conditions a given verb is envisaged. This may seem very technical and therefore we will here concentrate on just two moods:

Indicative – to express facts.

Subjunctive – to express wishes, possibilities, doubts, emotions, although its use is not entirely restricted to these areas.

Consider the sentence:

> **Elle est malade.**
> *She is ill.*

This is a simple statement of fact and we use the indicative mood of the verb **être** in the present tense.

Now let us look at the following sentence:

> **Je regrette qu'elle soit malade.**
> *I'm sorry that she is ill.*

It is still a fact that she is ill, but this fact is tinged by my personal reaction to it. The emotion expressed in **regretter que** triggers the use of the subjunctive mood.

The student is therefore faced with two problems – learning the verb forms and knowing when the subjunctive is required.

[To some it may come as a surprise that we use the subjunctive in English too, although its use is rarer in our language than in French. The sentence *If she **were** here she would agree* contains a subjunctive.]

The four tenses of the subjunctive in French are: present, perfect, imperfect and pluperfect. For the following reasons we intend to deal here only with the present and perfect tenses. The imperfect and pluperfect subjunctives are never spoken. Many respected, contemporary authors will often use a present or perfect subjunctive where in the past an imperfect or pluperfect would have been required. You should feel free to do likewise although your teachers may well expect you to recognise the subjunctive in all its tenses.

◆

First, we will deal with the formation of the **present subjunctive**.

The stem of the present subjunctive is **normally** formed by taking the **ils** form of the **present indicative**, **removing -ent** and adding the following endings, as shown here in green:

Examples

donner	finir
je donne	je finisse
tu donnes	tu finisses
il donne	il finisse
nous donnions	nous finissions
vous donniez	vous finissiez
ils donnent	ils finissent

With a regular **-er** verb, all three persons of the singular are identical to the present indicative. With all regular verbs, the third person plural is also the same as the present indicative.

The endings are the same for **every verb except avoir and être**, which we give below:

avoir	être
j'aie	je sois
tu aies	tu sois
il ait	il soit
nous ayons	nous soyons
vous ayez	vous soyez
ils aient	ils soient

However some verbs, **while they retain the regular endings**, have an irregular stem either throughout or in their **nous** and **vous** forms. We list the most important verbs below, highlighting the irregularities. You will note that in most cases the **nous** and **vous** forms of the present subjunctive are identical to the imperfect indicative.

aller	boire
j' aille	je boive
tu ailles	tu boives
il aille	il boive
nous allions	nous buvions
vous alliez	vous buviez
ils aillent	ils boivent

devoir	envoyer
je doive	j' envoie
tu doives	tu envoies
il doive	il envoie
nous devions	nous envoyions
vous deviez	vous envoyiez
ils doivent	ils envoient

faire	mourir
je fasse	je meure
tu fasses	tu meures
il fasse	il meure
nous fassions	nous mourions
vous fassiez	vous mouriez
ils fassent	ils meurent

pouvoir	prendre
je puisse	je prenne
tu puisses	tu prennes
il puisse	il prenne
nous puissions	nous prenions
vous puissiez	vous preniez
ils puissent	ils prennent

recevoir	rire
je reçoive	je rie
tu reçoives	tu ries
il reçoive	il rie
nous recevions	nous riions
vous receviez	vous riiez
ils reçoivent	ils rient

[**Rire** is not irregular, but we are including it because the **-ii-**, which we have seen in the imperfect, may seem strange.]

savoir	venir
je sache	je vienne
tu saches	tu viennes
il sache	il vienne
nous sachions	nous venions
vous sachiez	vous veniez
ils sachent	ils viennent

voir	vouloir
je voie	je <u>veuill</u>e
tu voies	tu <u>veuill</u>es
il voie	il <u>veuill</u>e
nous voyions	nous voulions
vous voyiez	vous vouliez
ils voient	ils <u>veuill</u>ent

falloir	pleuvoir
il faille	il pleuve

The **perfect subjunctive** is quite straightforward in its formation. You will remember the perfect indicative:

Elle a refusé. Elle est partie. Elle s'est blessée.
She refused. She left. She hurt herself.

To form the perfect subjunctive, we simply change the **auxiliary verb**, **avoir** or **être**, to the **present subjunctive**:

Je regrette qu'elle ait refusé. Je regrette qu'elle soit partie. Je regrette qu'elle se soit blessée.
I'm sorry that she refused. I'm sorry that she left. I'm sorry that she hurt herself.

While in English the word *that* may be omitted here, in French the omission of **que** is not possible.

All rules regarding word order and agreement of past participles remain the same. You will also notice that the use of the subjunctive does not for the most part affect the English translation.

◆

When to use the subjunctive

a) After verbs and adjectives expressing **emotion** – wish, desire, sorrow, happiness, preference, surprise etc:

Je m'étonne que vous parliez si bien le français.
I am astonished that you speak French so well.

Elle préfère que vous ne buviez pas d'alcool.
She prefers you not to drink alcohol.

Nous regrettons qu'elle veuille partir si tôt.
We are sorry that she wants to leave so soon.

Le professeur veut que vous fassiez de votre mieux.
The teacher wants you to do your best.

Elle est désolée qu'il refuse de manger.
She is sorry that he is refusing to eat.

(**Refuse** here *is* in the subjunctive, but it is identical to the present indicative.)

Nous sommes tristes qu'elle soit absente.
We are sorry that she is not here.

Je suis heureux que tu ailles **bien.**
I am happy that you are well.

Ils sont surpris que vous soyez **toujours là.**
They are surprised that you are still here.

Cela m'étonne que vous ayez parlé **sur ce ton-là.**
I am astonished that you spoke in that tone of voice.

Elle est désolée qu'il ait refusé **de manger.**
She is sorry that he has refused to eat.

Nous regrettons qu'elle soit tombée.
We are sorry that she has fallen.

Elle est contente que son fils se soit lavé **les mains.**
She is happy that her son has washed his hands.

Je suis heureux que vous n'ayez **pas** répondu **à cette lettre.**
I am happy that you didn't reply to this letter.

NB Generally speaking **espérer que** takes the indicative:

J'espère que vous allez bien.
I hope that you are well.

b) After expressions of **fear**:

We have not included verbs expressing fear in the above section. The reason is shown in the following sentence:

J'ai peur qu'elle ne **soit déçue.**
I am afraid that she is disappointed.

[You can see that we have highlighted the word **ne**. There is no negative sense to this sentence; **ne** has no meaning here, it is superfluous. It is sometimes referred to in English as a **pleonastic ne** and in French as a **ne explétif**. Be careful not to translate it. It is frequently found after verbs of fearing, but it is not obligatory, although your teachers may expect you to use it in formal written work.

Where the verb of fearing is itself in the negative or interrogative forms, the pleonastic **ne** is not used.

Je n'ai pas peur qu'il soit **en retard.**
I don't fear that he will be late.

Avez-vous peur qu'elle prenne **froid ?**
Are you afraid that she will catch cold?]

La serveuse se tient à la porte de peur qu'il ne **parte sans payer.**
The waitress is standing at the door for fear that he will leave without paying.

Je m'en vais de crainte que la police ne **vienne m'arrêter.**
I'm off for fear that the police are coming to arrest me.

Ils craignent que le général ne **meure sur le champ de bataille.**

This final sentence may be translated in several ways:

*They are afraid that the general **may die** on the battlefield.*

*They fear that the general **will die** on the battlefield. (The subjunctive has no future tense. The present here serves to describe a possible future event.)*

*They fear the general **is dying** on the battlefield.*

c) After verbs expressing **commands** – instruction, prohibition, prevention and permission:

Le directeur ordonne que nous respections **les professeurs.**
The headmaster orders us to respect the teachers.

Je commande qu'il se taise **immédiatement.**
I order him to shut up at once.

Le fermier défend que nous traversions **ses champs.**
The farmer forbids us to cross his fields.

Il empêche qu'elle réponde **à la question.**
He is stopping her from answering the question.

Nous permettons qu'il le fasse.
We let him do it.

d) After verbs of **thinking** and **believing**, but only when they are used in negative or interrogative forms:

There are numerous occasions in French where the subjunctive is used after a verb in its **negative** or **interrogative** form which can suggest a lack of certainty in the mind of the speaker. This is the key to understanding the use of the subjunctive, which, as we stated at the beginning of this section, is the mood of doubts and possibilities. So:

Je pense (Je crois) qu'il a **menti.**
I think (believe) that he has lied. (Indicative)

Je ne pense (crois) pas qu'il ait **menti.**
I don't think that he has lied.

Pensez-vous (Croyez-vous) qu'il ait **menti ?**
Do you think that he has lied?

We feel that you should treat this rule with caution. To use the subjunctive is to use more formal language, what the French would call **un français soutenu / soigné**. Such a level of language might well be out of place when speaking informally to a friend. We would tend to say, for example:

Tu penses que c'est **vrai ?**
Do you think it's true?

rather than ... que **ce soit** vrai.

e) After **douter que**:

Je doute que ses parents aient **compris.**
I doubt that his parents have understood.

But:

Il n'y a pas de doute que ses parents ont **compris.**
There is no doubt that his parents have understood.

In this second example, we are certain that the parents understood – it is a fact or we regard it as such. The uncertainty only exists when we actually doubt something.

f) After expressions of **possibility**:

Est-il possible qu'il dorme **toujours ?**
Is it possible that he is still asleep?

Il se peut que vous ayez **raison.**
It is possible that you are right.

Est-il vrai qu'il vende **la maison ?**
Is it true that he is selling the house?

[**Probability** can seem a complicated area:

Il est probable qu'elle reviendra ce soir.
It is likely that she will come back this evening. (The indicative is used here as her arrival is seen as more probable than possible.)

However, when her arrival is less likely, the subjunctive is used:

Il est peu probable qu'elle revienne ce soir.
It's not very likely that she will come back this evening.]

g) After the following expressions:

• **à condition que** – *on condition that*

J'accepte à condition que vous veniez me chercher à la gare.
I accept on condition that you come and fetch me from the station.

• **afin que**, **pour que** – *so that, in order that*

Il s'est arrêté afin qu'elle (pour qu'elle) puisse se reposer.
He has stopped so that she can rest.

• **à moins que** – *unless*

Je serai là à moins que je ne puisse pas trouver un baby-sitter.
I'll be there unless I can't find a babysitter.

Je passerai vous voir à moins qu'il (ne) pleuve.
I will come and see you unless it is raining. (Pleonastic **ne** is optional.)

• **avant que** – *before*

Faites-le avant qu'il (ne) soit trop tard.
Do it before it's too late. (Pleonastic **ne** is again optional. However, as we said earlier, in more formal written work your teachers may require it.)

[**Après que** (*after*) takes the indicative although you may often hear French speakers use the subjunctive. This should be avoided.]

• **bien que**, **quoique** – *although*

Bien que sa femme soit malade, il va tous les soirs au bistro.
Although his wife is ill, he goes to the café every evening.

Quoiqu'elle sache la vérité, elle ne dit rien.
Although she knows the truth, she says nothing.

• **il faut que** – *it is necessary that*

Il faut que je m'en aille.
I must be off.

• **il semble que** – *it seems that*

Il semble qu'elle n'ait rien reçu.
It seems that she has not received anything.

[But: **Il me semble que** etc is followed by an indicative:

Il nous semble qu'elle n'a rien reçu.
It seems to us …]

• **jusqu'à ce que** – *until*

Restez là jusqu'à ce que votre père soit de retour.
Stay there until your father gets back.

[NB In general, **to wait until** is simply translated as **attendre que**:

Le professeur attend que l'élève finisse ses devoirs.
The teacher is waiting for the pupil to finish his homework.]

- **non que** – *not that*

  Non que vous soyez coupable.
  Not that you are guilty.

- **pourvu que** – *provided that*

  Pourvu que vous ayez dit la vérité, on n'a rien à craindre.
  Provided that you have told the truth, we have nothing to fear.

- **sans que** – *without*

  Il est parti sans que j'aie le temps de tout expliquer.
  He left without my having the time to explain everything.

h) After **superlatives**:

  C'est le meilleur film que j'aie jamais vu.
  It's the best film I've ever seen.

  C'est le plus grand joueur que je connaisse.
  He's the greatest player I know.

We must point out here that **le premier, le dernier, le seul** count as superlatives:

  C'est le seul poète qui ait remporté ce prix.
  He is the only poet who has carried off this prize.

i) In certain set expressions:

  Vive la reine !
  Long live the Queen!

  Sauve qui peut !
  Every man for himself!

  Que le meilleur gagne !
  May the best man win!

  À Dieu ne plaise !
  God forbid!

◆

The subjunctive must <u>not</u> be used …

When an infinitive construction is possible.

This will always be the case where there is **no change of subject**:

  Il s'est arrêté pour (afin de) se reposer.
  He stopped so that he could rest. (He stopped to rest.)

  Il a peur d'avoir tort.
  He is afraid of being wrong.

  Je crains d'arriver en retard.
  I'm afraid of arriving late. (I'm afraid I'll be late.)

  Nous voulons devenir riches.
  We want to become rich.

Il regrette d'avoir fait cela.
He is sorry he did that.

Il a mangé avant de partir.
He ate before leaving.

Nous sommes heureux de vous revoir, mes amis.
We're happy to see you again, my friends.

Here are some similar examples, this time with **a change of subject**:

Il s'est arrêté pour que (afin que) nous nous reposions.
He stopped so that we could rest.

Il a peur qu'elle (n')ait tort.
He is afraid that she is wrong.

Je crains qu'il (ne) soit arrivé en retard.
I'm afraid that he arrived late.

Nous voulons que vous deveniez riches.
We want you to become rich.

Je regrette qu'ils aient fait cela.
I am sorry they have done that.

Il mange avant qu'elle (ne) parte.
He eats before she leaves.

Nous sommes heureux que vous soyez revenus, mes amis.
We are happy that you have come back, my friends.

NB We **must not** presume that all verbs followed by **que** and a change of subject require a subjunctive.

Je dis que vous avez raison.
I say that you are right.

J'affirme qu'il a dit cela.
I state that he said that.

We have to learn those verbs and expressions which trigger a subjunctive and in which circumstances.

Consider, for example, the sentence *She wants him to leave.* This cannot be translated into French using an infinitive construction as there is a change of subject. We will have to begin **Elle veut qu'il ...** and knowing that **vouloir que** triggers the subjunctive, we complete the translation with **parte. – Elle veut qu'il parte.**

◆

The subjunctive avoided

There are often other ways of expressing the same idea without using the subjunctive. **Un français soutenu / soigné** is not always appropriate.

It is, of course, possible to say:

À moins que vous (ne) soyez fatigué.
Unless you are tired.

We would almost certainly prefer to say:

Si vous n'êtes pas fatigué.
If you're not tired.

Bien qu'elle soit malade son mari continue de travailler.
Although she is ill her husband continues to work.

is likely to become:

Elle est malade mais son mari continue de travailler.
She is ill but her husband continues to work.

Je regrette qu'elle ait l'estomac dérangé.
I'm sorry that she has an upset stomach.

could become:

Elle a l'estomac dérangé. Quel dommage !
She has an upset stomach. What a pity!

or:

Elle a l'estomac dérangé. La pauvre !
She has an upset stomach. Poor girl (woman)!

Here are some further examples:

Je suis content qu'il ait eu son baccalauréat.
I'm happy that he has passed his baccalauréat.

Il a eu son bac. J'en suis content.
He's passed his bac. I'm pleased (about that).

Je vais écrire une lettre avant qu'il (n')arrive.
I'm going to write a letter before he gets here.

Je vais écrire une lettre avant son arrivée.
… before his arrival.

Nous allons manger avant qu'il (ne) parte.
We're going to eat before he leaves.

Nous allons manger avant son départ.
… before his departure.

Il est rentré à la maison sans que je le sache.
He came home without my knowing.

Il est rentré à la maison à mon insu.
… without my knowledge (unknown to me).

J'aime mieux que vous disiez la vérité.
I prefer you to tell the truth.

Dites la vérité – voilà ce que je préfère.
Tell the truth – that's what I prefer.

Il faut que nous rencontrions le directeur.
Il nous faut rencontrer le directeur.
We want to meet the headmaster.

◆

As you learn more French and perhaps spend some time in France, you will develop a feeling for whether the subjunctive is appropriate or not. Do remember, however, that there is no way round the use of the subjunctive after expressions such as **il faut que**.

TRAIL → 46
page 207

→ TRAIL 57

THE PASSIVE VOICE – LA VOIX PASSIVE

▶ TECHNICAL TERMS

Active and passive voices – A verb is said to be in the active voice when the subject carries out the action of the verb: *The dog **bit** the burglar.* A verb is in the passive voice when the subject receives the action of the verb: *The burglar **was bitten** by the dog.*

◆ ◆ ◆

The passive voice in French is formed in exactly the same way as the passive voice in English – a tense of the verb **être** followed by a past participle:

Elle	**sera**	**invitée**
She	*will be*	*invited*

What you will note here is that in French the past participle acts as an adjective and thus agrees with the subject (elle).

We give below the same example in the third person singular with each of the ten tenses:

Present: Elle est invitée.
She is invited.

[This should not be confused with

Elle a invité …
She invited …]

Perfect: **Elle a été invitée.**
*She has been (was *) invited.*

Imperfect: **Elle était invitée.**
*She was * invited.*

Pluperfect: **Elle avait été invitée.**
She had been invited.

Future: **Elle sera invitée.**
She will be invited.

Future perfect: **Elle aura été invitée.**
She will have been invited.

Conditional: **Elle serait invitée.**
She would be invited.

Conditional perfect: **Elle aurait été invitée.**
She would have been invited.

Past historic: **Elle fut invitée.**
*She was * invited.*

Past anterior: **Elle eut été invitée.**
She had been invited.

The verb **être** may be in the **infinitive**:

Les résultats viennent d'être publiés.
The results have just been published.

* Care must be taken here when translating **was**. The imperfect tense implies a regular or habitual action:

Elle était toujours invitée aux meilleurs restaurants.
She was always invited to the best restaurants.

The use of the perfect and past historic tenses would imply a single invitation. As you will remember, you will never find the past historic and past anterior tenses other than in written texts.

NB The past participle of **être** (**été**) never takes an agreement under any circumstances.

Here are some further examples of the passive, using different subjects, various tenses, negatives and questions:

Ils avaient été blessés.
They had been injured.

Elles n'ont pas été insultées.
They have not been (were not) insulted. (just on that occasion)

Les enfants seront-ils punis ?
Will the children be punished?

Nous n'aurions pas été battus.
We wouldn't have been beaten.

Les arbres furent abattus.
The trees were knocked down. (once)

Cette décision est prise par le Premier ministre.
This decision is taken by the Prime Minister.

You can see that in this last example we have mentioned the person carrying out the action. This person (it could also be a thing) is technically known as the **agent**. Often in French, the agent, provided that it is a noun, will be preceded by the word **par**:

Ils avaient été blessés par une voiture.
They had been injured by a car.

Elles ont été insultées par les videurs.
They were (have been) insulted by the bouncers.

Les enfants seront punis par le professeur.
The children will be punished by the teacher.

Nous aurions été battus par cette équipe-là.
We would have been beaten by that team.

Les arbres furent abattus par l'orage.
The trees were knocked down by the storm.

[Where the agent is a **pronoun** in English, the above sentence structure is no longer possible.

The mistake was made by her, for example, would best be translated as
C'est elle qui a fait l'erreur.]

However the agent is sometimes preceded by **de**:

a) After a verb expressing a **feeling**:

Cet homme était admiré de tous.
This man was admired by all.

b) When the verb is used in a **non-literal sense**:

Il est écrasé d'impôts.
He is crushed by taxes.

c) When the verb is one of **description**:

Le tapis est couvert de papiers.
The carpet is covered in papers.

◆

The passive is far less commonly used in French than in English and is often avoided in the following ways:

a) By preferring an **active voice**:

Instead of saying

Le facteur est mordu tous les jours par le chien.
The postman is bitten every day by the dog.

we could say

Le chien mord le facteur tous les jours.
The dog bites the postman every day.

It is worth pointing out that although both sentences mean virtually the same, the first places the emphasis on the postman and the second on the dog.

b) By the use of **on** when the agent is not mentioned directly but is **clearly human**:

Instead of saying

Les innocents ne seront pas punis.
The innocent will not be punished.

Les poires ont été vendues.
The pears were (have been) sold.

we could say

> **On ne punira pas les innocents.**
>
> **On a vendu les poires.**

c) By the use of a **pronominal verb**:

Instead of saying

> **Ce livre est vendu dans toutes les librairies.**
> *This book is sold in every bookshop.*

we could say

> **Ce livre se vend dans toutes les librairies.**

Here are some further examples using pronominal verbs:

> **Cela se dit souvent à Paris.**
> *That is often said in Paris.*
>
> **Ces erreurs s'éliminent facilement.**
> *These mistakes are easily eliminated.*
>
> **Cela s'entend.**
> *That is understood.*

◆

It is important to point out that not all English passives can be translated by a French passive. Only the **direct** object of a verb can become the subject of the equivalent passive sentence in French.

> **Le garçon a renversé la bouteille.**
> *The waiter knocked over the bottle.*

Now, we can take the direct object (la bouteille) and make it the subject of a passive sentence:

> **La bouteille a été renversée par le garçon.**
> *The bottle was knocked over by the waiter.*

Compare this with

> **Pierre a téléphoné à Marie.**
> *Pierre rang Marie.*

Now because Marie is an **indirect** object, indicated by **à**, a passive construction is not possible. The sentence *Marie was telephoned by Pierre* **cannot** be translated word for word into French if we wish to use the verb **téléphoner**.

You will have to be very careful when translating into French those sentences where the indirect object is **not** introduced by the word **to**:

The doctor sent the patient's wife a letter **really means** *The doctor sent a letter* **to** *the patient's wife.*

We can take the **direct** object (the letter) and make it the subject of a passive sentence:

> *A letter was sent to the patient's wife by the doctor.*

We can translate this word for word into French:

> **Une lettre a été envoyée à la femme du malade par le docteur.**

However, the sentence

> *The patient's wife was sent a letter by the doctor.*

cannot be treated in the same way as the wife is an **indirect** object – the letter was sent **to** her.

By far the most common way of translating sentences such as these is to use an active verb:

Le docteur a envoyé une lettre à la femme du malade.

Here are some further examples:

Every year the best pupil was given a book by the headmaster.
Tous les ans le directeur donnait un livre au meilleur élève.

You cannot say in French *The best pupil was given …*

The tourist was shown a map of the town by the policeman.
L'agent de police a montré au touriste un plan de la ville.

You cannot say in French *The tourist was shown …*

Further to this point, we draw attention to the following verbs where the person(s) addressed are **indirect objects** introduced by **à**:

- **conseiller** – *to advise*

  Le professeur a conseillé à l'élève de travailler dur.
  The teacher advised the pupil to work hard.

You cannot say in French *The pupil was advised to …*
However, it is possible to have **conseiller** followed by a direct object:

Le professeur a conseillé ses étudiants à propos de leurs examens.
The teacher advised his students regarding their examinations.

We can therefore have the passive sentence:

Les étudiants ont été conseillés par le professeur à propos de leurs examens.
The students were advised by the teacher regarding their examinations.

- **défendre** and **interdire** – *to forbid*

  Elle défend (interdit) aux enfants de jouer dans le jardin.
  She forbids the children to play in the garden.

You cannot say in French *The children are forbidden to …*

- **demander** – *to ask*

  Je vais demander à la femme de se taire.
  I will ask the woman to be silent.

You cannot say in French *The woman will be asked to …*

- **dire** – *to tell*

  Le patron a dit au client de sortir.
  The café owner told the customer to leave.

You cannot say in French *The customer was told to …*

- **ordonner** – *to command, to order*

  Le général a ordonné à ses hommes de se rendre.
  The general ordered his men to surrender.

You cannot say in French *His men were ordered to …*

- **permettre** – *to allow, to let*

Il avait permis à sa fille d'aller à la boum.
He had allowed his daughter to go to the party.

You cannot say in French *His daughter had been allowed to …*

- **promettre** – *to promise*

J'ai promis à mon père de rentrer avant minuit.
I promised my father that I would be back (to be back) by midnight.

You cannot say in French *My father was promised that …*

Let us take a further look at our example with the verb **conseiller**. We can never say, as we can in English, *The pupil was advised to work hard.* We remember that indirect objects cannot become the subject of a passive verb.

In our example we have **the teacher** as our subject. What are we to do when faced with the translation of *The pupil was advised to work hard?* Here, with no particular person mentioned as the advisor, we have no option but to use **on** – **On a conseillé à l'élève de travailler dur**.

If retranslating this sentence into English, we would of course avoid using *one* and simply say, as above, *The pupil was advised to work hard.*

Our following examples will show how this affects the other verbs in the list:

On a défendu (interdit) aux enfants d'écouter à la porte.
The children were forbidden to listen at the door.

On a demandé à la femme de s'asseoir.
The woman was asked to sit down.

On a dit au client de payer sa tournée.
The customer was told to pay his round.

On a ordonné aux touristes de rester à l'hôtel.
The tourists were ordered to stay at the hotel.

On a permis à la jeune fille de sortir avec son petit ami.
The girl was allowed to go out with her boyfriend.

On a promis à mon père que le livre serait rendu.
My father was promised that the book would be returned.

To help you with this topic, which we know many students find difficult, our exercises deal mainly with changing the active voice to the passive voice and vice versa.

TRAIL → 58
page 208

◆ ◆ ◆

→ TRAIL 61

THE PRESENT PARTICIPLE – LE PARTICIPE PRÉSENT

The present participle in English is the part of the verb which ends in **-ing** – *coming, proving, saying* etc.

[NB When dealing with a person's physical position – standing, kneeling, leaning etc – French uses the **past participle**:

Adossés contre le mur, ils regardaient passer les automobiles.
Leaning against the wall, they were watching the cars go by.

Couchée sur l'herbe, elle songeait à l'avenir.
Lying on the grass, she was thinking of the future.]

In every case, the ending of the present participle in French is **-ant** and in almost every case the stem is the **nous** form of the **present** tense without **-ons**. Thus we have **donn**ant, **fin**issant, **pren**ant, **fais**ant, **envoy**ant, **jet**ant.

There are only three exceptions:

être	ét**ant**
avoir	ay**ant**
savoir	sach**ant**

◆

These verb forms are invariable (that is to say they do not change, they take no endings):

Les professeurs étaient là portant **leurs livres.**
The teachers were there carrying their books.

Voulant **se reposer elle a pris une chaise.**
Wishing to rest she took a chair.

J'ai vu beaucoup de jeunes criant **et** riant.
I saw many young people shouting and laughing.

L'épreuve étant **très facile, personne n'a échoué.**
The test being very easy, nobody failed.

Les clients ayant **un chèque-restaurant peuvent manger tout de suite.**
Customers having a luncheon voucher can eat straight away.

Ayant followed by a **past participle** means *having done something*:

Ayant fini **son travail, il est allé au cinéma.**
Having finished his work, he went to the cinema.

Ayant payé **sa consommation, elle s'est assise.**
Having paid for her drink, she sat down.

[We could have conveyed the same meaning using the perfect infinitive:

Après avoir fini … **Après avoir payé** …]

Sachant qu'on avait besoin de lui, il est rentré à la maison.
Knowing that he was needed, he returned home.

◆

Sometimes in English, the present participle is the **subject** of the sentence. In this instance we must use an **infinitive** in French:

Voir c'est croire.
Seeing is believing.

Maîtriser une langue étrangère n'est jamais facile.
Mastering a foreign language is never easy.

Vivre en ville ne me plairait pas.
Living in town would not please me. (I wouldn't like living in town.)

◆

You will often see the present participle preceded by **en**. [You may like to note that this form of the verb is called in English **the gerund** and in French **le gérondif**.] The word **en** translates the English *by*, *while (whilst)*, *in* and *on* as in the following examples:

En travaillant vous ferez des progrès.
***By working** you will make progress.*

Il a pris froid en sortant sans veste.
*He caught cold **by going out** without a jacket.*

En écrivant son essai il écoutait de la musique.
***While writing** his essay, he listened (was listening) to music.*

Il a vu son ami en traversant la place.
*He saw his friend **while crossing** the square.*]

[You will often find **tout en** used to point out that the two actions are simultaneous:

Il a continué de travailler tout en mangeant ses sandwichs.
*He continued working **whilst eating** his sandwiches.*]

En défendant son ami il a fait preuve de beaucoup de courage.
***In (By) defending** his friend he showed great courage.*

En me levant si tard tous les matins je fâchais ma mère.
***In (By) getting up** so late every morning I upset my mother.*

En arrivant chez elle, elle a vu les pompiers.
***On arriving** home she saw the firemen.*

En buvant le vin ils se sont évanouis.
***On drinking** the wine they fainted.*

You will note that in each case the action of the present participle preceded by **en** is done by the subject of the sentence.

Il a vu son amie en revenant du marché.
He saw his friend coming back from the market.

We have deliberately offered here a translation which is confusing. However there is no confusion in the French. Here *he* is the person coming back from the market. If we omit the word **en** (**Il a vu son amie revenant du marché**), *she* is the one on her way back.

If we wish in English to avoid any misunderstanding, we would perhaps say: *As he was coming back from the market, he saw his friend.*

[Note that this rule may be broken in a set expression such as:

L'appétit vient en mangeant.
The more you have, the more you want.]

There are also occasions where **en** is used in French where in English we do not require *by*, *while*, *in* or *on*. This is so when the present participle expresses an action done at the same time as another verb and **draws attention to the manner in which this verb is carried out**:

Il a répondu en riant.
He replied laughing.

Elle est partie en pleurant.
She left weeping.

Ils sont entrés en criant.
They entered shouting.

◆

The present participle forms we have met so far have been verbs and have remained unchanged in their spelling. Often the same form may be used as an adjective and here the **rules of agreement** will be applied. As in our section on the adjective, we will use **bold green** and roman green to indicate **masculine** and feminine forms respectively:

un roman **intéressant** (*an interesting novel*) ; une histoire intéressante (*an interesting story*) ; des romans **intéressants** ; des histoires intéressantes

We give below some further examples of these adjectival forms:

une apparition saisissante (*a striking vision*) ; des nouvelles surprenantes (*surprising news*) ; des édifices **imposants** (*impressive buildings*) ; des hommes **charmants** (*charming men*)

How are we to tell whether we are dealing with a **verbal** use of the present participle, where it will remain invariable, or the **adjectival** use where agreement is required?

Here are some guidelines:

a) If the participle has an **object**, it is a **verb**:

Les femmes aimant **la boxe sont peu nombreuses.**
Women with a liking for boxing are few and far between.

b) If the participle is **negative**, it is a **verb**:

Elle se promenait, ne songeant **à rien de précis.**
She was walking, not thinking of anything in particular.

c) If the participle is a **pronominal** form it is a **verb**:

Elle restait là, se demandant **pourquoi son mari n'était pas arrivé.**
She stayed there, wondering why her husband had not arrived.

d) If the participle could be **replaced by qui** (*who, which*) **and a verb**, it is a **verb**:

J'ai vu des chiens courant **(qui couraient) à travers la forêt.**
I saw dogs running (which were running) through the forest.

e) If the participle **describes** a **noun** or a **pronoun**, it is an **adjective**:

Ils sont amusants.
They are funny.

Nos amies étaient accueillantes.
Our friends were welcoming (hospitable).

Attention aux trottoirs glissants !
Watch out for slippery pavements!

Sometimes you may find a participle acting as an adjective coming before the noun:

Il a pris une étonnante **décision.**
He took an astonishing decision.

◆

To end this section we must point out that the present participles of some verbs, whilst retaining the same pronunciation, have a different spelling when they are used as adjectives. Among these are **fatiguer, fatiguant,** fatigant; **communiquer communiquant,** communicant:

Ce cours fatiguant **tous les étudiants, le professeur a décidé de s'arrêter.**
As this lesson was tiring all the pupils, the teacher decided to stop.

Elle a reçu une lettre communiquant **le désespoir de son amie.**
She received a letter communicating her friend's despair.

But:

un travail fatigant (*tiring work*); **une journée** fatigante (*a tiring day*); **un couloir** communicant (*a connecting corridor*); **une porte** communicante (*a connecting door*).

TRAIL → 62
page 210

→ TRAIL 23

Until now, we have only used the most common negative **ne (n') ... pas**, about which we will mention some further points before moving on to other negative words.

First, a little revision. As you will remember, with the one-word tenses, **ne** and **pas** surround the verb:

Je n'aime pas regarder la télévision.
I don't like watching television.

Elle ne jouait pas au tennis.
She wasn't playing tennis.

Je ne voudrais pas vous déranger.
I wouldn't want to disturb you.

Mes collègues ne feront pas grève.
My colleagues won't strike.

Sa copine ne vint pas à la maison.
His girlfriend didn't come to the house.

You will note once more the position of **ne** when there is an object pronoun before the verb:

Elle ne les aime pas.
She doesn't like them.

Nous n'y allons pas.
We aren't going there.

Papa ne le fera pas.
Dad won't do it.

Ne leur en donnez pas !
Don't give them any!

We must also point out the position of **ne** and **pas** with negative questions (they cannot split words joined by hyphens):

Ne partez-vous pas ?
Aren't you leaving?

N'a-t-il pas d'argent ?
Hasn't he any money?

Ne viendront-ils pas ce soir ?
Won't they come this evening?

In the compound tenses, **ne** and **pas** surround the auxiliary verb (**pas** NEVER follows the past participle):

Maman n'est pas encore arrivée.
Mum hasn't arrived yet.

Nous ne sommes pas rentrés avant minuit.
We didn't get back before midnight.

Mon professeur n'avait pas dit au revoir.
My teacher hadn't said goodbye.

Mon père n'aurait pas permis à ma sœur de sortir.
My father wouldn't have allowed my sister to go out.

Again you will remember that where there are object pronouns, these will always follow **ne** and stand immediately before the auxiliary verb:

Je ne les ai pas vus.
I haven't seen them.

L'automobiliste ne s'était pas arrêté.
The car driver hadn't stopped.

Ne le lui a-t-elle pas envoyé ?
Didn't she send it to him (her)?

Elle n'y aurait pas pensé.
She wouldn't have thought of it.

We can now move on to our further points.

◆

- **making an infinitive negative**

Here *Hamlet* will be of use:
'To be or not to be'
« **Être ou ne pas être ... »**

As you can see, **ne** and **pas** now stand together before the infinitive. We give some more examples to illustrate the point:

Elle a décidé de ne pas partir.
She has decided not to leave.

Le médecin lui a conseillé de ne pas fumer.
The doctor advised him (her) not to smoke.

Je me suis décidé à ne pas le voir.
I made up my mind not to see him.

(Note the position of the object pronoun – immediately before the **verb of which it is the object**.)

Je préfère ne pas rester.
I prefer not to stay.

Il croit ne pas pouvoir sortir.
He believes he can't go out.

Il peut ne pas arriver à l'heure.
He may not arrive on time.

This word order also applies to the perfect infinitive, where the auxiliary verb (**être** or **avoir**) is in the infinitive:

Je regrette de ne pas avoir compris.
I'm sorry not to have understood. I'm sorry I didn't understand.

Elle était contente de ne pas l'avoir vu.
She was happy not to have seen him.

(Note the position of the object pronoun.)

Elle s'est excusée de ne pas s'être levée à mon arrivée.
She apologised for not having got up when I arrived.

However, another word order is possible with the perfect infinitive:

Je regrette de n'avoir pas compris.

Elle était contente de ne l'avoir pas vu.

Elle s'est excusée de ne s'être pas levée à mon arrivée.

◆

- **pas un, pas une** – *not one*

    Le professeur a posé sa question aux jeunes filles. Pas une n'a répondu.
    The teacher put his question to the girls. Not one of them replied. (**Ne** comes in its normal position.)

    Malgré les pertes, de nos soldats, pas un ne reculera.
    Despite the losses, of our soldiers, not a single one will retreat.

◆

- **pas de ...** – *no* **+ noun**

    J'ai perdu la clef de ma chambre. – Pas de problème.
    I've lost the key to my room. – No problem.

This is a frequently used shortened form of **il n'y a pas de problème**.

    J'arrive à l'école. Pas d'enfants !
    I arrive at school. No children!

- **pas de** is frequently used with **quoi** as in the following example:

    Merci beaucoup, monsieur. – Pas de quoi.
    Thank you very much, sir. – Think nothing of it. (Don't mention it.)

This is the short form of:

    Il n'y a pas de quoi me remercier.
    There is no reason to thank me.

◆

- **ne ... plus** – *no longer, not any longer, no more, not any more*

    Après sa maladie, il ne sort plus.
    After his illness, he no longer goes out.

    Mes amis ne sont plus revenus.
    My friends didn't come back any more.

    Mon père aurait voulu ne plus travailler à la banque.
    My father would have liked not to work at the bank any more.

    'Le Figaro', s'il vous plaît. – Désolé, monsieur, plus de journaux.
    'The Figaro', please. – Sorry, sir, no papers left.

As you can see, the word order with **ne ... plus** is the same as with **ne ... pas**.

[**Plus** is frequently used in combination with **non** to mean *neither do I, we, they* etc:

    Je n'aime pas cet homme-là. – Moi non plus. Et mes amis non plus.

    I don't like that man. Me neither. (Nor do I.) And neither do my friends.]

◆

• **ne ... rien** – *nothing, not anything*

> **Papa ne dit rien.**
> *Dad says nothing.*

> **Les hommes politiques n'avaient rien fait.**
> *The politicians hadn't done anything.*

> **Le pauvre enfant a choisi de ne rien manger.**
> *The poor child has chosen not to eat anything.*

Again, you will note that **ne ... rien** follows the same word order as **ne ... pas**, but **rien** can also act as the subject of a sentence:

> **Rien ne me fait peur.**
> *Nothing scares me.*

> **Rien n'a bougé.**
> *Nothing moved.*

Ne remains in its usual position.

Rien can also be used as a single-word reply:

> **Qu'est-ce que tu cherches ? – Rien.**
> *What are you looking for? – Nothing.*

We must point out that when **rien**, like **quelque chose**, is linked to an adjective, **de** is required:

> **Quoi de neuf ? – Rien de neuf.**
> *What's new? – Nothing new.*

> **Il n'a rien fait de bon.**
> *He has done nothing good.*

◆

• **ne ... jamais** – *never, not ever*

> **Elle ne vient jamais nous voir.**
> *She never comes to see us.*

> **Ils ne s'étaient jamais promenés dans la vieille ville.**
> *They had never walked through the old town.*

> **Il a décidé de ne jamais répondre à mes questions.**
> *He has decided never to answer my questions.*

If we wish to stress the idea of *never*, we can place **jamais** at the start of the sentence:

> **Jamais je ne partirai sans elle !**
> *Never will I leave without her!*

As with **rien**, **ne** remains in its usual position.

Jamais can also be used as a single-word reply:

> **Vous le ferez, n'est-ce pas ? – Jamais !**
> *You'll do it, won't you? – Never!*

◆

- **ne ... personne** – *nobody, not anybody, no one, not anyone*

    Je ne connais personne ici.
    I don't know anybody here.

    Elle n'a vu personne.
    She has seen nobody. (**Personne** is placed after the past participle.)

    Il est triste de n'inviter personne à la maison.
    It is sad not to invite anyone to the house. (Again, note the position of **personne** in relation to the infinitive.)

Personne can also act as the subject of the sentence:

    Personne ne vous empêche d'y aller.
    Nobody is stopping you from going there.

    Personne n'est venu.
    Nobody came.

(**Personne** as the subject of the sentence is masculine. Of course, **une personne** meaning *a person* is a feminine noun.)

Personne can also be used as a single-word reply:

    Qui avez-vous rencontré ? – Personne.
    Who(m) did you meet? – No one.

Where the verb requires an indirect object, you will also find **personne** introduced by the preposition **à**:

    Il n'écrit à personne.
    He doesn't write to anybody.

    Elle n'a téléphoné à personne.
    She didn't ring anyone.

Like **rien**, when **personne** is linked to an adjective, **de** is required:

    Je n'ai trouvé personne d'agréable à la réunion.
    I didn't find anyone nice at the meeting.

◆

- **ne ... que** – *only*

    L'école ne prend que les enfants les plus doués.
    The school takes only / only takes the most gifted children.

[It is, of course, possible to say here:
L'école prend seulement les enfants les plus doués.]

    Papa ne nous a donné que dix euros.
    Dad only gave us ten euros.

It is important to note here the position of **que** after the past participle. The use of **only** implies a restriction. In French, **que** is placed before that which is restricted. Let us consider this sentence:

    He only offered to give us one photo.
    Il n'a offert de nous donner qu'une photo.

The restriction here is the single photo, so **que** immediately precedes it. Consequently, **que** is often positioned at some distance from **ne**:

Il **ne** peut aller la voir à la maison de retraite **que** le mardi.
He can only go to see her at the home on Tuesdays.

Sometimes the restriction may be a condition:

Je **ne** vais réserver des places pour 'Le Malade Imaginaire' mercredi prochain **que** si vous m'envoyez de l'argent.
I'll only book seats for 'The Hypochondriac' next Wednesday if you send me some money. (An alternative translation, exactly matching the French, would be: I'll book seats for 'The Hypochondriac' next Wednesday only if you send me some money.)

The position of **que** relative to the infinitive follows the same pattern, preceding the restriction:

Le médecin lui a conseillé de **ne** travailler **que** deux jours par semaine.
The doctor advised him to work only two days a week.

Ne faire que + an **infinitive** translates the English *merely*:

Tu lui poses une question. Il **ne** fait **que** répondre non.
You ask him a question. He merely says no. (All he says is no. All he does is say no.)

Je **ne** fais **qu'**espérer qu'elle va toujours bien.
I only hope she's still OK.

[NB Where *only* restricts the subject of the sentence, **ne ... que** cannot be used:
Only non-smokers are allowed in.
Seuls les non-fumeurs sont admis.]

◆

- **ne ... ni ... ni ...** – *neither ... nor ...*

Je **ne** connais **ni** le père **ni** le fils.
I know neither the father nor the son.

Elle **n'**a vu **ni** le voleur **ni** son complice.
She saw neither the thief nor his accomplice.

Sometimes, you will see **ni ... ni ...** followed by nouns without articles when no specific noun is referred to:

Cet élève **n'**a **ni** cahier **ni** stylo.
This pupil hasn't got an exercise book or a pen.

Il **ne** portait **ni** chemise **ni** pantalon.
He was wearing neither shirt nor trousers.

When **ni ... ni ...** is used with two singular subjects of a sentence, the verb, unlike in English, may be singular or plural. Thus:

Ni l'un **ni** l'autre **ne** répond / **ne** répondent.
Neither the one nor the other answers.

Ni l'un **ni** l'autre **n'**a parlé / **n'**ont parlé.
Neither the one nor the other spoke / has spoken.

Ni lui **ni** elle **ne** refusera / **ne** refuseront.
Neither he nor she will refuse.

Where there is a plural subject, there is no choice:

Ni le professeur **ni** les élèves **n'**étaient contents.
Neither the teacher nor the pupils were happy.

[*Either … or …* is translated by **ou … ou …**:

Ou il t'a parlé ou il ne t'a pas parlé.
Either he spoke to you or he didn't (speak to you).]

◆

- **ne … aucun / aucune** – *not one, not at all* – a strong negative

In this negative, **aucun** is an adjective and will agree with its noun. As in our section on the adjective, we will use **bold green** and roman green respectively to distinguish between masculine and feminine.

Il n'y avait aucun doute.
There was no doubt. (There wasn't a single doubt. There was no doubt at all.)

[This is a stronger version of
Il n'y avait pas de doute.]

Je n'ai aucune envie de les voir.
I have no wish to see them.

Aucun(e) can accompany the subject of the sentence:

Aucun candidat ne se présenta.
Not a single candidate turned up. (Not one candidate …)

Aucune erreur ne sera tolérée.
No mistake at all will be tolerated.

Aucun(e) may also stand as a pronoun as a one-word answer:

Vous avez eu des problèmes ? – Aucun.
Did you have any problems? – Not one. (None.)

A-t-il vendu des maisons aujourd'hui ? – Aucune.
Did he sell any houses today? – Not a single one. (None.)

◆

- **ne … nulle part** – *nowhere, not anywhere*

Je ne les trouve nulle part.
I can't find them anywhere.

Nous ne l'avons vu nulle part.
We didn't see him anywhere.

(As you can see, **nulle part** is placed after the past participle.)

Nulle part can stand as a reply on its own:

Vous les avez trouvés, n'est-ce pas ? – Nulle part.
You found them, didn't you? – Nowhere.

◆

Negatives in combination

At the end of this section, for ease of reference, we give a table showing the word order when two negative words are used together. However, we feel that the best way to learn how these words combine is to study, and especially to listen to and repeat aloud, the example sentences. We will use examples of negatives with both simple and compound tenses:

- **ne ... plus, jamais, rien**

  Il n'y a plus rien **à faire.**
  *There is **nothing more** to do / to be done.*

  Il n'a plus rien **dit.**
  *He didn't say **anything more / else**.*

  Elle ne retournera plus jamais **dans cette ville.**
  *She will **never** go back **again** to that town.*

  Elle n'est plus jamais **retournée dans cette ville.**
  *She **never** went back to that town **again**.*

  (Also possible are: **Elle** ne retournera jamais plus **dans cette ville. Elle** n'est jamais plus **retournée dans cette ville.**)

  Ces garçons-là ne font jamais rien **pour nous aider.**
  *Those boys **never** do **anything** to help us.*

  Ces garçons-là n'ont jamais rien **fait pour nous aider.**
  *Those boys have **never** done **anything** to help us.*

  Elle ne dira plus jamais rien.
  *She will **never** say **anything any more**.*

  Elle n'a plus jamais rien **dit.**
  *She **never** said **anything else**.*

You will note that in English there is only **one negative word** in each sentence – *nothing, not, never*.

– Now we add **personne** to the above:

  Il n'y a plus personne **à la maison.**
  *There's **no one left** in the house. (There is **no longer anyone** at home.)*

  Je n'ai plus vu personne.
  *I didn't see **anyone any more**. (I **no longer** saw **anyone**.)*

  Je ne dirai rien à personne.
  *I will **not** say **anything** to **anyone**. (I will say **nothing to anybody**.)*

  Je n'ai rien dit à personne.
  *I said **nothing to anybody**. (I haven't said **anything to anyone**.)*

  Vous ne trouverez jamais personne **pour réparer cette voiture-là.**
  *You'll **never** find **anyone** to repair that car.*

  Nous n'avons jamais trouvé personne **qui parle le russe aussi bien qu'elle.**
  *We have **never** found **anyone** who speaks Russian as well as she does.*

– Here are some further possible combinations of negatives:

  Il n'y a pas que **toi.**
  *You're **not** the **only one**. (There is **not only** you.)*

  Il n'y a plus que **lui.**
  *He's the **only one left**.*

  Ils n'ont plus ni **chien ni chat.**
  *They **no longer** have a dog **or** a cat.*

  Mon arrière-grand-père n'avait jamais lu ni **un roman ni un poème.**
  *My great-grandfather had **never** read **either** a novel **or** a poem.*

Elle ne **boit** pas **de gin** ni **de whisky.**
She doesn't drink gin or whisky.

Elle n'a jamais **mangé de viande** ni **de poisson.**
*She has **never** eaten **either** meat **or** fish.*

Nous n'avons plus aucun **espoir.**
*We **no longer** have **any** hope **at all**.*

Elles n'avaient jamais eu aucune **intention de venir.**
*They had **never** had **any** intention of coming.*

Je ne **le trouve** plus nulle part.
*I **can't** find him **anywhere any more**.*

– Combinations where one negative word stands at the head of the sentence:

Rien n'est jamais **facile.**
***Nothing** is **ever** easy.*

Jamais **je** ne **retournerai** plus **dans cette boîte !**
***Never** will I go to that night club **again**!*

Ni **l'un** ni **l'autre** n'est jamais **arrivé à l'heure /** ne **sont** jamais **arrivés à l'heure.**
***Neither** one **nor** the other has **ever** arrived on time.*

Aucun **employé** n'aura jamais **l'autorisation de partir avant quatre heures.**
***No** employee will **ever** have permission to leave before four o'clock.*

Aucune **d'elles** n'en **parlera** jamais à personne.
***Not one** of them will **ever** tell **anyone** about it.*

Personne ne **mangera** plus jamais rien **dans ce restaurant !**
***No one** will **ever** eat **anything again** in this restaurant!*

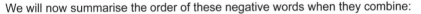

We will now summarise the order of these negative words when they combine:

	aucun(e)
	jamais *
	rien
ne ... plus	**personne**
	ni ... ni ...
	que
	aucun(e)
	rien
ne ... jamais	**personne**
	ni ... ni ...
	que
ne ... rien	**que**

* **jamais plus** is also possible

The sense of the negative is often introduced by **sans** (without):

Il est parti sans **faire de bruit.**
*He left **without** making **any** noise.* (You will recognise here the use of **de**, the form of the partitive article which normally follows a negative.)

Sans is often found in combination with other negatives:

Papa est entré sans rien **dire.**
*Dad came in **without** saying **anything**.*

L'élève écoutait attentivement sans jamais **faire de progrès.**
*The pupil would listen attentively **without ever** making progress.*

J'ai quitté l'église sans **voir** personne.
*I left the church **without** seeing **anybody**.*

« Sans aucun **doute », a-t-il répondu.**
*'**No** doubt,' he replied.*

Il a dit au revoir sans aucune **explication.**
*He said goodbye **with no** explanation.*

Il est arrivé à la gare sans **billet** ni **passeport.**
*He arrived at the station **without** ticket **or** passport.*

◆

We will close this section with reference to two negatives which you will meet less often.

- **ne ... guère** – *hardly, scarcely*

  Cela ne **se dit** guère **de nos jours.**
  That is hardly said these days.

  Elle n'a guère **d'amies.**
  She has hardly any friends.

- **Ne ... point**, which used to be regarded as a strong version of **ne ... pas**, is now seen as literary, archaic or regional.

It is perfectly possible to stress **ne ... pas** by the addition of **du tout**:

Elle n'est pas du tout **contente.**
She is not at all happy.

Pas du tout may stand alone:

Tu y vois un inconvénient ? – Pas du tout.
Do you see any problem here? – Not at all.

TRAIL → 24
page 210

→ TRAIL 3

▶ TECHNICAL TERMS

Noun – a naming word: a word used to name a person, place or thing. For example, the words *glass, tiger, courage* and *Belgium* are nouns.

Abstract noun – by contrast with **concrete** nouns (those recognised through the senses) such as *wind, scent, flavour, tree, tune,* **abstract** nouns are appreciated intellectually: *courage, evil, goodness, silence, knowledge.*

Definite article – the word *the.*

Indefinite article – *a* or *an.*

Partitive article – *some* or *any.* The first syllable of the word **partitive** indicates its meaning. We are dealing with a **part** of something or **some** of a quantity – *some cake, some cakes.*

Gender – whether a noun is grammatically masculine or feminine. (The neuter gender, which exists for example in German and Latin, is not found in French.)

Preposition – a word which indicates the position of one person or thing relative to another in time or space. *In, on, under, before, in front of, after, without, for* are examples of prepositions. Often in French a preposition will have no specific meaning: **Ce travail est facile** à **faire.** – *This work is easy to do.* Nevertheless its use here is grammatically necessary.

GENDER – LE GENRE

The gender of a noun in French generally follows that of the Latin noun from which it is derived. Masculine nouns in Latin tend to be masculine in French and feminine nouns tend to be feminine. Neuter nouns in Latin became, by and large, masculine in French, except for those which were more frequently used in their plural rather than their singular form. As this plural form ended in **-a** – eg *folia, arma* – these nouns were frequently mistaken for feminine singular nouns and have become feminine in French – une feuille (*leaf*), une arme (*weapon*).

In this section on gender, and in the section on the adjective, we will use **bold green** and roman green text to indicate masculine and feminine respectively.

In French, the gender of the noun determines which article we must use with it. As there are only a few occasions where a noun may appear without an article, it is essential to learn the gender of a noun in French. Therefore it is not sufficient to learn that **tasse** means *cup* and **tapis** means *carpet.* We have to learn that it is la tasse (or une tasse), **le tapis** (or **un tapis**). Naturally it would make little sense to learn **l'armoire** (*cupboard*) or **l'hôtel** as this would not remind you of the gender – rather we should learn une armoire and **un hôtel.**

85

The rules which you will find in most French grammars regarding the gender of nouns are subject to so many exceptions that they are of very little practical use. So: **ALWAYS LEARN THE GENDER AS YOU LEARN THE NOUN**.

Nevertheless, we can offer some hints regarding gender.

You probably know already that in French there is **le livre** (book) and la livre (pound – both in weight and in money). A special note should be made of the following nouns:

le manche *handle*

la manche *sleeve*

la Manche *the English Channel*

le mort *dead man*

la mort *death*

le poêle *stove*

la poêle *frying pan*

le poste *position* (job) / *set* (radio or television)

la poste *post office*

le somme *nap*

la somme *sum* (of money)

le tour *turn* (as in *my turn*) / *trick* / *walk* (as in **faire un tour** *to go for a walk*)

la tour – *tower*

le voile – *veil*

la voile – *sail* (of a boat)

Listening to the following sentences will help you to remember the genders of these nouns:

Il a saisi le manche **de son balai.**
He grabbed the handle of his brush.

Elle a déchiré la manche **de son manteau.**
She tore the sleeve of her coat.

Le premier homme à traverser la Manche **à la nage s'appelait Matthew Webb.**
(NB **M majuscule** *capital M*)
The first man to swim across the Channel was called Matthew Webb.

Le détective a trouvé le mort **derrière le canapé.**
The detective found the dead man behind the sofa.

« La mort **n'est pas la fin », dit le curé.**
'Death is not the end,' said the priest.

Ne mets pas la main sur le poêle, **mon petit.**
Don't put your hand on the stove, my boy.

Je vais faire une omelette. Passe-moi la poêle.
I'm going to make an omelette. Pass me the frying pan.

Il a perdu le poste **de directeur l'année dernière.**
He lost the position of director last year.

Je vais acheter des timbres à la poste.
I'm going to buy some stamps at the post office.

Le somme **de l'après-midi fait du bien.**
The afternoon nap does you good.

Un million d'euros par an ! La somme **est énorme comme salaire !**
A million euros a year! It's an enormous sum of money as a salary!

Il a fait le tour de la ville à vélo.
He cycled round the town.

Elle est allée voir la tour Eiffel.
She went to see the Eiffel Tower.

On ne voit plus le voile islamique au lycée en France.
The Muslim veil isn't seen any more in French schools.

La voile **triangulaire s'appelle le spinnaker.**
The triangular sail is called the spinnaker.

◆

We can offer guidance for certain categories of nouns.

Gender determined by meaning

* **always masculine**

Days of the week (NB no capital letters) – dimanche, mercredi etc

Months (NB no capital letters) – février, juillet, août etc

Seasons (NB no capital letters) – le printemps, l'été, l'automne, l'hiver

Languages (NB no capital letter) – le français, le latin

Names of trees and metals – le chêne (*oak*), le saule (*willow*) (but une aubépine – *hawthorn*), l'or (*gold*), l'argent (*silver*), le bronze

Names of colours – le rouge, le noir

* **always feminine**

Names of sciences – la physique, la chimie, la biologie, l'astronomie

Names of shops ending in **-erie** – la boulangerie, l'épicerie, la papeterie (*stationer's*), la quincaillerie (*ironmonger's*, *hardware shop*), la boucherie, la charcuterie (*pork butcher's*)

Gender determined by ending

* **generally masculine** (exceptions in brackets):

-age – le voyage, le village (la page, l'image, la cage, la rage *rabies*, la nage, la plage; there are a few other exceptions here, but you are unlikely to meet them)

-(e)au – le bureau, le seau *bucket* (l'eau, la peau *skin*), le joyau *jewel*, le noyau *fruit stone, nucleus*

-et – le paquet *parcel*, le billet *ticket, banknote*

-isme – le journalisme, le réalisme

-ment – le mouvement, le monument (la jument *mare*)

-oir – le soir, le loir *dormouse*

-phone – le téléphone, le xylophone

* **generally feminine** (exceptions in brackets):

-aison – la saison *season*, la raison *reason*

-ance, -ence – l'assistance, la chance *luck*, la prudence *caution*, la patience (**le silence**)

-ée – la soirée, la rentrée *return, start of term* (**le lycée**, **le musée** *museum*; again there are a few other exceptions)

-esse – la sagesse *wisdom*, la richesse *wealth*, la politesse *politeness*

-ette – la serviette *towel, briefcase*, la raquette *racket* (**le squelette** *skeleton*)

-ie – la partie *part*, la démocratie (**le génie** *genius*, **l'incendie** *fire*, **le parapluie** *umbrella*)

-tion – la question, la station *underground station* (**le bastion** *rampart, strong supporter*)

-té – la qualité, la liberté

-tude – la solitude, l'habitude *custom, habit*

-ure – la fermeture *closure*, la piqûre *injection, sting* (**le murmure**)

◆

People and animals

Nouns naming persons or animals of the male sex are almost always masculine. However certain nouns which may refer to either sex are always feminine in gender:

la victime *victim*

la personne *person*

la dupe *dupe* (informally *mug*)

la sentinelle *sentry*

la recrue *recruit*

la vedette *star* (of stage or screen)

la brute *brute, tyrant*

◆

Places

Nouns referring to places or geographical features are never easy – we ourselves have to check their gender quite often.

- **countries**

These are generally feminine if they end in an **-e**:

la France, l'Angleterre, l'Écosse *Scotland*, l'Allemagne *Germany*, la Grèce, l'Italie, la Belgique

Some exceptions are: **le Mexique**, **le Cambodge** *Cambodia*, **le Zaïre**, **le Zimbabwe**

The others are masculine:

le Portugal, **le Japon**, **le Canada**, **le Brésil**, **l'Afghanistan**, **le Vietnam**

- **regions of France**

Regions ending in an **-e** are feminine: la Bretagne, la Normandie, la Provence, la Picardie, la Bourgogne *Burgundy*

Masculine regions include: **le Languedoc**, **le Limousin**, **le Poitou**, **le Jura**, **le Roussillon**

[Most counties in Great Britain and Ireland are masculine:

Il vient de passer quinze jours dans le Yorkshire.
He's just spent a fortnight in Yorkshire.

Exception: Cornouailles *Cornwall* – is feminine.

Il y a bien des raisons pour aller en Cornouailles.
There are many reasons for going to Cornwall.]

- **towns**

Here the gender is not fixed. However if the name ends in an **-e**, the tendency is to consider it feminine:

Boulogne **est petite**, Dieppe **est belle**, **mais** Paris **est grand**.

We are, of course, more likely to hear:

Boulogne est une petite ville ; **Dieppe est une belle ville** ; **Paris est une grande ville.**

- **mountains and rivers**

Once more the gender is not fixed:

le Jura, le Caucase *Caucasus*, les Alpes, les Rocheuses *Rockies*

la Seine, la Loire, la Tamise *Thames*, l'Amazone, **le Rhône**, **le Rhin**, **le Nil**, **le Mississippi**, **le Pô**

◆

FORMING THE PLURALS OF NOUNS

Some French nouns are found only in the plural – **les environs** *surroundings*, **les gens** *people*, **les mœurs** *customs*, *habits*.

The general rule, as in English, is simply to add an **-s** – **un arbre**, **des** arbres; **le camping**, **les** campings.

However:

- Nouns ending in **-s**, **-x** and **-z** do not change in the plural – **un bras**, **des** bras; **une voix** *voice*, **des** voix; **le gaz**, **les** gaz.
- Nouns ending in **-eau**, **-au**, **-eu** form their plurals by adding **-x** – **un bateau**, **des** bateaux; **un joyau**, **des** joyaux; **un cheveu**, **des** cheveux. Exception: **un pneu** *tyre*, **des** pneus.

Nouns ending in **-al** form their plurals by changing the **-al** to **-aux** – **le journal**, **les** journaux; **le cheval**, **les** chevaux; **un hôpital**, **des** hôpitaux; **un animal**, **des** animaux. Some exceptions are: **un bal** *dance*, *ball*, **des** bals; **un carnaval**, **des** carnavals; **un festival**, **des** festivals.

- Nouns ending in **-ail** form their plurals by changing **-ail** to **-aux** – **un travail** *work*, **des** travaux; **un vitrail** *stained glass window*, **des** vitraux; **un soupirail** *cellar window*, **des** soupiraux; **le corail** *coral*, **les** coraux. BUT **un éventail** *fan* (for fanning the face), **des** éventails; **un portail** *portal*, *large door* or *gate*, **des** portails.
- Nouns ending in **-ou** generally add an **-s** – **un trou** *hole*, **des** trous – but there are seven which add an **-x** – **le bijou** *jewel*, **les** bijoux; **le caillou** *pebble*, **les** cailloux; **le chou** *cabbage*, **les** choux; **le genou** *knee*, **les** genoux; **le hibou** *owl*, **les** hiboux; **le joujou** *toy*, **les** joujoux; **le pou** *louse*, **les** poux *lice*.

The difficulty with compound nouns

It is not easy to give hard-and-fast rules about compound nouns. However, we can say that only those parts which are nouns or adjectives are made plural:

le chou-fleur – **les choux-fleurs** – *cauliflower*

la belle-mère – **les belles-mères** – *stepmother, mother-in-law*

le rouge-gorge – **les rouges-gorges** – *robin*

un sourd-muet – **des sourds-muets** – *deaf-mute*

Any part which is a verb, preposition or adverb will not change:

le tire-bouchon – **les tire-bouchons** – *corkscrew*

un garde-robe – **des garde-robes** – *wardrobe*

une arrière-pensée – **des arrière-pensées** – *afterthought*

un bien-pensant – **des bien-pensants** – *conformist*

un avant-coureur – **des avant-coureurs** – *forerunner*

But:

un porte-monnaie – **des porte-monnaie** – *purse*

un chasse-neige – **des chasse-neige** – *snowplough*

un pis-aller – **des pis-aller** – *last resort*

A few final points on plural nouns:

Note the following:

un œil – **des yeux** – *eye*

le ciel – **les cieux** (also **ciels**) – *sky*

(le) monsieur – **(les) messieurs**

madame – mesdames

mademoiselle – mesdemoiselles

Unlike English, names of families do not add an **-s** – **les Martin, les Chirac**.

TRAIL → 4
page 212

→ TRAIL 15

THE DEFINITE ARTICLE – L'ARTICLE DÉFINI (LE, LA, L', LES)

We will begin this section by stressing one aspect of the definite article which we have found to be a source of frequent error.

While we can happily say **à la** and **à l'**:

Elle est allée à la piscine.
She went to the baths.

Nous allons tous les dimanches à l'église.
We go every Sunday to church.

we do **not** use **à** with **le** or **les** before a noun. Here we have the contracted forms **au** and **aux**:

Veux-tu aller au cinéma ?
Do you want to go to the cinema?

Mes parents sont allés aux magasins.
My parents went to the shops.

Similarly, we may freely use **de la** and **de l'**:

En rentrant de la gare elle a vu son amie.
On returning from the station she saw her friend.

La porte de l'hôtel était fermée.
The hotel door was closed.

However we do **not** use **de** with **le** or **les** before a noun. We use instead the contracted forms **du** and **des**:

Les professeurs du collège sont en grève.
The teachers at the school are on strike.

Il est rentré des États-Unis.
He has come back from the United States.

[You **will** find **à + le**, **à + les**, **de + le** and **de + les** before an infinitive where **le** and **les** are **not** definite articles but personal pronouns:

Elle a commencé à le comprendre.
She began to understand him / it.

Nous sommes prêts à les recevoir.
We are ready to welcome them.

Elle a décidé de le voir.
She decided to see him.

Nous avons essayé de les contacter.
We tried to contact them.]

◆

French often uses the definite article (**le, la, l'** and **les**) where we will not find it in English.

a) Making a **general statement** about a noun:

Imagine that you are studying the wine list in a Parisian restaurant. You might well be tempted to say to the waiter:

Le vin est cher !

You would mean by this *The wine is expensive!*

The translation from English to French will cause no difficulty here – it is word for word.

Now suppose that you wish to make a statement about wine as a commodity. You would say *Wine is expensive*. Our previous method of word-for-word translation will not do. We are obliged to say once again **Le vin est cher**.

We need to be aware that French uses a definite article when making a **general comment** about a noun. Of course you may argue that not all wines are expensive. Here the speaker is not concerned with any particular wine but is making a global statement:

Les hommes sont plus grands que les femmes.
Men are taller than women.

J'aime les frites mais je déteste les chips.
I like chips but I hate crisps.

Le tabac t'abat.
Smoking (Tobacco) kills you.

L'argent ne fait pas le bonheur.
Money doesn't bring happiness.

L'eau est bonne pour la santé.
Water is good for your health.

As we have seen with **le bonheur** and **la santé** in the last two examples, exactly the same rule applies when dealing with **abstract** nouns:

Il nous faut réprimer l'ivresse.
We must put an end to drunkenness.

La sagesse est lente à venir.
Wisdom comes slowly.

La haine est toujours une émotion destructrice.
Hatred is always a destructive emotion.

J'adore la solitude le week-end après une semaine au bureau.
I love being alone at the weekend after a week at the office.

b) With the names of **countries** and **regions**:

la Suède *Sweden*, **le Portugal, la Normandie, l'Europe**

La Norvège est un très joli pays.
Norway is a very pretty country.

Le Canada est plus grand que le Japon.
Canada is bigger than Japan.

La Bretagne a beaucoup de ports de pêche.
Brittany has many fishing ports.

You will find a few exceptions to this rule. For example:

Israël a été fondé en 1948.
Israel was founded in 1948.

If we are talking about going *to* or being *in* a country, it is important to learn its gender. Feminine countries have **en** and no article, masculine countries for the most part retain the definite article:

Il va en Espagne.
He is going to Spain.

Elle travaille en Ecosse.
She works in Scotland.

Ils vont au Pays de Galles.
They are going to Wales.

Elles travaillent aux États-Unis.
They work in the United States.

(**au** and **aux** are the contracted forms of **à + le** and **à + les**)

Exceptions: **en** Israël, **en** Irak

c) With the names of **peoples** and **languages**:

We use the definite article in English with nouns of nationality where the noun does not end in a single **-s**. Thus we say *the French, the Irish*, but *Norwegians, Germans*. Of course with some nationalities we have a choice – *the Spanish* or *Spaniards*. French **always uses the definite article**:

people: **les Français, les Allemands** *Germans* (note the capitals)

languages: **le français, l'allemand** (no capitals)

Les Suisses parlent bien l'anglais.
The Swiss speak good English.

Il étudie l'italien.
He is studying Italian.

Il comprend le russe.
He understands Russian.

but:

Elle parle espagnol.
She speaks Spanish.

The article is omitted when **parler** is used **without an adverb**. The article must be retained if another verb is used (*study, understand* etc).

d) With **seasons** and **festivals**:

le printemps *spring*, **l'été** *summer*, **la Toussaint** *All Saints' Day*, **le jour de l'an** *New Year's Day*

L'hiver a été rigoureux.
Winter was harsh.

La Pentecôte est célébrée le septième dimanche après Pâques.
Whitsun is celebrated on the seventh Sunday after Easter.

However, as you can see in this last example, with **Pâques** (*Easter*) no definite article is used. This is also generally the case with **Noël**:

J'adore recevoir des cadeaux à Noël.
I love receiving presents at Christmas.

You may find **la Noël**, feminine here as it replaces **la fête de Noël**, in a sentence such as:

La Noël est une fête importante pour la famille.
Christmas is an important festival for the family.

The greeting *Happy Christmas* is always masculine – **Joyeux Noël**.

e) With days of the week to express the idea of **every week on that day**:

Le mardi je joue au foot.
On Tuesdays I play football.

Le mercredi soir on va au cinéma.
On Wednesday evenings we go to the cinema.

f) With **times of the day**:

 Le soir nous regardons la télé.
 In the evening we watch TV.

 L'après-midi elle reste à l'école.
 In the afternoon she stays at school.

g) With **people's titles**:

 Le président Chirac adresse ses vœux à la nation.
 President Chirac is sending his best wishes to the nation.

 Le pape Jean-Paul II était Polonais.
 Pope John Paul II was Polish.

h) With **colours**:

 Le brun est ma couleur préférée.
 Brown is my favourite colour.

 Elle a horreur du noir.
 She can't stand black.

i) To express **prices** and **measurements** where English uses *a* or *an*:

 J'ai payé deux euros le kilo.
 I paid two euros a kilo.

 C'est cinq dollars le mètre.
 It's five dollars a metre.

 Il roule à cent kilomètres à l'heure.
 He drives at a hundred kilometres an hour.

j) With **parts of the body** in cases where it is clear whose body is being referred to:

 Elle m'a pris le bras.
 She took my arm.

 Il s'est coupé la main.
 He cut his hand.

 Elle a hoché la tête.
 She nodded / shook her head.

 Il s'est lavé les cheveux.
 He washed his hair.

◆

We will close this section on the definite article with a brief reference to words in French which begin with the letter **h**. While the **h** is practically never pronounced, it is sometimes treated as a consonant, when it is known as an **aspirate h** (h aspiré).

With such words the full definite article is used:

le **hérisson** *hedgehog*, le **hibou** *owl*, la **haine** *hatred*, le **héros**, le **haricot** *bean*

You will have encountered rather more words beginning with a **mute h** (h muet) where to all intents and purposes the word is regarded as beginning with a vowel:

l'**hôtel**, l'**homme**, l'**heure**, l'**héroïne** *heroine / heroin*, l'**habitude** *custom / habit*, l'**habitant** *inhabitant*, l'**herbe** *grass*

You will, of course, find **les** before the plural forms of all of these and here we must raise an important point about pronunciation.

The final **-s** of a word is often pronounced when the next word begins with a vowel:

mes͜amis, les͜élèves

We refer to this as making a liaison. We can treat plurals beginning with a **mute h** in the same way:

les͜hôtels, les͜hommes

However, the liaison cannot be made with plurals beginning with an **aspirate h**, which is regarded as a consonant:

les haricots, les héros (NB no liaison ͜)

Here are some further sentences to illustrate the use of the aspirate h:

Il est parti à la hâte.
He left in haste.

Dans la vie il faut accepter les hauts et les bas.
In life we have to accept the ups and downs.

Le hamster s'est évadé.
The hamster has escaped.

Vous ne mangez pas le hors d'œuvre ?
Aren't you eating the starter?

Elle adore les harengs.
She loves herrings.

◆

THE INDEFINITE ARTICLE – L'ARTICLE INDÉFINI (UN, UNE, DES)

Once again, French will often use an indefinite article where none is found in English.

Although English and French are identical in a sentence such as:

Il a lutté avec courage.
He fought with courage (courageously).

French will have an indefinite article whenever the abstract noun is qualified by an adjective:

Il a lutté avec un courage étonnant.
He fought with astonishing courage.

Elle travaille avec patience.
Elle travaille avec une patience admirable.
She works with admirable patience.

Il a répondu avec humour.
Il a répondu avec un humour ironique.
He replied with ironic humour.

Ils ont fait des progrès rapides.
They made rapid progress.

The plural form of *a* or *an* – *some* or *any* – is frequently omitted in English. An example you will certainly recognise is:

C'est un livre.
It is a book.

Ce sont des livres.
They are books.

Here are some further sentences to illustrate the point:

Elle achète des journaux.
She buys newspapers.

(*Newspapers* here indicates *some* newspapers, not *the* newspapers which would be **les journaux**.)

Nous avons des amis en Belgique.
We have (some) friends in Belgium.

Je vois des étoiles dans le ciel.
I can see (some) stars in the sky.

However there is an occasion where English uses an indefinite article where French does not. Here we are referring to someone's job:

Elle est professeur.
*She is **a** teacher.*

(Also possible is: **C'est un professeur.**)

Il veut être médecin.
*He wants to be **a** doctor.*

THE PARTITIVE ARTICLE – L'ARTICLE PARTITIF (DU, DE LA, DE L', DES)

Here again, English often omits the words *some* and *any* while French rarely does.

Elle a acheté des pommes de terre.
She bought (some) potatoes.

Avez-vous des enfants ?
Do you have (any) children?

- **du** – used when the noun is masculine singular and begins with a consonant:

Ils boivent du vin.
They are drinking wine.

As-tu du fromage ?
Do you have any cheese?

- **de la** – used when the noun is feminine singular and begins with a consonant:

Veux-tu de la salade ?
Do you want some / any salad?

Il y a de la glace dans le frigo.
There is (some) ice cream in the fridge.

- **de l'** – used when a singular noun begins with a vowel or mute **h**:

Nous avons de l'argent.
We have (some) money.

De l'eau, s'il vous plaît.
(Some) water, please.

Je voudrais de l'huile.
I'd like some oil.

- **des** – used with all plural nouns, masculine and feminine and with the **s** pronounced before a vowel and mute **h**:

  Je connais des͜hôtels magnifiques.
  I know some splendid hotels.

  Avez-vous des papiers ?
  Have you any identification papers?

  J'ai des pièces de deux euros.
  I have some two-euro coins.

  Elle vend des͜œufs.
  She sells eggs.

[Note the pronunciation of **œufs**. The **f** is only pronounced in the singular – **un œuf**.]

But: in certain circumstances, each of the four forms above becomes **de** (**d'** before a vowel or mute **h**):

- After a negative:

  Avez-vous de l'argent ?
  Have you any money?

  Non, je n'ai pas d'argent.
  No I haven't any money / I have no money.

  Prenez-vous du vin, monsieur ?
  Are you having any wine, sir?

  Merci, je ne prends pas de vin.
  No thank you, I am not having wine.

[Strictly speaking, **merci** means *no thank you*. To avoid ambiguity we often add **oui** or **non**.]

  N'ont-ils pas d'eau ?
  Haven't they any water?

  Si, ils ont de l'eau.
  Yes, they have some water.

[Notice the use of **si** (*yes*) to contradict the negative.]

  Donnez-moi de la confiture.
  Give me some jam.

  Désolé, je n'ai pas de confiture.
  Sorry, I haven't any jam.

  A-t-il envoyé des fleurs ?
  Did he send some flowers?

  Non, il n'a pas envoyé de fleurs.
  No, he didn't send any flowers.

- After an expression of quantity:

  Avez-vous de l'argent ?
  Have you any money?

  Oui, j'ai beaucoup d'argent.
  Yes, I have lots (a lot) of money.

  Prenez-vous du vin, monsieur ?
  Are you having any wine, sir?

  Oui merci, je voudrais une bouteille de Bordeaux.
  Yes thank you, I'd like a bottle of Bordeaux.

  N'ont-ils pas d'eau ?
  Haven't they got any water?

  Si, ils ont un litre d'Evian.
  Yes, they have a litre of Evian.

  Donnez-moi de la confiture.
  Give me some jam.

  Volontiers, voilà un pot de confiture de fraises.
  Certainly, here is a pot of strawberry jam.

  A-t-il envoyé des fleurs ?
  Did he send any flowers?

  Oui, il a envoyé un bouquet de roses.
  Yes, he sent a bouquet of roses.

- Where there is a plural adjective **before** the noun:

  Voilà de belles photos !
  Here are some beautiful photos!

  Et voilà des photos merveilleuses !
  And here are some great photos!
  (Now the adjective **follows** the noun.)

  Je connais de bons restaurants à Paris.
  I know some good restaurants in Paris.

  Il a eu d'excellents résultats.
  He has had excellent results.

Two words of caution:

Sometimes the plural adjective and noun are seen as one entity. Here the partitive article **des** is retained:

   des jeunes gens, des grands magasins, des petits pois
   young people, department stores, garden peas.

In spoken French, there is a tendency to keep **des**, even when there is an adjective before the noun:

   Elle avait eu des bonnes notes.
   She had had good marks.

We would not say this ourselves!

◆

OMISSION OF THE ARTICLES IN FRENCH – OMISSION DES ARTICLES

- In lists:

  Venez au palais de Versailles. Vous verrez tout : sculptures, tableaux, dessins, meubles, tapisseries.
  Come to the Palace of Versailles. You will see everything: sculptures, paintings, drawings, furniture, tapestries.

  Allez tout de suite aux Galeries Lafayette ! Tout est à moitié prix ! Chemises, manteaux, chaussures, cravates.
  Go at once to the Galeries Lafayette (a chain of French department stores)! Everything is half price! Shirts, coats, shoes, ties.

- After certain verbal expressions:

  avoir besoin de
  J'ai besoin d'argent.
  I need money.

  [If we are talking about a specific sum of money, we would use the definite article in English – *I need **the** money which you owe me.* French too will use the article – **J'ai besoin de l'argent que tu me dois**.]

  avoir envie de
  Elle avait envie de se reposer.
  She wanted to rest.

  faire attention
  Ce garçon ne fait jamais attention.
  This boy never pays attention.

  rendre service
  Puis-je vous rendre service ?
  May I be of service to you?

- In certain expressions using a preposition:

  en hiver *in winter*, **en France**, **à pied** *on foot*, **avec plaisir** *with pleasure*, **par terre** *on the ground*, **sans issue** *no exit*

◆

Care should be taken when using articles in negative sentences. We have seen that the partitive article becomes **de**. However the definite article will not change. Compare:

Nous n'avons pas de livres. – *any books*

Nous n'avons pas les livres. – *the books*

The case of the indefinite article is perhaps more complicated. We say and write:

Je n'ai pas d'amis. – *any friends*

Je n'ai pas d'argent. – *any money*

But we can also have:

Je n'ai pas un ami. – *a (single) friend*

Je n'ai pas un sou.
I haven't a cent. (I'm completely broke.)

(Compare this to the English: *I haven't a penny to my name.*)

Retaining the indefinite article stresses our plight.

◆

SOME OCCASIONS WHERE THE ARTICLE IS RETAINED

- Generally after the verb **faire**:

  Elles font du sport.
  They do sport.

  Il faisait du yoga.
  He used to do yoga.

  Je ferai de la danse.
  I'll do dancing.

  On a fait des études à Paris.
  We studied in Paris.

  Elle a envie de faire du théâtre, mais lui, il va faire de la politique.
  She wants to act but he's going to go into politics.

  Elles avaient fait de l'aérobic.
  They had done aerobics.

- Sports and games – **jouer** à:

  Il jouait au football.
  He used to play football.

  Elle jouera au hockey.
  She'll play hockey.

  Elle veut jouer à la belote.
  She wants to play belote (a card game).

  Il préfère jouer aux échecs.
  He prefers to play chess.

- Instruments – **jouer** de:

  Elle joue du piano.
  She plays the piano.

  Je jouais de la guitare.
  I used to play the guitar.

  Je voudrais apprendre à jouer de l'accordéon.
  I would like to learn to play the accordion.

TRAIL → 16
page 212

→ TRAIL 27

We recognise that many pronouns present difficulties for the student. In this chapter we will attempt to break the subject down into manageable areas. Once again we stress the importance of listening to and repeating aloud the examples as this will reinforce what you read. This listening and repeating will give you a feel for the way pronouns are used in French.

Let us define once again the word **pronoun**. Pronouns are simply words which stand in place of nouns. **Je**, **tu**, **il**, **elle**, **on**, **nous**, **vous**, **ils**, **elles** are **personal pronouns** used as the **subject** of the **verb** and they have their equivalent **direct** and **indirect object** forms. They also have an **emphatic** (or **strong**) form used mainly after prepositions. You may find these indexed as **disjunctive pronouns** in some grammar books. In French they may be referred to as **pronoms toniques**.

First person singular – je

- subject

Je parle bien le français.
I speak French well.

NB **Je** is normally shortened to **j'** before a vowel. However, this is not the case in inverted question forms:

Puis-je entrer ?
May I come in?

- direct object

Mon oncle me voit tous les jours.
My uncle sees me every day.

Maman m'aime beaucoup.
Mum loves me very much.

Note that the object pronoun is placed **before the verb**.

M'entendez-vous ?
Can you hear me?

Vous ne m'entendez pas.
You can't hear me.

Ne m'entendez-vous pas ?
Can't you hear me?

Vous m'avez entendu(e).
You heard me.

M'avez-vous entendu(e) ?
Did you hear me?

Vous ne m'avez pas entendu(e).
You didn't hear me.

Ne m'avez-vous pas entendu(e) ?
Didn't you hear me?

In the perfect, as with all compound tenses, the object pronoun is placed **immediately before the auxiliary verb**; that is, before the part of **avoir**. Where the pronoun is a **direct** object, it will cause an agreement of the past participle and this explains our **(e)** above.

Il vient me **voir tous les jeudis.**
He comes to see me every Thursday.

Note that here the object pronoun is placed before the infinitive – **voir** – as it is the object of this verb.

Il refuse de m'**écouter.**
He refuses to listen to me.

Ils ne veulent pas me **rencontrer.**
They don't want to meet me.

• indirect object

Mon père me **montre sa collection de timbres.**
My father is showing me his stamp collection. (... is showing his stamp collection to me.)

L'agent de voyage m'**offre un séjour à Paris.**
The travel agent is offering me a holiday in Paris.

Me **parlez-vous ?**
Are you speaking to me?

Vous ne me **parlez pas.**
You don't speak to me.

Ne me **parlez-vous pas ?**
Aren't you speaking to me?

Vous m'**avez parlé.**
You spoke to me.

M'**avez-vous parlé ?**
Did you speak to me?

Vous ne m'**avez pas parlé.**
You didn't speak to me.

Ne m'**avez-vous pas parlé ?**
Didn't you speak to me?

There is no question of any agreement of the past participle here as **me (m')** is an **indirect** object.

• emphatic pronoun

Venez chez moi **!**
Come to my house!

Elle est partie sans moi.
She left without me.

We prefer the term emphatic pronoun since it is the pronoun used to give emphasis. Consider the English sentence:

I didn't order the book.

You can see how we stress the subject pronoun. In the printed form we use a different script. In writing we could underline the word and in speech we simply give the word a different tone of voice. This is rarely done in French. The emphatic pronoun is used **together with the subject pronoun** to give the same sense:

Moi, je n'ai pas commandé le livre.
I didn't order the book.

Emphatic forms are often seen linked by a hyphen to **même(s)** (*self*) to give *myself, yourself* etc:

Je l'ai fait moi-même.
I did it myself.

Second person singular – tu

- subject

  Tu peux regarder cette émission.
  You can watch this programme.

- direct object

  Le chien te suit.
  The dog is following you.

  Ton père t'accompagne à l'hôpital.
  Your father is going with you to the hospital.

  Elle t'a pris pour un imbécile.
  She took you for a fool.

  Je vais te mettre au courant.
  I'll bring you up to date.

- indirect object

  Je te répète encore une fois, non !
  I'm telling you once again, no!

  Ton frère t'a lancé le ballon.
  Your brother threw the ball to you (threw you the ball).

- emphatic pronoun

  Je n'ai pas peur de toi.
  I'm not afraid of you.

  Toi, tu vas rester à la maison !
  You will stay at home!

  Tu feras cela toi-même.
  You will do that yourself.

Third person singular masculine – il

- subject

  Il ennuie tout le monde.
  He's annoying everybody.

- direct object

  Elle le connaît.
  She knows him.

  Son oncle l'a mené en voiture au cinéma.
  His uncle took him in the car to the cinema.

Elle le boit.
She drinks it.

Nous le mangeons.
We are eating it.
(Here the meaning is clearly **it**.)

Je ne l'ai pas vu.
I haven't seen him / it.

Je voudrais bien le voir.
I should really like to see him / it.

- indirect object

    Je ne lui parle pas.
    I don't speak to him.

    Lui a-t-elle envoyé le paquet ?
    Did she send him the parcel? (Did she send the parcel to him?)

- emphatic pronoun

    Elle est assise près de lui.
    She is sitting near him.

    Lui, il bavarde sans arrêt !
    He never stops talking.

    Il a sauvé sa fille lui-même.
    He saved his daughter himself.

Third person singular feminine – elle

- subject

    Elle appelle son amie tous les jours.
    She calls her friend every day.

- direct object

    Nous devons aller la voir.
    We must go and see her.

    Je l'attends depuis une heure.
    I've been waiting for her for an hour.

    Je ne l'ai pas vue.
    I haven't seen her / it.

    La glace. Elle ne veut pas la manger.
    *The ice cream. She doesn't want to eat it. (Again the meaning is clearly **it**.)*

- indirect object

    Je ne lui parle pas.
    I don't speak to her.

    Lui a-t-elle envoyé le paquet ?
    Did she send her the parcel? (Did she send the parcel to her?)

(We have intentionally kept here the examples used above with the masculine form to show that **lui** means both *to him* and *to her*.)

- emphatic pronoun

  Il le fera pour elle.
  He will do it for her.

  Elle, elle ne va pas sortir avec lui.
  She is not going to go out with him.

  Elle s'est chargée elle-même de l'enquête.
  She dealt with the investigation herself.

The indefinite pronoun – on

On is only ever used as the subject of a verb and can only refer to a person or persons. It will always take the third person singular form of the verb.

- subject

  On craint le pire.
  We fear the worst.
  (It is very unlikely that you will need to use the word one to translate **on**.)

  On avait injurié mes parents.
  My parents had been insulted.

- direct object

  On s'est vite habillé(e)s.
  We got dressed quickly.

  On s'est levé(e)s de bonne heure.
  We got up early.

Where agreement is necessary, the past participle will show the number and gender of the person or persons represented by **on**. In the two examples above, **s'** is the preceding direct object.

- indirect object

  On s'est fait couper les cheveux.
  We have had a haircut.

  On s'était demandé la raison de votre refus.
  We had wondered why you refused (about the reason for your refusal).

Here there is no agreement as **se (s')** is the **indirect** object.

- emphatic pronoun

  On rentre chez soi à la tombée de la nuit.
  People return home at nightfall.

  Ici, on fait tout pour soi-même.
  Here people do everything for themselves.

Soi is also used to refer to other indefinite subjects:

  Chacun pour soi !
  Every man for himself!

First person plural - nous

- subject

  Nous prenons le bus de sept heures dix.
  We catch the ten-past-seven bus.

- direct object

  Il ne peut pas nous sentir.
  He can't stand us.

  Il ne nous avait pas vu(e)s.
  He hadn't seen us.

- indirect object

  Il nous avait parlé.
  He had spoken to us.

  Elle nous téléphonait toutes les deux heures.
  She phoned / used to phone us every two hours.

- emphatic pronoun

  Derrière nous il y avait une foule immense.
  Behind us there was a huge crowd.

  Nous, nous ne savons pas quel âge elle a.
  We don't know how old she is.

  Nous voulons nous-mêmes gagner le sommet de la montagne.
  We want to get to the top of the mountain ourselves.

You will have been pleased to note that **nous** retains the same form for all these uses.

Second person plural - vous

- subject

  Vous écrirez encore une lettre ?
  You will write yet another letter?

- direct object

  L'avocat vous recevra dans son bureau.
  The lawyer will receive you in his office.

  Je suis heureux de vous connaître.
  I am happy to know you.

- indirect object

  Je vous ai dit pourquoi.
  I told you why.

  Vos parents vous auraient donné la permission de sortir.
  Your parents would have given you permission to go out.

- emphatic pronoun

  Il faut que nous arrivions avant vous.
  We must arrive before you.

Vous, vous m'embêtez !
You're getting on my nerves!

Vous avez vu vous-même(s) comment il se comportait.
You saw yourself / yourselves how he was behaving.

Once again, happily, **vous**, like **nous**, remains the same throughout.

Third person plural masculine – ils

- subject
  Ils sourient constamment.
  They are always smiling.

- direct object
  Je les ai lus.
  I've read them.

  Ne les avait-il pas reçus ?
  Hadn't he received them?

- indirect object
  Je leur ai expliqué mes raisons.
  I explained my reasons to them.

  Allez leur montrer le chemin.
  Go and show them the way.

- emphatic pronoun
  Je ne veux pas vivre avec eux.
  I don't want to live with them.

  Eux, ils sont innocents.
  They are innocent.

  Ils ont répondu eux-mêmes à la menace.
  They responded themselves to the threat.

Third person plural feminine – elles

- subject
  Elles ne partent pas avant demain matin.
  They aren't leaving before tomorrow morning.

- direct object
  Je les ai lues.
  I've read them.

  Ne les avait-il pas reçues ?
  Hadn't he received them?

- indirect object
  Nous leur aurions donné à boire.
  We would have given them something to drink.

Est-ce que tu vas leur téléphoner ?
Are you going to ring them?

- emphatic pronoun

  Il a couru à elles.
  He ran to them.

  Elles, elles se sont trompées de jour.
  ***They** got the wrong day.*

  Elles seraient revenues elles-mêmes si elles avaient su que vous étiez malade.
  They would have come back themselves if they had known that you were ill.

For ease of reference, we give below a table, setting out the pronouns we have covered so far:

SUBJECT	DIRECT OBJECT	INDIRECT OBJECT	EMPHATIC
je	me	me	moi
tu	te	te	toi
il	le	lui	lui
elle	la	lui	elle
on	se	se	soi
nous	← nous →		
vous	← vous →		
ils	les	leur	eux
elles	les	leur	elles

TRAIL → 28
page 214

→ TRAIL 35

The pronoun y

Students are introduced to **y** as a pronoun meaning *there*. They are familiar with such sentences as:

Allez-vous à Paris ? – Oui, nous y allons.
Are you going to Paris? – Yes, we're going there.

In our view, it is better to think of **y** as the pronoun which replaces **à + noun.** You will find that there are several possible ways of translating it:

Vous vous intéressez à la politique ? – Oui, je m'y intéresse. (Non, je ne m'y intéresse pas.)
Are you interested in politics? – Yes, I am (No, I am not) interested in it.

Est-ce qu'il s'habitue à sa nouvelle vie ? – Non, il ne s'y habitue pas.
Is he getting used to his new life? – No, he's not getting used to it.

Pensez-vous souvent à cette nuit-là ? – Oui, j'y pense toujours.
Do you often think about that night? – Yes, I'm always thinking about it.

Il joue aux échecs ? – Oui, il y joue tout le temps.
Does he play chess? – Yes, he plays all the time. (Sometimes there is no need to translate **y**.)

Ne répondez pas à cette lettre ! N'y répondez pas !
Don't answer that letter! Don't answer it!

However, **y** is rarely used to refer to people:

Vous vous intéressez à cet homme ? – Oui, je m'intéresse à lui.
Are you interested in that man? – Yes, I'm interested in him.

Vous pensez souvent à cette jeune femme ? – Oui, je pense souvent à elle.
Do you often think about that young woman? – Yes, I often think of her.

With people, we should use **à + the emphatic pronoun.**

Of course, to return to our first point, **y** will often mean **there**:

Vous travaillez depuis longtemps dans cette usine-là ? – Oui, j'y travaille depuis dix ans.
Have you been working in that factory for a long time? – Yes, I've been working there for ten years.

◆

The pronoun en

Meaning *some, any, of it* or *of them*, **en** replaces **de + noun**:

Avez-vous de l'argent ? – Oui, j'en ai.
Have you any money? – Yes, I have some.

Je n'en ai pas.
I haven't any.

Avez-vous mangé de ce jambon ? – Oui, j'en ai pris une tranche.
Have you tried this ham? – Yes, I've had a slice (of it).

Est-ce qu'il a acheté une cravate ? – Oui, il en a acheté une.
Has he bought a tie? – Yes, he's bought one (of them).

Avez-vous des frères ? – J'en ai deux.
Have you any brothers? – I've got two (of them).

A-t-elle des amies ? – Oui, elle en a beaucoup.
Has she any friends? – Yes she has a lot (of them).

The word **en** in the last three examples, although not necessarily translated into English, **cannot be omitted in French**.

Generally speaking, **en** is not used to refer to people. Our last two examples represent an exception to this rule when dealing with a **number** or **quantity** of people.

La situation en Afrique du Sud ? Qu'en pensez-vous ?
The situation in South Africa? What do you think of / about it?

Le Premier ministre ? Que pensez-vous de lui ?
The Prime Minister? What do you think of / about him?

[You will have noticed that we have used the verb **penser** in two ways – with **à** in our section on **y** and now with **de** in this section. It is important to distinguish between these two uses. **Penser à** means *to think of* in the sense of *to have in mind*; **penser de** means *to think of* in the sense of *to have an opinion about*.]

Vous vous souvenez de notre séjour à Paris ? – Oui, je m'en souviens.
Do you remember our holiday in Paris? – Yes, I remember it.

Vous vous souvenez de cette vieille dame ? – Oui, je me souviens d'elle.
Do you remember that old lady? – Yes, I remember her.

Parle-t-elle de ses affaires ? – Oui, elle en parle sans cesse.
Does she talk about her business? – Yes, she talks about it endlessly. (She never stops talking about it.)

Parle-t-elle de son ami ? – Oui, elle parle sans cesse de lui.
Does she talk about her friend? – Yes, she's always talking about him.

Avez-vous besoin de ce livre ? – Non, je n'en ai pas besoin.
Do you need this book? – No, I don't need it.

Avez-vous besoin de ces étudiants ? – Non, je n'ai pas besoin d'eux.
Do you need these students? – No, I don't need them.

You will notice that with **people** we use **de + the emphatic pronoun**.

◆

The pronouns **me, te, nous** and **vous** are also used in pronominal verbs, where they may sometimes require translation into English but often not:

Je me cache.
I'm hiding.

Tu te laves.
You are having a wash.

Nous nous sommes levé(e)s de bonne heure.
We got up early.

Ne vous étiez-vous pas endormis avant minuit, messieurs ?
Hadn't you gone to sleep before midnight, gentlemen?

To these we add **se**, which accompanies the third persons of pronominal verbs as we saw earlier with **on**:

Elle s'est promenée.
She went for a walk.

Ils se sont habillés.
They got dressed.

Il s'est tué.
He killed himself.

Elles ne se sont pas parlé.
They didn't speak to one another.

◆

We are now in a position to show you, in the form of a table, the order in which these pronouns come when two of them are combined in a sentence:

me te se nous vous	le la les	lui leur	y	en

Our examples will show the replacement of nouns, which we will put in italics, with pronouns, given in coloured text.

Il m'enverra *les lettres*. Il me les enverra.
He will send me the letters. He will send them to me. (He'll send me them.)

Mes parents ont envoyé *le cadeau à ma grand-mère*. Mes parents le lui ont envoyé.
My parents sent the present to my grandmother. My parents sent it to her.

L'agent de police verra *les voleurs devant la banque*. L'agent de police les y verra.
The policeman will see the thieves outside the bank. The policeman will see them there.

Nous avons donné *des fleurs à nos parents*. Nous leur en avons donné.
We gave some flowers to our parents. We gave them some.
(Remember that the past participle never agrees with **en**.)

Il nous racontait *des histoires*. Il nous en racontait.
He told us (some) stories. He told us some.

Je ne montre pas *le livre à ma sœur*. Je ne le lui montre pas.
I'm not showing the book to my sister. I'm not showing it to her.

Elle n'a pas donné *d'argent au vieillard*. Elle ne lui en a pas donné.
She didn't give any money to the old man. She didn't give him any.

Avez-vous parlé *à ces enfants de leur absence* ? Leur en avez-vous parlé ?
Did you speak to those children about their absence? Did you speak to them about it?

Va-t-il te prêter *l'argent* ? Va-t-il te le prêter ?
Is he going to lend you the money? Is he going to lend it to you?

As you listen to the recordings of these examples they will help you retain the position and order of pronouns.

Certain combinations of these pronouns are not seen. We do not use together pronouns from columns 1 and 3 or 3 and 4 of the above table:

Il nous présentera *au directeur*. Il nous présentera à lui. (Not **nous lui**.)
He will introduce us to the headmaster. He will introduce us to him.

Elle avait téléphoné *à ses amies à Paris.* **Elle** leur **avait téléphoné** à Paris. (Not leur y.)

She had phoned her friends in Paris. She had phoned them in Paris.

Let us briefly recapitulate the rules:

a) When two pronouns from the table are used, they always **stand together**.

b) They stand **before the verb**, except with positive commands, as we will see shortly.

c) In compound tenses they stand **before the auxiliary verb**.

d) They stand before the verb to which they are logically connected. This can mean placing them **before an infinitive: Il ne va pas** me les **donner.** *He is not going to give them to me.*

◆

Negative commands

With **commands** which are **negative**, we can follow the pattern shown above:

Ne parle pas *à cet homme-là de l'affaire* ! **Ne** lui en **parle pas** !
Don't speak to that man about the matter! Don't speak to him about it!

N'envoyez pas *d'argent aux enfants* ! **Ne** leur en **envoyez pas** !
Don't send any money to the children! Don't send them any!

Ne lui rends pas *le journal* ! **Ne** le lui **rends pas** !
Don't give him back the newspaper! Don't give it him back! (Don't give it back to him!)

Ne me donnez pas *de soupe* ! **Ne** m'en **donnez pas** !
Don't give me any soup! Don't give me any!

Ne montrons pas *le plan aux agents* ! **Ne** le leur **montrons pas** !
Let's not show the map to the police! Let's not show it them!

Ne m'en **veux pas** !
Don't hold it against me!

The command form of the verb **en vouloir à quelqu'un** (*to bear someone a grudge*) follows this rule.

◆

Positive commands

This is the **only** circumstance where these pronouns come after the verb. With their weak vowel sounds **me** and **te** cannot be the final element of a command and here **moi** and **toi**, the emphatic forms, are used:

Donne-moi **de l'argent** !
Give me some money!

Parlez-moi **d'amour** !
Speak to me of love!

Cache-toi **!**
Hide!

Lève-toi **tout de suite** !
Get up at once!

Where two of these pronouns appear together in a positive command they follow one of the following two possible combinations:

1.

				moi / toi
		le		lui
verb	-	la	-	nous
		les		vous
				leur

Donne *la carte à ton père* ! **Donne**-la-lui !
Give the map to your father! Give it to him!

Envoyez-*nous les nouvelles* ! **Envoyez**-les-nous!
Send us the news! Send it to us!

Montrons *le tableau à nos amis* ! **Montrons**-le-leur !
Let's show the painting to our friends! Let's show it to them!

Passez-*moi le sel* ! **Passez**-le-moi !
Pass me the salt! Pass me it!

2.

		m' / t'		
		lui		
verb	-	nous	-	en
		vous		
		leur		

Donne-*moi de l'argent* ! **Donne**-m'en !
Give me some money! Give me some!

Envoyons *des fleurs à nos parents* ! **Envoyons**-leur-en !
Let's send some flowers to our parents! Let's send them some!

Va-t'en ! **Allez**-vous-en !
Clear off!

(The command forms of the verb **s'en aller** (*to go away*) follow this rule.)

You will have noticed the **hyphens** which will always **link these pronouns to the verb when they follow it**.

In positive commands, combinations such as **m'y, t'y, l'y, nous-y, vous-y** are rare. However you will find **les-y**:

Mettez *les livres sur la table* ! **Mettez**-les-y !
Put the books on the table! Put them there!

TRAIL → 36
page 215

◆ ◆ ◆

→ TRAIL 39

The relative pronoun – Le pronom relatif

The relative pronoun is so called because it relates back to something, a noun or pronoun, which has already been mentioned. *I know the man* **who** *is reading the paper.* **Who** relates back to **the man**. *They noticed the letter* **which** (**that**) *Pierre had put on the sideboard.* **Which** (or **that**) relates back to **the letter**.

We can, in English, often omit the relative pronoun: *I know the man reading the paper; They noticed the letter Pierre had put on the sideboard.* We must stress here that the relative pronoun can NEVER be omitted in French: **Je connais l'homme qui lit le journal; Ils ont remarqué la lettre que Pierre avait mise sur le buffet.**

Here are some examples to show the uses of **qui** and **que**. As you will see, **qui is never shortened before a vowel**, whereas **que will become qu'**:

Va consulter la carte qui est sur le mur.
Go and look at the map (which is) on the wall.

C'est l'agent de police qui vient souvent chez nous.
He is the policeman who often comes to our house.

Il ne connaît pas cette vieille dame qui a parlé hier à mes parents.
He doesn't know that old lady who spoke to my parents yesterday.

C'est elle qui étudie l'allemand.
She is the one studying German.

We have used **qui** in our examples here because the word to which it refers is the **subject** of the following verb. The map *is* on the wall; it is the policeman who *comes* to our house; the old lady *spoke* to my parents; it is she who *studies* German.

Montre-moi les chaussures que ton père t'a achetées.
Show me the shoes (which / that) your father bought you.

C'est cet homme-là que tu as vu hier ?
Is that the man (who(m) / that) you saw yesterday?

Tous les livres qu'il a écrits sont épuisés.
All the books (which / that) he wrote are out of print.

C'est lui qu'elle rencontre souvent.
He is the one she often meets.

In this second group of examples, we have used **que**, as the word to which it refers is the **object** of the following verb. What was *bought* ? – the shoes. Who was *seen*? – the man. What was *written*? – the books. Who does she often *meet*? – him.

To sum up, let us suppose that we must give this sentence in French:

Here is the wine we prefer.

First, we know that the sentence will have to read: *Here is the wine **which** / **that** we prefer*. Secondly, what is the relationship between *wine* and *prefer*, subject or object? Clearly it is the **object**, so we write:

Voilà le vin que nous préférons.

Now suppose that the sentence had been:

*Here is the wine **which** interests you.*

What is the relationship between *wine* and *interests*, subject or object? It can only be the **subject** as it is the thing doing the interesting, so we have:

Voilà le vin qui vous intéresse.

We must stress that **qui** and **que** may each refer to people **or** things. It is their **relationship to the following verb** – as subject or object – which must be determined.

- **dont** – *of which, of whom, whose*

First read and listen to the following sentences:

Voilà le livre dont vous avez besoin.
Here is the book (which / that) you need.
*(to need – **avoir besoin de**)*

C'est lui dont elle a peur.
He is the one she is afraid of.
*(to be afraid of – **avoir peur de**)*

Mon fils m'a montré le travail dont il était fier.
My son showed me the work (which / that) he was proud of.
*(to be proud of – **être fier de**)*

C'était un résultat dont elle était très satisfaite.
It was a result (that / which) she was very satisfied with.
*(to be satisfied with – **être satisfait de**)*

Il m'a fait un compliment dont j'étais bien content.
He paid me a compliment (which / that) I was very happy with.
*(to be happy with – **être content de**)*

Je n'aime pas ce professeur dont vous parlez toujours.
I don't like that teacher (who / whom) you are always talking about.
*(to talk about – **parler de**)*

J'ai beaucoup de timbres dont deux sont très rares.
I have a lot of stamps two of which (of which two) are very rare.

Voilà la dame dont je connais les enfants.
There is the lady whose children I know. (*whose* means the same as *of whom*)

You can see that, as with **qui** and **que**, **dont** relates back to a noun or a pronoun – **livre**, **lui**, **travail** etc. It is used here because it links the noun or pronoun to an expression involving the preposition **de**, although we do not always use the word *of* in our translation, eg *Here is the book you need*. Literally: *Here is the book of which (**dont**) you have need*.

We must make two further points concerning the use of **dont** to mean *whose*:

a) **Dont** is never used to ask a question:

Whose is this shirt?
À qui est cette chemise ?

Whose were those old clothes?
À qui étaient ces vieux vêtements ?

b) The word order in French following **dont** is not always the same as the English:

Vous connaissez cet homme dont les enfants habitent en face ?
Do you know that man whose children (of whom the children) live opposite?

No problem here.

But:

Ils sont pénibles, ces enfants dont vous voyez souvent les parents !
They are a nuisance, those children whose parents you often see!

The order of words after **dont** is subject – verb – object:

L'homme dont j'ai déchiré la veste s'est mis en colère.
The man whose jacket I tore became angry.

However in a sentence where the noun is preceded by a preposition, it is not possible to use **dont**:

*The man **on whose jacket** I poured some wine (**whose jacket** I poured some wine **on**) became angry.*
L'homme sur la veste de qui j'ai versé du vin s'est mis en colère.

[NB *The way in which* is always **la façon / manière dont**:

La façon dont il parle ne laisse pas de doute.
The way (in which) he speaks leaves no doubt.

La manière dont il s'habille me fait penser aux années quatre-vingts.
The way (in which) he dresses reminds me (makes me think) of the eighties.]

◆

- **ce qui, ce que, ce dont** – *that which, that of which*

Let us now look at the relative pronouns **qui**, **que** and **dont**, preceded by the pronoun **ce**, which is required when referring to **ideas** or **situations**. (**Qui, que** and **dont** on their own can only relate to **nouns** or **pronouns**.)

Je ne sais pas ce qui s'est passé.
I don't know what happened. (that which happened)

Dites-moi ce que vous avez fait.
Tell me what you did. (that which you did)

Répète ce qu'il t'a dit.
Repeat what he said to you. (that which he said to you)

Expliquez au directeur ce dont vous avez besoin.
Explain to the headmaster what you need. (what you need means the same as what you have need of – that of which you have need)

- **ce qui** – subject

Je vais vous dire ce qui m'inquiète.
I am going to tell you what is worrying me.

- **ce que** – object

  Montre-moi ce que **tu tiens à la main.**
  Show me what you are holding in your hand.

- **ce dont** – *that of which* (ie incorporating **de**)

  Elle t'expliquera ce dont **elle se souvient.**
  She will explain to you what she remembers. (*to remember* – **se souvenir** de)

Thus, in these sentences, we provide **qui**, **que** and **dont**, which must relate back to something, with the pronoun **ce**.

To draw attention to the second part of the sentence, these pronouns can be placed at the start:

  Ce qui **m'énerve, c'est qu'il refuse de travailler.**
  What annoys me is that he refuses to work.

  Ce que **nous n'aimons pas, c'est qu'elle ne dit jamais la vérité.**
  What we don't like is that she never tells the truth.

  Ce dont **il a honte, c'est qu'il a abandonné ses amis.**
  What he is ashamed of is that he abandoned his friends.

You will also find **ce à quoi**:

  Ce à quoi **vous pensez ne m'intéresse pas.**
  What you are thinking about is of no interest to me.

These pronouns may be preceded by **tout** to express *everything, all that*:

  Je vais vous dire tout‿ce qui **lui est arrivé.**
  I am going to tell you everything that happened to him.

  Il vous donnera tout‿ce que **vous voulez.**
  He will give you everything you want.

  Tout ce dont **il a envie c'est d'aller au cinéma.**
  All he wants to do is go to the cinema. (All he wants is to go ...)
  (NB *to want ...* – **avoir envie** de ...)

◆

- **lequel, laquelle, lesquels, lesquelles** – *which*

These relative pronouns, combining the definite article and the adjective **quel**, generally refer back to things or animals, from which they take their number and gender, and are preceded by a preposition.

In French, **it is not possible to end a sentence with a preposition**. By definition, a preposition is positioned **before** its noun(s) or pronoun(s). Therefore *That is the table (which) he hid under* has to become *That is the table **under which** he hid* (**C'est la table** sous laquelle **il s'est caché**).

  Où est le stylo avec lequel **j'écris mes lettres d'amour ?**
  Where is the pen with which I write my love letters? (one pen, masculine)

  La table sur laquelle **il a mis la tasse était bancale.**
  The table he put the cup on was wobbly.

  Les murs derrière lesquels **ils se cachaient étaient peints à la chaux.**
  The walls they hid behind were whitewashed.

Les maisons devant lesquelles **se tenait une foule immense avaient été détruites.**
The houses outside which a huge crowd was standing had been destroyed.

Je ne sais pas la raison pour laquelle **il est parti.**
I don't know why (the reason for which) he left.

It is often possible to substitute the word **où** (*where*) for **lequel** when we are referring to a place:

La rue dans laquelle **se trouve la maison des Dupont est à cent mètres d'ici.**

is equivalent in meaning to:

La rue où **se trouve la maison des Dupont ...**
The street where the Dupont's house is is a hundred metres from here.

- **who(m)** with a preposition

Although **lequel** is possible, it is far more frequent to use **qui** with **people** to mean **who(m)** after prepositions:

Le jeune homme avec qui **elle sort est énormément riche.**
*The young man **with whom** she is going out is extremely rich.* (We would be more likely to say: *The young man (who) she is going out with ...*)

We feel it necessary to mention the word *whom* although it is used infrequently these days. Generally we use *who* or simply leave the word out in English, although this is not possible in French:

Le patron pour qui **il travaille est souvent difficile.**
The boss he works for is often difficult.

C'est un collègue sur qui **vous pouvez compter.**
He is a colleague you can count on.

However, with the prepositions **parmi** (*among*) and **entre** (*between*), **qui** is not used:

Les femmes parmi lesquelles **elle se trouvait étaient très bien habillées.**
The women she found herself among were very well dressed.

Les agents entre lesquels **il se tenait étaient énormes.**
The policemen he was standing between were huge.

- with **à** and **de**

We must be particularly careful with **lequel** when using the prepositions **à** and **de**. While we can say **à laquelle** and **de laquelle**, as **à** combines with **le** to make **au** and with **les** to make **aux**, so it combines with **lequel** to make **auquel**, with **lesquels** to make **auxquels** and with **lesquelles** to make **auxquelles**:

C'était un incident auquel **il pensait constamment.**
It was an incident he thought about constantly.

Voilà les chats sauvages auxquels **la vieille femme donne du lait.**
Here are the wild cats the old woman gives milk to.

Vous connaissez les règles du jeu auxquelles **il faut faire attention.**
You know the rules of the game which you must observe. (NB ... **la règle du jeu à laquelle...**)

Similarly, we have the forms **duquel**, **desquels** and **desquelles** when **de** is the preposition:

Il a traversé le lac au milieu duquel **se trouvait une île.**
He crossed the lake in the middle of which there was an island.

Les immeubles près desquels **on a construit l'autoroute sont invendables.**
The flats near which the motorway was built are impossible to sell (unmarketable).

Tout le monde regardait les Ferraris à côté desquelles il y avait une vedette de cinéma.
Everyone was looking at the Ferraris beside which there was a film star.
(NB **...la Ferrari à côté** de laquelle...)

TRAIL → 40
page 216

→ TRAIL 43

Our next sections will deal with pronouns which have corresponding adjectives.

The possessive pronoun – Le pronom possessif

À qui est ce stylo ?
Whose is this pen?

C'est le mien. **C'est** le tien / le vôtre. **C'est** le leur.

*It's **mine**; it's **yours**; it's **theirs**.*

Possession is far more frequently expressed by **à + emphatic pronoun: Il est à moi / à toi / à vous / à eux / à elles**. This is also the way to emphasise the owner:

C'est mon portefeuille à moi.
*It's **my** wallet.*

C'est son père à elle qui a dit ça.
*It's **her** father who said that.*

Here are the forms of the possessive pronoun:

mine:	
le mien	la mienne
les miens	les miennes

yours:	
le tien	la tienne
les tiens	les tiennes

his / hers:	
le sien	la sienne
les siens	les siennes

ours:
le nôtre
les nôtres

la nôtre
les nôtres (NB masculine
<u>and</u> feminine form)

yours:
le vôtre
les vôtres

la vôtre
les vôtres (NB masculine <u>and</u>
feminine form)

theirs:
le leur
les leurs

la leur
les leurs (NB masculine <u>and</u>
feminine form)

Note that **les nôtres, les vôtres** and **les leurs** are used to refer to both masculine and feminine nouns.

À qui est cette maison ? *Whose is this house?*

C'est la mienne.	or	**Elle est à moi.**
C'est la sienne.	or	**Elle est à lui / à elle.**
C'est la nôtre.	or	**Elle est à nous.**
C'est la leur.	or	**Elle est à eux / à elles.**

À qui sont ces chemises ? *Whose are these shirts?*

Ce sont les tiennes.	or	**Elles sont à toi.**
Ce sont les siennes.	or	**Elles sont à lui / à elle.**
Ce sont les vôtres.	or	**Elles sont à vous.**
Ce sont les leurs.	or	**Elles sont à eux / à elles.**

[For the distinction between **ce** and **il(s) / elle(s)** as the subject of **être**, see Section H.]

Here are some further examples of the use of the possessive pronoun:

Mes parents sont en vacances à Rome. Et les tiens ?
My parents are on holiday in Rome. And (how about) yours?

Avez-vous vu mes résultats ? – Non, mais j'ai vu les leurs.
Have you seen my results? – No, but I've seen theirs.

À la tienne **! À** la vôtre **!**
Cheers! Good health!

Est-ce que je peux emprunter ton auto ? La mienne **est en panne.**
Can I borrow your car? Mine's broken down.

◆

The interrogative pronoun – Le pronom interrogatif : lequel

lequel, laquelle **?** – *which one?*

lesquels, lesquelles **?** – *which ones?*

Une des jeunes filles vient de casser un carreau. – Laquelle **?**
One of the girls has just broken a window. – Which one?

(Here, had we wished to ask which window had been broken, we would have used **lequel**.)

Voici deux tableaux. Lequel préférez-vous ?
Here are two pictures. Which (one) do you prefer?

Deux accusés se sont échappés. – Lesquels ?
Two of the accused have escaped. – Which ones?

Je vais acheter des roses pour ma femme, mais lesquelles ?
I'm going to buy some roses for my wife, but which ones?

◆

The demonstrative pronoun – Le pronom démonstratif

celui, celle – *this (one) / that (one) / the one*

ceux, celles – *these (ones) / those (ones) / the ones*

You will probably remember the demonstrative adjective (**ce, cet**, cette, ces) meaning **this** or **that**, **these** or **those**, and **followed by a noun**. The demonstrative pronoun stands **in place of a noun** as our examples below will show:

Aimez-vous mieux ce pull-ci ou ce pull-là ? – Celui-ci.
Do you prefer this sweater or that sweater? – This one.

Vous choisissez cette robe-ci ou cette robe-là ? – Celle-là.
Are you choosing this dress or that dress? – That one.

Prenez-vous ces magazines-ci ou ces magazines-là ? – Ceux-là.
Are you taking these magazines or those? – Those (ones).

Vous achetez ces chaussures-ci ou ces chaussures-là ? – Celles-ci.
Are you buying these shoes or those? – These (ones).

In the above examples, we have used **-ci** and **-là** to show clearly which sweater is preferred, which dress is chosen etc. The demonstrative pronoun **never stands on its own**. It may also be followed by several prepositions, of which the most common is **de**, by a relative pronoun or by a past participle:

Ton stylo ne marche pas. Prends celui de mon frère.
Your pen's not working. Take my brother's (the one of my brother).

Ma veste est brune, celle de Jean est noire.
My jacket is brown, Jean's is black.

Je n'aime pas ces gâteaux ! Ceux de ma mère sont meilleurs.
I don't like these cakes! My mother's are better.

N'achète pas ces pommes-là. Celles de M. Dupont sont moins chères.
Don't buy those apples. M. Dupont's are cheaper.

Vous cherchez quel livre ? – Celui qui était sur la table ce matin.
Which book are you looking for? – The one which was on the table this morning.

Que pensez-vous de cette robe ? – Je préfère celle que vous avez achetée hier.
What do you think of this dress? – I prefer the one (which / that) you bought yesterday.

Vous parlez de quels amis ? – De ceux à qui je dois de l'argent.
Which friends are you talking about? – The ones I owe money to.

Des cartes ? Voilà celles dont tu as besoin.
Cards? There are the ones (which / that) you need.

J'ai tous mes livres sauf celui perdu **dans le déménagement.**
I have all my books except the one lost when we moved house.

J'aime recevoir des lettres. Celles écrites **par mon oncle sont passionnantes.**
I love to receive letters. The ones written by my uncle are exciting.

To conclude our section on the demonstrative pronoun, we must mention a further meaning of **celui-ci, celle-là** etc. They are used in the sense of *the former ... the latter.* **Celui-ci** (*this one, the nearer*) means *the latter*, **celui-là** (*that one, further away*) means *the former.*

Son oncle est arrivé en même temps que le facteur. Celui-ci avait des cadeaux pour la famille.
His uncle arrived at the same time as the postman. The latter (ie the postman) *had presents for the family.*

[It is possible to use **ce dernier** or cette dernière to mean the latter.]

Il a rendu visite à sa tante et à sa cousine. Celle-là **était malade depuis une semaine.**
He visited his aunt and his cousin. The former (ie his aunt) *had been ill for a week.*

The indefinite pronouns – Les pronoms indéfinis

* **chacun**, chacune – *each (one)*

There is no difference in meaning between **chaque livre** (*each book*) and **chacun des livres** (*each of the books*).

Les étudiants ont apporté chacun **son portable.**
Each of the students has brought his laptop.
(More frequently you will hear: **Chaque étudiant a apporté son portable**.)

Ces glaces coûtent deux euros chacune.
These ice creams cost two euros each.

* **quelqu'un**, quelqu'une – *someone*, **quelques-uns**, quelques-unes – *some, a few*

This pronoun is related to the adjective **quelque** *some*.

J'ai entendu quelqu'un **à la porte.**
I heard someone at the door.

Quelqu'une **de vos amies a laissé un message.**
One of your friends has left a message.
(**Une de vos amies** ... is the much more likely alternative nowadays.)

Avez-vous trouvé de vieux livres ? – Oui, j'en ai trouvé quelques-uns.
Did you find any old books? – Yes, I found some (a few).

J'aime quelques-unes **de ces photos.**
I like some of these photos.

If we wish to use an adjective with **quelqu'un**, the adjective will be preceded by **de**:

Il y avait quelqu'un de célèbre **devant l'ambassade.**
There was someone famous outside the embassy.

An interesting use of the pronoun is:

Elle se croit quelqu'un (masculine form)**.**
*She thinks she **is** someone.*

- **tout, tous**, toutes – *all, everything, everyone*

This pronoun is related to the adjective **tout**, toute, **tous**, toutes *all / every*.

Tout est bien qui finit bien.
All's well that ends well.

Nous avons tout prévu.
We've thought of everything.

Ils sont tous contents.
All of them are happy. (They are all happy.)

The **s** of the pronoun is pronounced, but not that of the adjective:

Tous les jeunes sont contents.
All the youngsters are happy.

Hommes, femmes, enfants, tous sont sortis en courant.
Men, women, children, all came running out.

Elles me faisaient toutes **peur.**
They all frightened me.

Je vous le dis une fois pour toutes **!**
I'm telling you once and for all!

Tout le monde *(everybody / everyone)* takes a singular verb as in English:

Tout le monde était déçu.
Everybody was disappointed.

[If we wish to say *the whole world*, we need to use **le monde entier.**]

◆

The interrogative pronoun – Le pronom interrogatif : qui, que, quoi, etc

The form that the interrogative pronoun will take depends on the part it plays in the sentence and on whether it refers to a **person** or a **thing**. Here once again we will find that English usage is far looser than the French.

	SUBJECT	OBJECT
PERSON	Qui Qui est-ce qui	Qui + Inversion Qui est-ce que
THING	- - - Qu'est-ce qui	Que + Inversion Qu'est-ce que

You will note that in the longer forms of these pronouns, the first element is **qui** for a **person**, **que** for a **thing**; the final element is **qui** for the subject, **que** for the object. [Here the interrogative pronoun differs from the relative pronoun where, as we saw, **qui** and **que** are both used to refer to people **and** things.]

- person, subject – *who?*

Qui:

Qui se trouve derrière ce mur ?
Who is behind this wall?

Qui **étaient les premiers à arriver ?**
Who were the first to arrive?

or

Qui est-ce qui:

Qui est-ce qui **a assassiné le roi ?**
Who killed the king?

Qui est-ce qui **est l'auteur de cette lettre ?**
Who is the author of this letter?

- person, object – *who(m)?*

Qui, followed by the inverted form of the question:

Qui **avez-vous vu à la gare ?**
Who did you see at the station?

Qui **regardez-vous ?**
Who are you looking at?

or

Qui est-ce que (ie **qui** followed by the other method of asking a question):

Qui est-ce que **vous voulez voir ?**
Who do you want to see?

Qui est-ce que **ces hommes craignent ?**
Who are those men afraid of?

The major source of confusion here, as with the relative pronoun, is that in modern (especially spoken) English we rarely make the distinction between *who* and *whom*, preferring to use *who* as both subject and object: **Who** *do you want to see?* **Who** *are those men afraid of?* **Who** *did they visit?*

- thing, subject – *what?*

Qu'est-ce qui:

Qu'est-ce qui **se passe ?**
What's going on?

Qu'est-ce qui **te fait penser à ton grand-père ?**
What makes you think of your grandfather?

Qu'est-ce qui **vous surprend le plus ?**
What surprises you the most?

- thing, object – *what?*

Que, followed by the inverted form of the question:

Que **veut-il nous dire ?**
What does he want to tell us?

Qu'y **a-t-il à faire ?**
What is there to do?

Que **voulez-vous que je fasse ?**
What do you want me to do?

or

Qu'est-ce que (ie **que** followed by the other method of asking a question):

Qu'est-ce que **vous en pensez ?**
What do you think about it?

Qu'est-ce qu'on va leur dire ?
What are we going to tell them?

Qu'est-ce que les Allemands aiment faire le dimanche ?
What do Germans like to do on Sundays?

Once again we must be aware that the English usage of the word *what* as both subject **and** object may cause confusion.

• person with a preposition – *who(m)*?

Qui, followed by the inverted form of the question:

Avec qui vient-elle ?
Who is she coming with?

Pour qui faites-vous ce travail ?
Who are you doing this work for?

Chez qui vas-tu passer la semaine ?
Who are you going to spend the week with? (At whose house are you going to spend the week?)

or

Qui est-ce que (ie **qui** followed by the other method of asking a question):

Derrière qui est-ce que mes amis doivent s'asseoir ?
Who do my friends have to sit behind?

Sans qui est-ce qu'il faut travailler ?
Who do we have to work without?

À qui est-ce que vous allez donner le prix ?
Who are you going to give the prize to?

We feel we should remind you that, while in English we can say: **Who** *is she coming* with? **Who** *are you doing this work* for? **Who** *are you going to give the prize* **to**?, this is not possible in French. Here the preposition must follow the rule (and the rule simply translates the word **pre-position**) of being placed **directly before the word it is associated with**: *With whom is she coming? For whom are you doing this work? To whom are you going to give this prize?*

Exactly the same rule applies in the next section:

• thing, following a preposition – *what*?

Quoi, followed by the inverted form of the question. We also give a less formal alternative:

Avec quoi va-t-on ouvrir la bouteille ? / On va ouvrir la bouteille avec quoi ?
What are we going to open the bottle with?

À quoi pensez-vous ? / Vous pensez à quoi ?
What are you thinking about?

Dans quoi ont-ils mis les billets de banque ? / Ils ont mis les billets de banque dans quoi ?
What did they put the banknotes in?

De quoi avez-vous besoin ? / Vous avez besoin de quoi ?
What do you need?

De quoi as-tu peur ? / Tu as peur de quoi ?
What are you afraid of?

[The word **pourquoi** (*why*, literally *for what*) follows this rule, but it is so common that its two parts have become fused.]

or

Quoi est-ce que (ie **quoi** followed by the other method of asking a question):

Sur quoi est-ce que **mes amis vont se reposer ?**
What are my friends going to rest on?

À quoi est-ce qu'**elles pensent ?**
What are they thinking about?

Sous quoi est-ce que **vos amis vont cacher les papiers ?**
What are your friends going to hide the papers under?

TRAIL → 44
page 217

→ TRAIL 19

▶ TECHNICAL TERMS

Adjective – a word which says, indicates or asks something about a noun – *a green carpet*, **my old** *friend*, **this** *car*, **which** *town* – or about a pronoun – *he is* **tall***, those are* **cheap.**

Agreement – in French, nouns (and therefore pronouns which stand in their place) are either masculine or feminine, singular or plural. An adjective which accompanies a noun or pronoun must match the noun or pronoun in gender and number. This 'match' is commonly referred to as **agreement**. Un petit garçon, une petite fille, deux petits garçons, deux petites filles.

Throughout our section on the adjective, we will use **bold green** for masculine forms and roman green for feminine forms. Where the masculine and feminine forms are the same, we will simply use **bold black**.

There are several types of adjectives and we will make a start with the **possessive adjective – l'adjectif possessif** – *my, your, his, her, our, their* – which indicates ownership of a particular noun.

Here is the possessive adjective set out in table form (masculine, feminine and plural below refer to the **noun possessed**, not to the person or persons possessing it):

	M	F	PL
my	mon	ma	mes
your (**tu**)	ton	ta	tes
his / her / its	son	sa	ses
our	notre		nos
your (**vous**)	votre		vos
their	leur		leurs

As we said above, it is the number and gender of the **noun** which determines the form of the adjective. Thus we have:

mon père, ma mère

This applies whether the person speaking is male or female.

In our experience, the most common error made with the possessive adjective is with *his* and *her*, where French uses the same word for both:

son père, sa mère

This may mean both *his* father and *her* father, *his* mother and *her* mother.

We would also like to draw your attention to the forms **notre, votre, leur**, which describe singular nouns:

notre <u>maison</u>, votre <u>auto</u>, leur <u>pays</u> (*country*)

and **nos, vos, leurs** – which describe plural nouns:

nos <u>enfants</u>, vos <u>décisions</u>, leurs <u>livres</u>, leurs <u>élèves</u>.

There is one final point to note. Ma, ta and sa cannot be placed before a **vowel** or a **mute h**. The masculine forms are used here, even though the noun is feminine:

mon amie, ton histoire, son école.

◆

The **demonstrative adjective – l'adjectif démonstratif** – this, that, these, those – indicates, or points to, a noun:

	M	F	PL
this / that	**ce** *	cette	**ces**

* **Ce** cannot be used before a **vowel** or **mute h**. In its place, **cet** is used: **cet arbre** (*tree*), **cet hôtel**.

Cette is used before any singular feminine noun, even one which begins with a vowel or mute h: cette **assiette** (*plate*), cette **histoire**.

You will sometimes find **-ci** or **-là** attached to a noun described by a demonstrative adjective:

ce livre-ci, cet homme-là, cette **fille-ci, ces autos-ci, ces messieurs-là** – *this book, that man, this girl, these cars, those gentlemen*.

These additions are used to distinguish objects which are **near** to us (*this, these*) from those **further away** (*that, those*) where the distinction would otherwise be unclear.

[**-ci** is a shortened form of **ici** (here), **-là** you already know to mean *there* as an alternative to **y**. Compare this to **voici** and **voilà**.]

◆

The **interrogative adjective – l'adjectif interrogatif**, as you would expect, is used to ask a **question**. In English, this is best expressed as: *which book?, which shoes?*, etc, although in speech these days we will often hear: *what book?, what shoes?* This will cause more difficulty to the foreigner learning English than to an English person learning French.

	M	F
Singular	**quel**	quel<u>le</u>
Plural	**quels**	quel<u>les</u>

Generally, as you will hear, these are all identically pronounced. However the final **-s** of **quels** and quelles is sounded before a **vowel** and a **mute h**:

quel livre ? quelle **fille ? quels journaux ?** quelles **chaussures ? quels‿enfants ?** quelles‿**histoires ?**

This adjective is also used in exclamations:

Quel désastre !
What a disaster!

Quelle **journée !**
What a day!

You will have noted that in French there is here **no indefinite article** (*a* or *an*).

Quels grands chevaux !
What big horses!

Quelles belles **tasses !**
What fine cups!

◆

As you will have seen in the examples above, if you are going to make correct agreements of the adjective, you will need to know the gender of the noun it describes.

We will now look at the agreement of the adjective in general.

Most adjectives are **regular** in that we add an **-e** to form the feminine and an **-s** to form the plural. The agreement of the past participle is made in the same way.

Thus we have:

	M	F
Singular	**petit**	petit<u>e</u>
Plural	**petit<u>s</u>**	petit<u>es</u>

However where an adjective ends in an **-e** in its masculine singular, the feminine forms will be identical to the masculine ones:

	M	F
Singular	**jeune**	jeune
Plural	**jeune<u>s</u>**	jeune<u>s</u>

This will not apply where the masculine singular ends in **-é**:

	M	F
Singular	**fatigué**	fatigué<u>e</u>
Plural	**fatigué<u>s</u>**	fatigué<u>es</u>

There are no French words ending in **-ee**.

With regard to **irregular** adjectives, we set out below a series of rules regarding the formation of the **feminine singular** forms.

The plural forms of all of these feminines simply add an -s to the singular forms.
You should remember that our aim, as in the whole of the book, is not to produce exhaustive lists, but to draw attention to common difficulties. You should be aware that many adjectives will have other meanings than the one(s) we give here. A good dictionary will be your best guide to usage.

- Adjectives ending in **-f** have a feminine form ending in **-ve**:

actif	→	acti<u>ve</u>	*active*
fictif	→	ficti<u>ve</u>	*fictitious*
juif	→	jui<u>ve</u>	*Jewish*
naïf	→	naï<u>ve</u>	*naive*
neuf	→	neu<u>ve</u>	*brand new*

Exception:

bref	→	br<u>è</u>ve	*brief, short*

- Adjectives ending in **-ier** and **-er** add an **-e** and also take a **grave accent**:

dernier	→	derni<u>ère</u>	*last*
léger	→	lég<u>ère</u>	*light*
premier	→	premi<u>ère</u>	*first*
régulier	→	réguli<u>ère</u>	*regular*
saisonnier	→	saisonni<u>ère</u>	*seasonal*

- Adjectives ending in **-et** may double the **t** and add an **-e**:

muet	→	mue<u>tte</u>	*dumb, mute*
net	→	ne<u>tte</u>	*clear, precise*
seulet	→	seule<u>tte</u>	*alone*
sujet	→	suje<u>tte</u>	*subject (to)*

or they may take a **grave accent** and add an **-e**:

complet	→	compl<u>ète</u>	*complete*
discret	→	discr<u>ète</u>	*discreet*
inquiet	→	inqui<u>ète</u>	*anxious*
secret	→	secr<u>ète</u>	*secret*

- Adjectives ending in **-eux** change **x** to **s** and add an **-e**:

affreux	→	affreu<u>se</u>	*awful*
heureux	→	heureu<u>se</u>	*happy*
paresseux	→	paresseu<u>se</u>	*lazy*
peureux	→	peureu<u>se</u>	*fearful*

- Adjectives ending in **-el**, **-eil**, **-ien**, **-ul** and **-on** double the consonant and add an **-e**:

cruel	→	cruel<u>le</u>	*cruel*
pareil	→	pareil<u>le</u>	*similar*
chrétien	→	chrétien<u>ne</u>	*Christian*
nul	→	nul<u>le</u>	*hopeless*
bon	→	bon<u>ne</u>	*good*

- Adjectives ending in **-il** normally follow the general rule of adding an **-e**:

civil	→	civile	*civil*
subtil	→	subtile	*subtle*
vil	→	vile	*vile*

Exception:

gentil	→	genti<u>lle</u>	*kind*

- Adjectives ending in **-c** fall into two distinct groups:

grec	→	grec**que**	*Greek*
public	→	publi**que**	*public*
turc	→	tur**que**	*Turkish*

and

blanc	→	blan**che**	*white*
franc	→	fran**che**	*frank*
sec	→	sè**che**	*dry*

- Ten adjectives ending in **-eur** simply add an **-e**:

antérieur	→	antérieure	*anterior*
extérieur	→	extérieure	*exterior*
inférieur	→	inférieure	*inferior*
intérieur	→	intérieure	*interior*
majeur	→	majeure	*major*
meilleur	→	meilleure	*best*
mineur	→	mineure	*minor*
postérieur	→	postérieure	*posterior*
supérieur	→	supérieure	*superior*
ultérieur	→	ultérieure	*ulterior*

but most, like some feminine nouns, change the ending to **-euse**:

flatteur	→	flatt**euse**	flattering
menteur	→	ment**euse**	*lying*
prometteur	→	promett**euse**	*promising*

- Some adjectives ending in **-teur** have feminines as follows:

destructeur	→	destruc**trice**	*destructive*
dévastateur	→	dévasta**trice**	*devastating*
innovateur	→	innova**trice**	*innovative*
révélateur	→	révéla**trice**	*revealing*

- Adjectives ending in **-s** double the **s** and add an **-e**:

bas	→	bas**se**	*low*
épais	→	épais**se**	*thick*
gras	→	gras**se**	*fatty*
gros	→	gros**se**	*big, fat*
las	→	las**se**	*tired*

Exception:

| frais | → | fraî**che** | *fresh, cool* |

- The following feminine forms, which follow no distinct rule, should be carefully noted:

doux	→	dou**ce**	*soft, gentle*
faux	→	fau**sse**	*false*
favori	→	favor**ite**	*favourite*
jaloux	→	jalou**se**	*jealous*

long	→	lon**gue**	*long*
malin	→	mali**gne**	*malicious*
roux	→	rou**sse**	*red-haired*
sot	→	sot**te**	*stupid, daft*
beau	→	be**lle**	*beautiful*
nouveau	→	nouve**lle**	*new*
vieux	→	vie**ille**	*old*

- These final three adjectives require a special mention. They have a second **masculine singular** form which is used before a noun beginning with a **vowel** or a **mute h**:

beau	→	bel	un **bel** hôtel
nouveau	→	nouvel	le **nouvel** an
vieux	→	vieil	un **vieil** arbre

NB This special form is only used before a **singular** noun.

One final point concerns the use of the **tréma** (*dieresis*). This is a sign consisting of two dots placed above a vowel. Where an adjective ends in **-gu**, eg **aigu** (*acute*, *sharp*), **ambigu** (*ambiguous*), the feminine form will have the tréma: aigüe, ambigüe. This is to show that the **u** must be pronounced, unlike in the word **ligue** (*league*).

[Some dictionaries may place the **tréma** over the **e**. We are following the change in spelling recommended by the Académie française.]

◆

Our next section, still dealing with **irregular** adjectives, and covering the change from the **masculine singular** form to the **masculine plural**, is far less complex:

- Adjectives ending in **-s** and **-x** make no change in the masculine plural:

chanceux	→	chanceux	*lucky*
gras	→	gras	*fatty*
gris	→	gris	*grey*
gros	→	gros	*big, fat*
heureux	→	heureux	*happy*
peureux	→	peureux	*scared*

- Adjectives ending in **-al** have plurals ending in **-aux**:

brutal	→	brutaux	*brutal*
loyal	→	loyaux	*loyal*
mondial	→	mondiaux	*worldwide*

Exceptions include:

fatal	→	fatals	*fatal*
final	→	finals	*final*
naval	→	navals	*naval*

- The following two adjectives add **-x** to form the plural form:

beau	→	beaux	*handsome, beautiful*
nouveau	→	nouveaux	*new*

◆

We feel it important to make two further points. The first is very simple:

Plusieurs (*several*) never changes:

plusieurs garçons ; plusieurs filles

The second is somewhat more complicated. Here we deal with the adjective **tout** (all):

	M	F
Singular	**tout**	toute
Plural	**<u>tous</u>**	toutes

Many students misspell the masculine plural form – note that the **-t-** is dropped.

tout le gâteau
the whole cake, all (of) the cake

toute **la classe**
the whole class, all (of) the class

tous les étudiants
all (of) the students, all students

toutes **les femmes**
all (of) the women, all women

Note that while in English we distinguish between *all the women* and *all women*, French always retains the definite article.

Similarly, the definite article is retained when translating *both (of them)*, *all three (of them)* etc:

Ils sont partis tous les deux.
*They **both** left. **Both** of them have left.*

Toutes les trois **sont arrivées en même temps.**
All three (of them) arrived at the same time.

The English word *everybody* or *everyone* becomes in French *all the world* – **tout le monde**:

Il a donné un baiser à tout le monde.
He gave everyone a kiss.

As the subject of a verb, **tout le monde** takes a singular verb as **everyone** does in English:

Tout le monde est content.
Everyone is happy.

Tout le monde a mangé.
Everybody has eaten.

Tout le monde était parti.
Everyone had left.

We are giving a special mention to the word **tout** (*all*) as it has other uses besides being an adjective:

a) **Tout** may also serve as a pronoun meaning *everything* (both as subject and object):

Tout **s'est bien passé.**
Everything went well.

Tout est possible.
Everything is possible.

Il a tout fait.
He did everything.

Elle vend tout.
She's selling everything.

You will see from the above examples that **tout** does not change, it is invariable.

b) **Tout** also serves as an **adverb** to qualify an adjective in much the same way that we use the word *quite* to mean *completely*:

Here again, **tout** will remain invariable for the most part:

Il était tout fatigué.
He was quite tired.

Ils étaient tout charmants.
They were quite delightful.

However, we must point out the following examples regarding feminine adjectives:

Marie est toute haletante.
Marie is quite out of breath.

Elles étaient toutes fatiguées.
They were quite tired.

You will note that in these two examples **tout** is made to agree. This is the rule when the adjective (in the feminine) begins with a **consonant** or with **aspirate h**. The following examples illustrate the case with adjectives beginning with a **vowel** or **mute h**:

Elle était tout étonnée.
She was quite surprised.

Elles auraient été tout heureuses.
They would have been quite happy.

In these last two examples, the final **-t** is pronounced as the liaison is made, automatically giving the same sound as the feminine form.

◆

While we do not wish to introduce too many complications, we feel we ought to point out some cases where the adjective will **not agree** with the noun.

a) Where the adjective is in fact a **noun** in French:

Elle a les cheveux marron.
She has reddish-brown / auburn hair.
(**marron** *chestnut*)

J'aime bien les maillots orange de mon équipe.
I like my team's orange shirts.

However, the adjective **rose** (*pink*) does agree:

Elle a les joues roses.
She has pink cheeks.

b) Where the colour is qualified:

Elle vient d'acheter une jupe bleu clair.
She has just bought a light blue skirt.

Il porte une chemise vert foncé.
He is wearing a dark green shirt.

TRAIL → 20
page 218

→ TRAIL 65

POSITION OF ADJECTIVES – LA PLACE DE L'ADJECTIF

The vast majority of adjectives in French **follow the noun** and point out its distinguishing features:

Apportez-moi de l'eau froide !
Bring me some cold water! (not tepid or hot)

Je vais acheter le pantalon bleu.
I'm going to buy the blue trousers. (not the brown ones)

C'est une voiture française.
It is a French car. (not German)

NB Adjectives of nationality in French do not have a capital letter.

Il a fait des efforts considérables pour réussir.
He made great efforts to succeed.

Here we are drawing attention to the quality of the efforts he made in order to succeed.

There are, however, a number of commonplace adjectives, of only one or two syllables, which are placed before the noun. These include:

bon, mauvais, grand, gros,

jeune, joli, long, haut,

méchant, petit, beau,

vaste, vieux, vilain, sot.

The adjective excellent, although it has three syllables, is also placed before the noun:

Il m'a recommandé un excellent **hôtel près de la gare.**
He recommended an excellent hotel near the station.

◆

Whilst it is the case that you can say **un panorama magnifique** or **un magnifique panorama** (*a magnificent view*), **un séjour agréable** or **un agréable séjour** (*a pleasant stay*), adjectives which express our feelings have greater intensity when placed before the noun. We therefore offer on occasions **nos sincères condoléances** (*our sincere condolences*).

◆

You will also need to be aware that some adjectives have different meanings depending on whether they come before or after the noun. We will list the most common of these:

Un **ancien** ami (*old, of some years' standing*)
Une maison ancienne (*old, ancient*)

Un **brave homme** (*good, honest, upright*)
Une femme brave (*courageous*)

Un **certain** charme (*certain, indefinable*)
Une guérison (*cure*) certaine (*certain, definite, sure*)

Mon **cher** ami (*dear, well-liked*)
Une auto chère (*expensive*)

[However, to express the loss of someone close, there is an exception to the above rule: **Il a perdu un ami cher.**]

Le **dernier** lundi du mois (*last, final*)
La semaine dernière (*last, most recent*)

Un **grand** homme (*great, famous*)
Une jeune fille grande (*tall*)

Un **pauvre** enfant (*poor, unfortunate*)
Une famille pauvre (*poor, penniless*)

Le **prochain** village (*next, nearest*)
L'année prochaine (*next, to come*)

Mon **propre château** (*own, my property*)
Une maison propre (*clean*)

Un **vrai** ami (*true, genuine, real*)
Une histoire vraie (*true, not fictitious*)

◆

THE COMPARATIVE ADJECTIVE – L'ADJECTIF COMPARATIF – MAKING COMPARISONS

Il est plus riche que son frère.
He is richer than his brother.

Il est aussi riche que son frère.
He is as rich as ...

Il est moins riche que son frère.
He is less rich than (not as rich as) ...

Elles sont plus douées **que lui.**
They are more gifted than he.

Elles sont aussi douées **que lui.**
They are as gifted as ...

Elles sont moins douées **que lui.**
They are less gifted than (not as gifted as) ...

As you can see, when we are comparing two of anything, we simply place the French for *more*, *as* or *less* before the adjective, which of course still agrees.

Less may be expressed in another way:

Il n'est pas aussi / si riche que son frère.

Elles ne sont pas aussi / si douées **que lui.**

You will also note that the second half of the comparison is always introduced by **que** in French (in English by *as* or *than*).

However, we need to be careful with the comparatives *better* and *worse*.

a) **Meilleur** – *better*

While it is correct to use **aussi bon** and **moins bon**, **plus** will never accompany this adjective. Instead, the English **better** is translated by **meilleur**:

C'est un meilleur restaurant.
It's a better restaurant.

J'ai une meilleure **idée.**
I have a better idea.

Ses efforts sont meilleurs qu'hier.
His efforts are better than yesterday.

The French for *much better* is **bien meilleur** – **beaucoup** is **not used** in this context.

b) **Plus mauvais / Pire** – *worse*

Votre traduction est plus mauvaise **que la précédente.**
Your translation is worse than the previous one.

La situation est pire que la semaine dernière.
The situation is worse than last week.

Plus mauvais is used to imply that something is more defective, more imperfect. **Pire** marks a greater degree of intensity and can indicate that something is morally worse:

Son frère est pire que lui.
His brother is worse than he is.

THE SUPERLATIVE ADJECTIVE – L'ADJECTIF SUPERLATIF – EXPRESSING BEST, WORST, LEAST, MOST

Voilà la fille la plus intelligente **de la classe.**
*There is the **most intelligent** girl in the class.*

Voilà la fille la moins intelligente **de la classe.**
*There is the **least intelligent** girl in the class.*

Ce sont les garçons les plus aimables du groupe.
*They are the **nicest** boys in the group.*

Ce sont les garçons les moins aimables du groupe.
*They are the **least nice** boys in the group.*

Simone est mon amie la plus chère.
*Simone is my **dearest** friend.*

As you can see, the definite article is repeated or added to form the superlative adjective. We have chosen here adjectives which normally follow the noun they describe – **la fille** intelligente, **les garçons aimables**.

However, where the adjective is normally placed before the noun – **une** belle **fille**, un cher **ami** – we can **still follow the same pattern** with the superlative:

Voilà la plus belle **fille de la classe.**
Here is the most beautiful girl in the class.

Pierre est le plus cher **ami de la famille.**
Pierre is the dearest friend of the family.

or express it in the same way as our earlier examples:

Voilà la fille la plus belle **de la classe.**

Pierre est l'ami le plus cher **de la famille.**

Similarly, when we talk about the youngest pupils we may have:

Les plus jeunes élèves ...

Les élèves les plus jeunes ...

While we have the choice of construction with adjectives which come before the noun, there is only the one possibility with those which follow it:

Thus, because we would talk about **un élève** attentif, we are obliged to say:

les élèves les plus attentifs

when speaking of the most attentive pupils.

Remember that when the superlative is placed after the noun, there is a **repetition or addition of the definite article**.

One further point to be noted is the use of the word **de** which here translates the English **in** or **from**:

C'est la plus belle **ville** du **monde.**
It's the most beautiful city in the world.

Je connais le meilleur **restaurant de la ville.**
I know the best restaurant in town.

Ce sont les plus beaux **souvenirs de l'enfance du poète.**
They are the most beautiful memories from the poet's childhood.

C'est le plus grand homme des États-Unis.
He is the greatest man in the United States.

Le patron ne boit que le champagne le plus cher de Reims.
The boss only drinks the most expensive champagne from Reims.

La plus jeune de la famille, c'est Charlotte.
The youngest in the family is Charlotte.

As with the comparative forms **meilleur** and **pire**, we must again take care:

a) **Le meilleur** – *the best*

Il porte son meilleur veston.
He is wearing his best jacket.

Je cherche la meilleure solution.
I'm looking for the best solution.

Ils achètent toujours les meilleurs chocolats.
They always buy the best chocolates.

b) **Le pire** – *the worst*

Cet homme est devenu son pire ennemi.
This man has become his worst enemy.

Il envisage toujours la pire des difficultés.
He always imagines the worst of difficulties.

À mon avis ce sont les pires excuses.
In my opinion they are the worst excuses.

Il craint le pire.
He fears the worst.

Where we are describing the **most defective** or **imperfect**, we should use **plus mauvais**:

Malheureusement, il ne reste que les plus mauvaises places (les places les plus mauvaises).
Unfortunately, only the worst seats are left (… there remain only the worst seats).

◆

Generally, the use of two adjectives does not pose a problem. We can say:

une belle jeune fille, une jolie maison blanche, un bel homme français

On those occasions where both adjectives follow the noun, they are linked by **et**:

Un étudiant travailleur et intelligent ...
A hard-working, intelligent student ...

TRAIL → 66
page 221

→ TRAIL 71

We recognise that this is a difficult aspect of French grammar to teach. It is only over a period of time that students come to appreciate that a given verb or adjective will require a particular preposition when preceding an infinitive while some verbs will take no preposition at all.

Let's consider the following sentences:

Elle veut vous voir.
She wants to see you.

Elle s'est arrêtée pour **vous voir.**
She stopped to see you.

Elle est prête à **vous voir.**
She is ready to see you.

Elle était contente de **vous voir.**
She was happy to see you.

From the first example we can see that **vouloir** does not require a preposition when linked to an infinitive. The second sentence demonstrates that where the first action is carried out in order that another will follow, the two are joined by **pour** (in order to). The adjectives **prêt** and **content** take the prepositions **à** and **de** respectively before the infinitive.

◆

We will begin by offering some advice on the use of **pour**:

Il s'est assis pour **se reposer.**
He sat down in order to rest. (More simply: *He sat down to rest.*)

Papa avait téléphoné pour **me dire que maman était malade.**
Dad had rung to tell me that mum was ill.

Nous avons acheté une carte de la région pour **être sûrs de la route à prendre.**
We have bought a map of the area to be sure of the route to take.

However, **pour** is not required if the first verb is **aller** or **venir**:

Ils sont allés dire bonjour à leurs copains.
They went and said hello to their pals. (*They went to say ...*)

Elle est venue m'offrir des conseils.
She came to give me some advice.

With other verbs of motion, **partir, retourner, entrer, rentrer, revenir, sortir, monter, descendre** and with the verb **rester**, **pour** is frequently omitted:

Elle est sortie parler à sa voisine.
She went out to speak to her neighbour.

Pour is also used, simply meaning *to*, after an adjective qualified by **assez** or **trop**:

Mon oncle est assez **riche** pour **nous offrir des billets.**
My uncle is rich enough to give us some tickets.

Il est trop **sage** pour **faire cela.**
He is too well behaved to do that.

◆

In this section we will concentrate on the verbs that require no preposition when linked to an infinitive and those verbs and adjectives which require **à** or **de** when followed by an infinitive.

It is not our intention to produce exhaustive lists but to offer guidance and to highlight prepositional usage with some verbs and adjectives that you will meet frequently.

[NB The preposition **en** is followed by the present participle:

Il est arrivé en **courant.**
He came running. (He arrived at a run.)

All other prepositions are followed by the infinitive.]

◆

We will first deal with those common verbs which require **no preposition** before the infinitive:

* **aimer**
  Nous aimions nous coucher avant minuit.
  We used to like to go to bed before midnight. (**Aimer à** may be used in formal language.)

* **aimer mieux**
  Il aimerait mieux être respecté.
  He would prefer to be respected.

* **aller**
  Va dire au revoir à ce monsieur.
  Go and say goodbye to that gentleman.

* **désirer**
  Nous désirons vous rendre service.
  We want to be of service to you.

* **devoir**
  Ils doivent faire un effort, ces enfants !
  These children must make an effort!

* **espérer**
  J'espère te revoir le plus tôt possible.
  I hope to see you again as soon as possible.

- **faillir**

  Elle a failli tomber.
  She almost fell.

- **falloir**

  Il nous a fallu rentrer tout de suite.
  We had to return immediately.

- **laisser**

  Je les laisserai partir tranquillement.
  I will let them leave in peace.

- **oser**

  Il n'osera pas refuser.
  He will not dare (to) refuse.

- **paraître**

  Il ne paraît pas savoir que faire.
  He doesn't seem (appear) to know what to do.

- **penser**

  Elle pense avoir compris.
  She thinks she has understood. (**Pensez à le faire.** *Don't forget to do it.*)

- **pouvoir**

  Je ne peux pas vous le dire.
  I can't tell you.

- **préférer**

  Ils préfèrent rester ici.
  They prefer to stay here.

- **savoir**

  Bien sûr elle sait nager.
  Of course she can (knows how to) swim.

- **souhaiter**

  Je souhaitais les récompenser.
  I wanted (wished) to reward them.

- **valoir mieux**

  Il vaut mieux travailler dur.
  It is better to work hard.

- **venir**

  Le général est venu annoncer la victoire.
  The general came and announced (to announce) the victory.

- **vouloir**

  Elles veulent passer une heure dans le parc.
  They want to spend an hour in the park.

[Although *and* is a conjunction, not a preposition, it is used in English to link *go* and *come* to another verb:

  *Go **and** buy a newspaper.*

  *He came **and** had dinner with us.*

Here the word *and* is **not translated** into French:

  Va acheter un journal.

  Il est venu dîner avec nous.]

◆

We have not found any completely reliable rule about the use of **à** and **de** followed by an infinitive. However, we do feel that, despite many exceptions, it may help you to think of **à** in terms of positive, ongoing actions, whereas **de** often indicates preventing, stopping, restricting.

◆

a) Some adjectives and verbs which are followed by à + infinitive:

Adjectives:

- **assis à**

  Elle était assise à faire un mots-croisés.
  She was sitting doing a crossword.

- **décidé à**

  Il est décidé à donner sa démission.
  He is determined to resign. (also **déterminé à**)

- **dernier à**

  Mes amis seront les derniers à partir.
  My friends will be the last to leave.

- **disposé à**

  Elle est disposée à vous inviter.
  She is willing to invite you.

- **premier à**

  C'était la première voiture à arriver.
  It was the first car to arrive. (also **deuxième à, troisième à,** etc)

- **prêt à**
  Nous sommes prêts à vous suivre.
  We are ready to follow you.

- **seul à**
  Elle était la seule à répondre.
  She was the only one to reply.

Verbs:

- **aider à**
  Papa aidera maman à faire le ménage.
  Dad will help mum to do the housework.

- **s'amuser à**
  Il s'amuse à dire des bêtises.
  He enjoys saying silly things.

- **apprendre à**
  Elle apprend à jouer du piano.
  She is learning to play the piano.
  Elle leur apprend à jouer du piano.
  She is teaching them to play the piano.

- **arriver à**
  J'arrive enfin à comprendre.
  I'm finally getting the gist of it.

- **aspirer à**
  Elle aspire à avoir une jolie maison à la campagne.
  Her ambition is to have a nice house in the country. (She aspires to owning ...)

- **s'attendre à**
  Il s'attend à recevoir sa lettre.
  He is expecting to receive his / her letter.

- **avoir à**
  J'ai une course à faire.
  I have an errand to do.
  Nous avons à repasser tout ce linge ce soir.
  We have all these clothes to iron this evening.

- **chercher à**
  Elle avait cherché à découvrir son secret.
  She had sought (tried) to discover his / her secret.

- **commencer à**

  Soudain il a commencé à pleuvoir.
  Suddenly it started to rain.
  (**Commencer de** is also possible.)

- **continuer à**

  Il continue à nous faire des surprises.
  He continues to spring surprises on us. (**Continuer de** is also possible.)

- **se décider à**

  Je me suis décidé à ne plus fumer.
  I have made up my mind to give up smoking (not to smoke any more).

- **demander à**

  Le directeur demande à vous voir dans son bureau.
  The headmaster is asking to see you in his office.

- **encourager à**

  Le professeur nous a encouragés à lire cet article.
  The teacher has encouraged us to read this article.

- **s'ennuyer à**

  Il s'ennuie à mourir.
  He's bored to death.

- **hésiter à**

  Elle hésitera à dire oui.
  She will hesitate to say yes.

- **inviter à**

  Je vous invite à passer la nuit chez moi.
  I am inviting you to spend the night at my house.

- **s'occuper à**

  Papa s'occupe à faire les corvées ménagères.
  Dad is busy doing the housework.

- **parvenir à**

  Il est enfin parvenu à comprendre le subjonctif.
  He's finally managed to understand the subjunctive.

- **passer du temps à**

  Nous avons passé deux heures à regarder cette émission.
  We spent two hours watching that programme.

- **persister à**
  Elle persistait à mentir.
  She went on (persisted in) lying.

- **pousser à**
  Elle nous pousse à les suivre.
  She is urging us to follow them.

- **prendre plaisir à**
  Il prenait plaisir à se promener à la campagne.
  He used to enjoy (take pleasure in) walking in the countryside.

- **renoncer à**
  Il avait renoncé à collectionner les timbres.
  He had given up collecting stamps.

- **réussir à**
  Il a réussi à trouver un bon poste.
  He has succeeded in finding a good job.

- **se mettre à**
  Elle s'est mise à faire du repassage.
  She got down to doing some ironing. (She began to do some ironing.)

- **se préparer à**
  Nous nous préparons à passer un examen de français.
  We are preparing to take a French exam.

- **servir à**
  Un aspirateur sert à nettoyer la maison.
  A vacuum cleaner is used (serves) to clean the house.

- **songer à**
  Elle songe à retourner aux États-Unis.
  She is thinking of going back to the United States.

◆

b) Some adjectives and verbs which are followed by de + infinitive:

Adjectives:

- **capable de**
  Bien sûr vous êtes capable de le faire !
  Of course you can do it!

- **certain de**
  Il est certain de réussir.
  He is certain (sure) to succeed. (also **sûr de**)

- **curieux de**
  Nous sommes curieux de savoir pourquoi.
  We are curious to know (interested in knowing) why.

- **désolé de**
  Elle était désolée de quitter son amie.
  She was sorry to leave her friend.

- **heureux de**
  Maman sera heureuse de vous revoir.
  Mum will be happy to see you again. (also **content de**)

- **libre de**
  Elle aurait été libre de partir.
  She would have been free to leave.

- **ravi de**
  Elle était ravie de sortir avec lui.
  She was delighted to go out with him.

- **triste de**
  Je suis triste d'entendre la nouvelle de sa mort.
  I am sad to hear the news of his / her death.

Verbs:

- **accepter de**
  Elle a accepté de recevoir vos enfants.
  She has agreed to take your children.

- **arrêter de**
  Il a arrêté de boire.
  He has stopped drinking. (also **s'arrêter de**)

- **avoir raison de**
  Il avait raison de se taire.
  He was right to keep silent.

- **avoir tort de**
  Elle a tort de protester.
  She is wrong to protest.

- **cesser de**

  Il a cessé de pleuvoir.
  It has stopped raining.

- **se charger de**

  Il s'est chargé de prendre contact avec les membres.
  He has undertaken (taken it on himself) to contact the members.

- **choisir de**

  Papa a choisi de louer une Renault.
  Dad chose to hire a Renault.

- **craindre de**

  Le voleur craignait de dire la vérité.
  The thief was afraid to tell the truth. (also **avoir peur de**)

- **décider de**

  L'arbitre a décidé de siffler la fin du match.
  The referee decided to blow (the whistle) for the end of the match.

- **se dépêcher de**

  Dépêchons-nous de traverser la rue !
  Let's hurry across the street! (also **se hâter de**)

- **empêcher de**

  Vous ne m'empêcherez pas de répondre.
  You will not prevent (stop) me from replying.

- **s'empêcher de**

  Je ne pouvais pas m'empêcher de rire.
  I couldn't stop myself (from) laughing. / I couldn't help laughing.

- **essayer de**

  Il essaie toujours de faire de son mieux.
  He always tries to do his best. (also **tâcher de, tenter de**)

- **éviter de**

  J'ai évité de lui expliquer mes raisons.
  I avoided explaining my reasons to him / her.

- **faire semblant de**

  Il faisait semblant de dormir.
  He was pretending to be asleep. (also **feindre de**)

- **finir de**

  Ils ont fini de regarder la télévision.
  They have finished watching television.

- **menacer de**

  Le directeur a menacé de la mettre à la porte.
  The director threatened to dismiss (sack) her.

- **offrir de**

  Ma tante a offert de me payer un café.
  My aunt has offered to buy me a coffee.

- **oublier de**

  Elle avait oublié de me rappeler.
  She had forgotten to call me back.

- **promettre de**

  Ma cousine a promis de venir.
  My cousin promised to come.

- **refuser de**

  Elle refuse de répondre à la lettre.
  She refuses to answer the letter.

- **regretter de**

  Je regrette d'entendre cela.
  I'm sorry to hear that. (also **être désolé de**)

◆

Points to bear in mind

- When an adjective introduces an infinitive (*difficult to open, easy to learn, interesting to read, pleasant to hear etc*), two constructions are possible:

a. noun – part of être – adjective – à – infinitive

b. il est / c'est – adjective – de – infinitive

  Cette bouteille est difficile à ouvrir.
  This bottle is difficult to open.

  Il est / C'est difficile d'ouvrir cette bouteille.

[The version using **il est** is more formal than that using **c'est**.]

  Cette langue est facile à apprendre.
  This language is easy to learn.

  Il est facile d'apprendre cette langue.

Cet article serait intéressant à lire.
This article would be interesting to read.

Il serait intéressant de lire cet article.

La musique était agréable à entendre.
The music was pleasing to hear.

Il était agréable d'entendre la musique.

- Care must be taken when using verbs which express compulsion:

  forcer à / obliger à:

  Je les forcerai à dire oui.
  I will force them to say yes. (I'll make them say yes.)

  Il m'a obligé à répondre en français.
  He made me answer in French.

  But:

  être forcé de / être obligé de:

  Nous sommes forcés de tirer la même conclusion.
  We are forced to draw the same conclusion.

  Elle avait été obligée de rendre le portefeuille.
  She had been forced (obliged) to give back the wallet.

[The same constructions apply to **contraindre à** and **être contraint de** which also mean *force, compel, oblige, constrain*.]

After verbs of beginning and ending, **par** followed by an **infinitive** is used to mean *by (do)ing*:

Elle a commencé par dire qu'elle n'en savait rien.
She began by saying that she knew nothing about it.

Ils ont fini par avouer qu'ils avaient été à la banque ce jour-là.
They ended by confessing (In the end they confessed) that they had been at the bank that day.

[In other circumstances, *by (do)ing* is translated by **en** and the **present participle**:

Il a réussi en travaillant jour et nuit.
He succeeded by working day and night.]

- As well as knowing whether a verb takes **à** or **de** before an infinitive, it is important to remember which verbs take **direct** and which **indirect** objects.

Compare the following pairs of sentences:

J'ai demandé à la jeune fille de venir me voir.
I asked the girl to come and see me.

J'ai invité la jeune fille à venir me voir.
I invited the girl ...

Nous avons conseillé aux étudiants de finir le travail.
We advised the students to finish the work.

Nous avons aidé les étudiants à finir le travail.
We helped the students ...

Nous leur avons dit d'aller la voir.
We told them to go and see her.

Nous les avons encouragés à aller la voir.
We encouraged them ...

[You will find further examples of verbs which take indirect objects in our section on the passive.]

Knowing how to consult a good dictionary is the key to using any given verb correctly. With this in mind, we offer some guidance in our section entitled Dictionaries.

TRAIL → 72
page 222

→ TRAIL 25

▶ TECHNICAL TERM

Adverb – a word which tells us more about (qualifies) a verb, adjective or other adverb. *She stood up **slowly**. He was **seriously** ill. He speaks **extremely quickly**.* Most adverbs in English end in the letters **-ly** and in French in **-ment**.

FORMATION OF ADVERBS

Please be aware that, as with the adjectives, we will not be giving every meaning of the adverbs.

As a general rule, adverbs are formed from the feminine singular form of the corresponding adjective:

anxieux		
anxieuse	**anxieusement**	*anxiously*
doux		
douce	**doucement**	*gently*
fort		
forte	**fortement**	*strongly*
fou		
folle	**follement**	*madly*
heureux		
heureuse	**heureusement**	*happily*
lent		
lente	**lentement**	*slowly*
sage		
sage	**sagement**	*wisely*

vif

vive	**vivement**	*eagerly*

Where the adjective ends in **-i**, **-é** or **-u**, the adverb is formed by adding **-ment** to the masculine singular form:

absolu	**absolument**	*absolutely*
aisé	**aisément**	*easily*
poli	**poliment**	*politely*
vrai	**vraiment**	*really*

Exception:

gai

gaie	**gaiement**	*cheerfully*

Where the adjective ends in **-ant** or **-ent** the adverb will end in **-amment** or **-emment** respectively (note the double m). As with the adjective endings, these adverb endings are all pronounced in the same way:

abondant	**abondamment**	*abundantly*
constant	**constamment**	*constantly*
courant	**couramment**	*fluently*
évident	**évidemment**	*obviously*
prudent	**prudemment**	*wisely*
récent	**récemment**	*recently*

Exception:

lent	**lentement**	*slowly*

Other irregular adverbs include:

aveugle	**aveuglément**	*blindly*
bref	**brièvement**	*briefly*
énorme	**énormément**	*hugely*
gentil	**gentiment**	*kindly*
précis	**précisément**	*precisely*
profond	**profondément**	*deeply*

NB The English *seriously*, *gravely* when applied to illness or injury is translated as follows: **grièvement blessé** (*seriously injured*) BUT **gravement malade** (*gravely ill*).

Note also these two very important adverbs:

bon	**bien**	*well*
mauvais	**mal**	*badly*

Some adjectives, in their masculine singular form, may be used as adverbs. You need to be aware that all adverbs are **invariable**:

Compare:

Ces livres pèsent lourd (adverb, invariable).
These books weigh a lot.

Ces valises sont lourdes (adjective, agreement).
These suitcases are heavy.

Ces autos coûtent cher.
These cars are expensive.

Ils parlaient fort.
They were speaking loudly.

Elles chantent faux ces enfants-là.
Those children are singing out of tune.

Nous voyons clair maintenant.
We can see clearly now.

N'oubliez pas de travailler dur.
Don't forget to work hard.

La viande sent bon.
The meat smells good.

◆

Before mentioning the position of the adverb in the sentence, we will point out the difference between **meilleur** and **mieux**, which we know can cause problems as each can mean both *better* and *best*.

Meilleur is an adjective and must have a noun or pronoun which it describes and with which it will agree:

C'est une meilleure boutique.
It's a better shop.

Ce sont les meilleurs films de l'année.
They are the best films of the year.

Mieux is the adverb and as such remains invariable:

Elle va mieux.
She is better (in terms of health).

C'est elle qui joue le mieux.
She is the one who plays the best.

◆

Comparative and superlative adverbs are straightforward and, although of course they do not agree, are similar to the corresponding adjectives:

Elle parle plus vite que son frère.
She speaks more quickly than her brother.

Cette expression s'emploie moins couramment aujourd'hui.
This expression is not used as much today.

Le voleur a ouvert la porte aussi doucement que possible.
The thief opened the door as quietly as possible.

C'est ma sœur qui parle le plus/moins vite.
It's my sister who speaks the quickest/slowest.

◆

POSITION OF ADVERBS – LA PLACE DE L'ADVERBE

There are few hard-and-fast rules here. The position of the adverb may be changed to suit the rhythm and balance of the sentence and may depend on the emphasis the speaker or writer wishes to convey.

In our view, you will not go wrong if you place the adverb after the verb:

Il arrive généralement avant neuf heures.
He usually arrives before nine.

Elle parlait extrêmement vite.
She was speaking extremely quickly.

Le professeur n'aime pas tellement ses élèves.
The teacher does not much like his pupils.

Il viendra probablement ce soir.
He will probably come this evening.

Mes parents regardent souvent la télé le soir.
My parents often watch TV in the evening.

With the compound tenses, many adverbs are placed before the past participle:

Ils avaient bien joué.
They had played well.

J'ai déjà vu ce film-là.
I've already seen that film.

Nous avons toujours été contents de son travail.
We have always been happy with his / her work.

Ils ont mal compris la situation.
They misunderstood the situation.

Je regrette d'en avoir trop dit.
I regret having said too much about it.

Nous avons enfin payé nos dettes.
We have finally paid off our debts.

J'ai toujours voulu visiter Paris.
I've always wanted to visit Paris.

Elle a maintenant compris pourquoi.
She has now understood why.

Je les ai souvent vus devant le cinéma.
I have often seen them outside the cinema.

However, despite our last four examples, adverbs of **time** and **place** generally follow the past participle:

Elle est revenue hier.
She came back yesterday.

Nous avons cherché partout.
We looked (searched) everywhere.

Maman est partie aussitôt sans rien dire.
Mum left straight away without saying anything.

Nous sommes rentrés ici à deux heures cinq.
We came back here at five past two.

Ma copine et moi avons mangé dehors.
My friend and I ate outside.

Similarly, long adverbs tend to be placed after the past participle:

Ils ont pris simultanément **la décision de déménager.**
They simultaneously took the decision to move house.

Elle avait agi follement.
She had acted madly.

Often it is neater to replace a long adverb by a phrase:

Les avocats ont plaidé sa cause avec éloquence. (rather than **éloquemment**)
The lawyers pleaded his case eloquently.

Il s'est exprimé avec élégance. (rather than **élégamment**)
He expressed himself elegantly.

To end this section, you should note the following:

Much better as an adjective is **bien meilleur**. *Much better* as an adverb is **beaucoup mieux**:

Cette pièce est bien meilleure **que l'autre.**
This play is much better than the other one.

À la suite de son opération ma mère va beaucoup mieux.
Following her operation my mother is much better.

Très and **beaucoup** are also adverbs:

Il est très **sûr de lui.**
He is very sure of himself.

Mon père a beaucoup **travaillé pour réussir.**
My father has put in a lot of work to succeed.

However they cannot be used together. To translate: *He likes the cinema **very much***, we might say:

Il aime bien (beaucoup) le cinéma. / Il adore le cinéma. / Le cinéma, c'est sa passion.

TRAIL → 26
page 223

→ TRAIL 63

▶ **TECHNICAL TERMS**

Complement – the verb être cannot have a direct object. However, it is most frequently followed by a noun, pronoun or adjective known as its **complement**.

We all remember our early days of learning French. The teacher would ask the question **Qu'est-ce que c'est ?** and hold up a pen. We would chorus **C'est un stylo.** In doing so, we learned the names of classroom objects and picked up our first notions of gender. But did we really register a further very important point? **When the complement of the verb être is a noun (or a pronoun), ce (c') is its subject:**

C'est une règle.
It's a ruler.

Ce sont des règles.
They are rulers.

C'est moi.
It's me. (Some would insist on the more formal *It is I.*)

C'est toi.
It's you.

C'est lui.
It's him.

C'est elle.
It's her.

C'est nous.
It's us. (although **nous** is clearly plural)

C'est vous.
It's you.

Ce sont eux.
It's them. (note **ce sont**)

Ce sont elles.
It's them.

[**C'est eux / elles** is often found in speech.]

C'est le mien.
It's mine.

Ce sont les miens.
They're mine.

C'est celui-ci que je préfère.
It's this one / This is the one I prefer.

Ce sont celles-là qu'elle va acheter.
It is those / Those are the ones she is going to buy.

Of course, the same applies in the other tenses of **être**:

C'était la tienne.
It was yours.

C'étaient les tiennes.
They were yours.

Ce sera moi qui le prendrai.
I'll be the one who'll take it.

Ce seront eux qui accueilleront le maire.
They'll be the ones who will welcome the mayor.

Although it may at first sight look strange, we also use **ce** with the compound tenses of **être**:

Ç'aurait été une bonne affaire.
It would have been a good deal.
(Note the cedilla)

Therefore, in answer to the question:

À qui est ce livre ?
Whose is this book?

there are two possible ways to say that it belongs to me:

C'est le mien.

Il est à moi.

In the first answer, **c'est** is used because it is directly followed by the possessive pronoun **le mien**. In the second answer, **il** is used because the verb is not directly connected to the pronoun which follows the preposition **à**.

Let us now return to our early days of French, when we would follow **c'est un stylo** by **il est bleu**. **Bleu** is neither a noun nor a pronoun, so we use **il est** as **stylo** is masculine. Here are some further examples to take you back to the past:

Qu'est-ce que c'est ?
– C'est une gomme. Elle est bleue.
It's a rubber. It's blue.

Qu'est-ce que c'est ?
– Ce sont des crayons. Ils sont verts.
They're pencils. They're green.

Qu'est-ce que c'est ?
– Ce sont des trousses. Elles sont vertes.
They're pencil cases. They're green.

However, you WILL find **il** (or **elle**) **est** followed by a noun:

a) When telling **the time**:

Il est midi. Il est deux heures.

b) When stating someone's **occupation**:

Elle est professeur. Il est médecin.

Note that here the word *a* is not translated. However if there is any qualification to the profession, **c'est** is used together with the indefinite article:

C'est un médecin distingué.
He is a distinguished doctor.

It is possible to use **il / elle + être + noun**. When we do so, we wish to emphasise whether we mean *he* or *she*:

> **Elle est son mauvais ange.**
> *She is a bad influence on him / her.*
> (**un ange** *angel*, always masculine)

Consider also the following:

> **Qui est-ce ?** – C'est **Monsieur Dubois.**
> *Who is it? – It's M. Dubois.*
>
> **Qui est-il ?** – Il est **mon père.**
> *Who is he? – He's my father.*

◆

Il est or c'est + adjective

You will have encountered the problem of translating **it is** when followed by an **adjective**. We will revisit our waiter and his wine to illustrate an important point.

If he were to ask you what you thought of the wine, you would answer **il est bon** (if that was your opinion). The complement of **être** is neither noun nor pronoun, so we use **il** as the subject. Similarly, our opinion of his ice cream might be **elle est bonne**. Notice that here the waiter is asking about a **specific** wine or ice cream.

Does this mean, therefore, that we can never say **c'est bon**? Not at all. It is used to make general statements:

> **Tu aimes les escargots ?**
> – **Oui, c'est bon.** (snails **in general**)

But:

> **Tu aimes ces escargots ?**
> – **Oui, ils sont bons. (these specific** snails)
>
> **Que pensez-vous de la crème anglaise ?**
> *What do you think of custard? –* C'est **délicieux.** (custard in **general**)
>
> **Que pensez-vous de notre crème anglaise ?**
> *What do you think of our custard? –* Elle **est délicieuse. (our** custard in particular)

An adjective following **c'est** is always in the masculine singular form:

> **La haine, c'est dangereux !**
> *Hatred is a dangerous thing!*
> (Equally possible is: **C'est dangereux, la haine !**)

Consider the following:

> **Il est difficile de savoir ce qu'il veut dire.**
> *It is difficult to know what he means.*
>
> – **Oui, c'est difficile.**
>
> **Il est évident qu'il était responsable de sa mort.**
> *It is obvious that he was responsible for his / her death.*
>
> – **Oui, c'est évident.**

Il n'est pas toujours facile de traduire cet auteur.
It is not always easy to translate this author.

– Non, ce n'est pas toujours facile.

In formal language, and this applies particularly to written French, **il est** stands before an adjective which is going to be defined (we will be told what is difficult, what is obvious, what is not always easy). Informal language would have **c'est** (or **ce n'est pas**) at the head of our examples. Where the adjective comes as the last word (is not further defined) and sums up a previous idea, **c'est** is always used:

Il est possible de découvrir la vérité. (Formal)
C'est possible de découvrir la vérité. (Informal)
It is possible to discover the truth.

– Oui, c'est possible. / Non, ce n'est pas possible. (In all circumstances)

◆

C'est is also used to refer back to geographical names:

Tu aimes la Belgique ?
Do you like Belgium ?
– Oui, c'est beau.

Que penses-tu des Caraïbes ?
What do you think of the Caribbean?
– C'est magnifique.

Où se trouve Antibes ? – C'est sur la Côte d'Azur.
Where is Antibes? – It is on the French Riviera.

TRAIL → 64
page 224

→ TRAIL 47

▶ TECHNICAL TERMS

Inversion – where the normal word order (subject – verb) is inverted to become (verb – subject): **Parlez-vous français ?**

We have, of course, discussed inversion with regard to asking questions in our section on Verbs.

Direct Speech – where the actual words of a speaker are quoted and would be placed within inverted commas. [Although many French authors now use the same inverted commas as we do, we have used the traditional **guillemets** in our French sentences.]

Our intention in this section is to provide help with the rules for the use of inversion in circumstances other than questions.

1. Within or after direct speech

Where *he said*, *she replied*, *they shouted* etc occurs within or after direct speech, only the inverted form is permissible in French:

> **Il a dit, « Je serai de retour vers sept heures. »**
> *He said, 'I will be back about seven.'*

Here there is no inversion as the words quoted come **after** *he said*.

> **« Je serai de retour, a-t-il dit, vers sept heures. »**
> **« Je serai de retour vers sept heures », a-t-il dit.**

In our last two examples, *he said* comes **within** or **after** the words quoted.

Here are some further examples:

> **« Ça m'est égal, répond-elle, tu peux faire ce que tu veux. »**
> *'It's all the same to me,' she answers, 'you can do what you want.'*

[As you can hear, when a liaison is made with a **-d** and a following vowel, the **d** is sounded as a **t**. The same applies to the **-d** of **quand**:

> **Quand il est arrivé, j'étais sous la douche.**
> *When he arrived, I was in the shower.*]

> **« Non, a-t-elle répondu, je ne le ferai pas ! »**
> *'No,' she replied, 'I will not do it!'*

> **« Vive le Président ! » ont-ils crié.**
> *'Long live the President!' they shouted.*

> **« C'est moi qui commande ici ! » s'est écrié mon père.**
> *'I'm the one who gives the orders here!' cried my father.*

« **Nous n'avons rien pris** », avaient protesté les voleurs.
'We didn't take anything,' the thieves had protested.

[Inversions with **noun** subjects, as in our last two examples, are not possible when asking questions.]

2. **Peut-être** and **sans doute**

Sans doute is the equivalent of *probably*. If you want to say *without a doubt* or *doubtless*, use **sans aucun doute**.

In formal French, inversion is required if **peut-être** or **sans doute** come before the verb:

Peut-être arrivera-t-il demain.
Perhaps he will arrive tomorrow.

Sans doute viendra-t-elle ce soir.
She will probably come this evening.

Where the subject is a noun, care is needed:

Peut-être mon oncle arrivera-t-il demain.
Perhaps my uncle will arrive tomorrow.

Sans doute ma cousine viendra-t-elle ce soir.
My cousin will probably come this evening.

Peut-être ce volume vous a-t-il intéressé.
Perhaps this book interested you.

Sans doute ce chien avait-il mordu le facteur.
This dog had probably bitten the postman.

Both **peut-être** and **sans doute** can be placed at the end of the sentence even in formal French and here there is no inversion:

Ce volume vous a intéressé peut-être.

Ce chien avait mordu le facteur sans doute.

In less formal language, both **peut-être** and **sans doute** may be followed by **que**, in which case there is no inversion:

Peut-être que ton ami te passera un coup de fil demain.
Perhaps your friend will ring you tomorrow.

Sans doute qu'il a raison de le dire.
He's probably right to say so.

3. After certain adverbs

In formal French, inversion is usual after the following when they stand at the head of the clause:

• **ainsi** – *in this way*

Ainsi parlait ma mère.
My mother used to speak in this way.
Ainsi parlait-elle.

- **aussi** – *that is why*

Ma mère était en colère. Aussi mon père ne l'a-t-il pas écoutée.
My mother was angry. So my father did not listen to her.

- **à peine** – *hardly, scarcely*

À peine le voleur fut-il descendu de l'autobus que l'agent de police l'arrêta.
Hardly (Scarcely) had the thief got off the bus when the policeman arrested him.
[NB **que** translates *when* here.]

- **du moins** – *at least*

Si nous ne sommes pas riches, du moins avons-nous de quoi manger.
If we're not rich, at least we have food to eat.

[**Du moins** often indicates a restriction, modifying what has just been said, and is close
in meaning to *nevertheless*. **Au moins**, which also means *at (the) least*, may also
modify or contradict but is closer in meaning to *at a minimum* as it often has a bearing
on quantity:

Parmi tous les étudiants, Pierre au moins a réussi à l'examen.
Of all the students, Pierre at least passed the exam.

It is less frequently followed by an inversion than **du moins**:

Au moins il voudrait / voudrait-il savoir ce qui s'est passé.
At least he would like to know what happened.]

- **encore** – *nevertheless, furthermore*

Encore vaudrait-il mieux ne rien dire.
Nevertheless it would be better not to say anything.

- **en vain / vainement** (*in vain*)

En vain le directeur avait-il essayé de faire taire les élèves.
The headmaster had tried in vain to get the pupils to shut up.

- **toujours est-il que** – *nevertheless*. This expression contains its own inversion:

Toujours est-il qu'elle n'était pas contente.
Nevertheless she wasn't happy.

4. Relative clauses after **ce que**

Where the subject is not **on**, **ce** or a **personal pronoun**, inversion is often seen, but is
not obligatory:

Je me demande ce que le patron a dit. / Je me demande ce qu'a dit le patron.
I wonder what the boss said.

As a matter of style, inversion is always preferred when a short verb accompanies a long
subject:

Je ne sais pas ce que dit le ministre de l'Intérieur.
I don't know what the Home Secretary is saying.

Essayez de découvrir ce qu'en pensent les conseillers municipaux.
Try to find out what the town councillors think about it.

It is difficult to be categorical about some inversions. It is often possible to place an adverb after the verb as we have seen with **peut-être** and **sans doute**, in which case there would be no inversion. The use of a good dictionary will point you in the right direction.

TRAIL → 48
page 225

→ TRAIL 49

▶ TECHNICAL TERMS

A **direct question** gives the actual words spoken and is followed by a question mark:

'What are you doing?' he asked. 'What do you want?'

An **indirect question** reports but does not quote the actual words used. There is no question mark:

He asks what you are doing. He doesn't know what you want.

There are many other verbs which can introduce an indirect question – *to understand, to tell, to show, to wonder, to explain, to be unaware of* etc.

It is the use of the word **what** in sentences such as these which causes difficulty for many students of French. We will concentrate on solving this problem.

You will see from the table that **qui** and **que** (in bold) are subject and object of the verb respectively:

DIRECT QUESTION	INDIRECT QUESTION
What are you doing?	*I want to know **what** you are doing.*
What frightens you?	*I want to know **what** frightens you.*
What do you need?	*I want to know **what** you need.*
*What are you thinking **about**?*	*I want to know **what** you are thinking **about**.*

DIRECT QUESTION	INDIRECT QUESTION
Que **faites-vous** ? Qu'est-ce que **vous faites** ?	**Je veux savoir** ce que **vous faites.**
Qu'est-ce qui **vous fait peur** ?	**Je veux savoir** ce qui **vous fait peur.**
De quoi **avez-vous besoin** ?	**Je veux savoir** ce dont **vous avez besoin.** *
À quoi **pensez-vous** ?	**Je veux savoir** ce à quoi **vous pensez.** **

* In informal French you may come across: **Je veux savoir** de quoi **vous avez besoin**.

** Also possible in informal French is: **Je veux savoir** à quoi **vous pensez**.

Note also:

Qu'est-ce ? / Qu'est-ce que c'est ?
What is it?

Je veux savoir ce que **c'est.**
*I want to know **what** it is.*

Although all the questions in the table are translated using the word *what*, it may be easier with indirect questions to remember to insert **ce** if you think of **ce qui** and **ce que** as *that which* and **ce dont** as *that of which*.

Used for the purpose of emphasis

Ce qui m'intéresse, c'est son rôle dans l'affaire.
What interests me is his rôle in the matter.

Ce que je n'aime pas, c'est qu'il refuse de travailler.
What I don't like is that he refuses to work.

Ce dont j'avais besoin, c'était de savoir la vérité.
What I needed was to know the truth.

Ce à quoi je pense, c'est à l'avenir.
What I'm thinking about is the future.

What we are emphasising here are the words which follow **c'est** or **c'était**. In the last two examples, note that there are no alternatives to **ce dont** and **ce à quoi**.

TRAIL → 50
page 225

→ TRAIL 29

- **depuis** – the action, having begun at a specified time, is still ongoing.

We saw in our section on verbs under the present and imperfect tenses that **depuis** is used when an action is or was still going on:

Elle étudie le japonais depuis deux ans.
*She has been studying Japanese **for** two years* (and she is still doing so).

Il pleuvait depuis cinq jours, tous les champs étaient inondés.
*It had been raining **for** five days, all the fields were flooded.*

- **pour** – used with future time to imply intention:

Je suis là pour quinze jours.
*I'm here **for** a fortnight.*

Elle sera aux États-Unis pour deux mois.
*She will be in the States **for** two months.*

- **pendant**

a) for completed actions in the past:

Hier soir elle a lu pendant une heure.
*Last night she read **for** an hour.*

La semaine dernière il a plu pendant deux jours.
*Last week it rained **for** two days.*

b) for actions in the present tense:

Il rentre chez lui, il regarde la télé pendant une heure, puis il monte dans sa chambre.
*He comes home, watches TV **for** an hour, then he goes up to his room.*

TRAIL → 30
page 226

→ TRAIL 69

We are treating **où** separately as it has several uses (note the grave accent which distinguishes it from **ou** meaning *or*):

1. *Where* (adverb)

    Où va-t-il ? – Je ne sais pas où il va.
    Where is he going? – I don't know where he is going.

    D'où venez-vous ?
    Where do you come from?

    Où en sommes-nous ?
    Where are we up to?

Note the use of **partout** and **là** with **où** at the head of the sentence:

    Partout où il va, son chien le suit.
    Everywhere he goes, his dog follows him.

    Là où il travaille on voit peu de touristes.
    Where he works you don't see many tourists.

2. *Where / In which* (relative pronoun)

    L'appartement où elle est née n'existe plus.
    The flat where she was born no longer exists.

Où often replaces **dans lequel, à laquelle** etc.:

    L'école où je vais est loin de chez moi.
    The school I go to is a long way from my house.

    Les jardins où il se promenait étaient pleins de fleurs.
    The gardens where he used to walk were full of flowers.

    La boîte où elle a mis ses photos se trouve sous la table.
    The box in which she put her photos is under the table.

3. **Où** is used to mean *when* after a noun expressing time which is preceded by a **definite article**:

    Au moment (À l'instant) où il est venu, le téléphone a sonné.
    (At) the moment he came the phone rang.

    Le jour où il s'est marié ne sera jamais oublié.
    The day (when) he got married will never be forgotten.

    La police voulait savoir l'heure où elles sont parties.
    The police wanted to know the time (when) they left.

[NB **que** (not **où**) is used after **fois**:

La première fois que je l'ai vu je faisais du repassage.
The first time I saw him I was doing some ironing.]

Also when the noun indicating time is preceded by an **indefinite article**, **que** is generally used to mean *when*:

Un jour que je me promenais en ville j'ai perdu mon portefeuille.
One day when I was strolling in town I lost my wallet.

4. **Où que** + subjunctive – *wherever*

Où que tu ailles, tu verras la même chose.
Wherever you go, you will see the same thing.

[Also:

Qui que vous soyez c'est inacceptable.
Whoever you are it is not acceptable.

Quoi que vous fassiez vous ne réussirez pas.
Whatever you do you will not succeed.

These are called **concessive clauses** and take the **subjunctive** in French.]

TRAIL → 70
page 227

→ TRAIL 67

In this section, we will concentrate on areas where French usage differs from English.

- **Price**

In English we use the **indefinite article**:

*This wine is £5 **a** bottle. I paid £2.50 **a** kilo. Our pizza is 50p **a** slice. Crisps are 30p **a** packet.*

In French, the **definite article** is used:

Ce vin se vend à € 7 la bouteille. J'ai payé € 3.50 le kilo. Notre pizza c'est 70 centimes la part. Les chips sont à 45 centimes le paquet.

(In place of **le kilo**, you will sometimes find: **au kilo**, **par kilo** and even **du kilo**. We prefer the standard expression.)

Where in English we use *each*, for example on a greengrocer's stall we might see:

*Melons – £1.25 **each**,*

French uses **la pièce**, again retaining the **definite article**:

Melons – € 1.75 la pièce.

- **Payment**

You will find several ways of expressing earnings:

On gagne € 10 l'heure.
We earn €10 an hour.

On gagne € 10 par heure.

or, more rarely,

On gagne € 10 à l'heure.

You may even come across in speech:

On gagne € 10 de l'heure.

If the verb **payer** is used, it is accompanied by the preposition **à**:

On est payé à € 10 l'heure.

*He earns x euros **per** day* (week, month, year) or *so much **a** day* becomes:
Il gagne x euros par jour (semaine, mois, an).

- **Speed**

Again the indefinite article is not used in French:

Il roulait à 120 kilomètres à l'heure.
*He was travelling at 75 miles **an hour**.*

Le cycliste fera 25 km/h.
*The cyclist will do 15 **mph**.*

- **Measurement**

While you will find several ways of expressing measurement, we prefer to keep things simple and suggest:

Cette table fait deux mètres de long.
This table is two metres long.

Ce fleuve fait cinquante mètres de large.
This river is fifty metres wide.

Le tapis faisait trois mètres de long sur deux mètres de large.
The carpet was three metres (long) by two (metres wide).

Cette montagne fait trois mille mètres de haut.
This mountain is three thousand metres high.

NB While we can use the adjectives **long, large** and **haut** in this way, the nouns **profondeur** (*depth*) and **épaisseur** (*thickness*) are used in the following:

La mine fait deux cents mètres de profondeur.
The mine is two hundred metres deep.

Le livre fait trois centimètres d'épaisseur.
The book is three centimetres thick.

[You may also find the verb **avoir** used in place of **faire** in all the above examples.]

The question *How long (wide, high, deep, thick) is ...?* becomes **Quelle est la longueur (largeur, hauteur, profondeur, épaisseur) de ... ?**

Quelle est la hauteur de ce mur ?
How high is this wall?

– Elle est de cinq mètres.
– It's five metres high.

Quelle est la longueur de cette rivière ?
How long is this river?

– Elle est de trente kilomètres.
– It is thirty kilometres long.

**TRAIL → 68
page 228**

→ TRAIL 37

In French, expressions of quantity are generally followed by **de (d')**:

Combien d'argent avez-vous ?
How much money do you have?

Combien de frites a-t-il mangées ?
How many chips has he eaten?

Nous avons assez d'œufs.
We have enough eggs.

Il a tant de soucis.
He has so many worries.

Je n'ai jamais vu tant de pluie !
I have never seen so much rain!

Ma mère prend autant de sucre que mon père.
My mother takes as much sugar as my father.

Elle a autant d'amies que moi.
She has as many friends as me (or more formally: as I).

Je n'ai pas trop de regrets.
I don't have too many regrets.

Il a reçu beaucoup de cadeaux.
He received many (a lot of, lots of) presents.

Ma tante écrit peu de lettres.
My aunt writes few letters.

Il a eu moins de chance que nous.
He had less luck than we (had). (He hadn't as much luck as us.)

De nos jours il y a plus de magasins ouverts le dimanche.
These days there are more shops open on Sundays.

◆

La plupart (*most of, the majority of*) is also followed by **de**:

La plupart de ceux-là sont contents.
Most of those are happy.

However, the definite article is included where the meaning is *most of the ...*

La plupart de la classe a bien travaillé.
Most of the class worked well.

La plupart des enfants aiment le chocolat.
Most children (Most of the children) like chocolate. (The majority of children like chocolate.)

La plupart des Allemands boivent de la bière.
Most Germans (Most of the Germans) drink beer.

Note the use of the plural verb in these last two examples, dictated by the plural nouns **enfants** and **Allemands**.

◆

An alternative to **beaucoup de** is **bien des**:

Bien des étudiants font de leur mieux pour réussir.
Many students do their best to succeed.

◆

Encore (*more*) is followed by the partitive article:

Encore du vin, monsieur ?
More wine, sir?

Nous avons encore des escargots.
We have more snails.

TRAIL → 38
page 228

→ TRAIL 55

Impersonal verbs, although they have **il** as their subject, do not refer to any person. You are already acquainted with impersonal constructions concerning the weather:

Il pleut aujourd'hui, il fera beau demain, il a fait froid hier et il avait neigé pendant la nuit.
It's raining today, it will be fine tomorrow, it was cold yesterday and it had snowed during the night.

You will be equally used to seeing **il y a**:

Il y a un livre dans le tiroir.
There is a book in the drawer.

Il y avait des enfants à la porte.
There were (some) children at the door.

Il y aura des problèmes.
There will be problems.

Here it is in all its tenses:

- present
  il y a
  there is / are

- perfect
  il y a eu
  there was / were (on one occasion), there has / have been

- future
  il y aura
  there will be

- future perfect
  il y aura eu
  there will have been

- imperfect
  il y avait
  there was / were

- pluperfect
  il y avait eu
  there had been

- conditional
  il y aurait
  there would be

- conditional perfect
  il y aurait eu
  there would have been

- past historic
  il y eut
  there was / were (on one occasion)

- **past anterior**
  il y eut eu
  there had been

We should stress the position of **ne ... pas**:
Il n'y a pas de haricots.
There are no beans.

Il n'y a pas eu de problème.
There was no problem. / There has been no problem.

We would draw your particular attention to this construction in its infinitive form. Take the sentence: *There must be a book in the drawer.* Using the verb **devoir**, we would need to say:
Il doit y avoir un livre dans le tiroir.

It is also worth learning
il peut y avoir
there may be
Il peut y avoir une solution.

[When followed by an expression of time, **il y a** means *ago*: **il y a deux jours** *two days ago*. In the imperfect tense, **il y avait** means *before, earlier* or *previously*: **il y avait quinze jours** *a fortnight earlier*.]

Another impersonal verb you will have met is **falloir**:
- present
  il faut

- perfect
  il a fallu

- future
  il faudra

- future perfect
  il aura fallu

- imperfect
  il fallait

- pluperfect
  il avait fallu

- conditional
  il faudrait

- conditional perfect
  il aurait fallu

- past historic
  il fallut

- past anterior
  il eut fallu

You will note that we have offered no translations here. While **falloir** means *to be necessary* and **il faut** means *it is necessary*, this will not always be the best way of translating it. You will often prefer to use *must* or *have to* and a **personal pronoun** to fit in with the context.

A teacher speaking to pupils may well say:

Il faudra travailler dur, mes enfants.

Literally, this means *It will be necessary to work hard, children.* A better translation would be *You will have to work hard, children.*

Again, according to the circumstances, **Il faut partir** could mean *We **must** leave*, *We'll have to leave*, *I'll have to go*, *You'll have to go*.

If there is any confusion, a pronoun is added in French: **Il nous faut partir, il leur faut partir.**

NB

Il le faut.
It's / That's necessary.

Il faut may be followed by a noun:

Il faut un passeport.
A passport is required. / You (I / We / They etc) need a passport.

◆

- **il s'agit de**

  De quoi s'agit-il ?
  What is it about?

  Il s'agit du roman que je t'ai prêté.
  It's about the novel I lent you.

The subject, as with all impersonal verbs, must be **il**. Therefore, if we wish to say *This article is about the European Community*, the French will be:

Il s'agit dans cet article de la Communauté européenne.

NB

> **Je ne sais pas** ce dont il s'agissait.
> *I don't know what it was about.*

- **il importe**

  > **Il importe de rester calmes.**
  > *We (You) must keep calm.*

  > **Peu importe.**
  > *It's of little importance.*

  > **N'importe.**
  > *It doesn't matter.*

  > **N'importe où.**
  > *Anywhere at all.*

  > **N'importe quand.**
  > *Any time at all.*

  > **N'importe qui.**
  > *Anyone at all.*

  > **N'importe quoi.**
  > *Anything at all.*

- **il reste**

This impersonal verb expresses what is left, what is the only option remaining:

  > **Il reste bien des choses à faire.**
  > *There are lots of things left to do (still to do). / There remain lots of things to do.*

  > **Il restait cinq euros.**
  > *There were five euros left.*

  > **Que reste-t-il à manger ?**
  > *What's left to eat?*

  > **Il ne nous restait qu'à partir.**
  > *All that remained to be done (could be done / we could do) was to leave.*

- **il arrive**

  > **Il est arrivé un malheur.**
  > *There has been a mishap. / Something nasty has happened.*

  > **Il m'arrive d'acheter un journal de temps en temps.**
  > *I sometimes buy a newspaper.*

  > **Il m'est arrivé de dîner dans ce restaurant-là.**
  > *I've had dinner in that restaurant.*

  > **Il arrive souvent qu'elle soit en retard.**
  > *She often turns up late.*

  > **Quoi qu'il arrive, je serai toujours là pour toi.**
  > *Whatever happens, I'll always be here for you.*

While **il arrive** is the equivalent of *it happens*, we will only rarely translate it in this way.

Two other verbs which may be used impersonally and which also convey the idea of *happening* are:

- **il se produit**

  Il s'est produit **un accident.**
  There has been an accident. / An accident has happened.

- **il se passe**

  Il se passe **des choses extraordinaires.**
  Extraordinary things are happening (going on).

TRAIL → 56
page 229

▶ TECHNICAL TERM

Factitive verb – a verb whose subject does not perform the action but causes it to be done. Thus we can say:

I am going to paint the wall (myself).
Je vais peindre le mur.

Or, using the factitive verb:

*I am going to **have** the wall **painted*** (by someone else).
Je vais faire peindre le mur.

There are several ways of expressing this idea in English. Consider the sentence

Je les ferai comprendre.

This may be translated as:

I will make them understand. / I will have them understand. / I will get them to understand.

You should note the position of the direct object pronoun, **les**. With this construction, **all** object pronouns are linked to the verb **faire** and will generally precede it. However, as we have seen with positive commands, object pronouns follow the verb:

Faites-les comprendre !
Make them understand!

◆

We should like to make a number of points about this important construction.

1. **Se faire** + infinitive

Il se fait couper les cheveux tous les deux mois.
He has a haircut (He has his hair cut) every two months.

Elle n'aime pas se faire remarquer.
She doesn't like to be noticed (to get herself noticed).

Nous voulons nous faire respecter.
We want to be respected (to have ourselves respected).

Notice in the last two examples that a simple passive (*to be* + past participle) is often the best English translation.

2. Compound tenses – no agreement

Je les ai fait venir.
I sent for them.

Ma montre, je l'ai fait réparer.
My watch, I had it repaired.

Mes parents les auraient fait quitter ma chambre.
My parents would have had them leave my room.

3. Direct or indirect object?

If the following infinitive does not itself have an object, **faire** will have a *direct object*:

Je les faisais travailler dur.
I made them work hard.

Le professeur le fera rester jusqu'à cinq heures.
The teacher will make him stay until five o'clock.

Ma sœur ? Mon père la fait monter dans sa chambre quand elle est méchante.
My sister? My father makes her go up to her room when she is naughty.

However, where the following infinitive has a direct object, **faire** will have an *indirect object*:

Je leur faisais finir les exercices.
I had them finish the exercises.

Le professeur lui fera comprendre son erreur.
The teacher will make him / her understand his / her mistake.

Ma sœur ? Mon père lui fait faire le ménage quand elle est méchante.
My sister? My father makes her do the housework when she is naughty.

This same rule applies when instead of a noun, it is a **clause** which follows the infinitive:

Je leur faisais comprendre qu'il était nécessaire de travailler.
I made them understand that it was necessary to work.

Le professeur lui fera voir que son attitude est insupportable.
The teacher will make him / her see that his / her attitude is intolerable.

Ma sœur ? Mon père lui fait savoir qu'elle est souvent méchante.
My sister? My father lets her know that she is often naughty.

So far, our examples have used pronouns to indicate the person who is being made to act in some way. The same rules apply when we use a noun instead:

Direct object:

J'ai fait venir le médecin.
I sent for the doctor.

Faites-vous parler vos élèves en français ?
Do you make your pupils speak in French?

Indirect object:

Faites-vous parler français à vos élèves ?
Do you make your pupils speak French?
(Now the language is the **direct** object of **parler**.)

J'ai fait voir à mon ami qu'il avait tort.
I made my friend see that he was wrong.

Mon père fait savoir la vérité à ma sœur.
My father lets my sister know the truth.

Now suppose we have the sentence

I will make him read the newspaper.

As *read* has a direct object, we must say: **Je lui ferai lire le journal.**

If we later wished to say

*I will make him read **it**.*

our sentence would become

Je **le lui** ferai lire.

NB Both the object pronouns are placed before the verb **faire**.

4. **Faire voir** (an alternative to **montrer**)

Il m'a fait voir son appartement.
He showed me his flat.

Faites voir votre passeport.
Show (me) your passport.

Fais voir ta main !
Show (me) your hand!

5. **Faire + pronominal verb in the infinitive**

Nous les avons fait s'asseoir.

Nous les avons fait asseoir.

As you can see from these two sentences, both of which mean *We had them sit down*, it is possible to retain or omit the reflexive pronoun. Similarly:

Elle le fera se lever.
Elle le fera lever.
She'll make him get up.

If there is any confusion, the reflexive pronoun is retained:

Papa les a fait arrêter.

could mean *Dad had them arrested*. If we simply mean *Dad got them to stop*, we would say:

Papa les a fait s'arrêter.

◆

[To *make* ... + adjective – **rendre**

Ces huîtres nous ont rendus malades.
These oysters have made us ill.

Parler français me rend bien content.
Speaking French makes me very happy.]

TRAIL → 42
page 230

→ TRAIL 53

The major difficulty which students find with this verb is the variety of ways in which it may be translated into English:

- present tense

Il doit sortir.
He has to go out. / He must go out.

Mon père doit rentrer ce soir.
My father is (due) to return this evening.

Il me doit 100 euros.
He owes me 100 euros.

In its present tense, **devoir** may also mean *should* when making a **general moral statement**:

Les enfants doivent respecter leurs parents.
Children should respect their parents.

- perfect tense

Il a dû laver la voiture de son père.

This has three possible meanings:

He had to (on one particular occasion) wash his father's car.
He must have washed his father's car.
He has had to wash his father's car.

Elle a dû partir.

Again this has three possible meanings:

She had to leave.
She must have left.
She has had to leave.

- imperfect tense

Quand il était jeune il devait laver la voiture de son père.
When he was young he had to (regularly) wash his father's car.

Il me devait 100 euros.
He owed me 100 euros.

Mon père devait rentrer ce soir-là.
My father was (due) to return that evening.

- conditional tense

Il devrait aller voir son ami.
He should (ought to) go and see his friend.

- conditional perfect tense

Elle aurait dû y penser.
She should (ought to) have thought about it.

Nous n'aurions pas dû les quitter.
We should not have (ought not to have) left them.

[NB Where **devoir** implies **obligation**, it is possible to substitute the impersonal verb **falloir** or the expression **être obligé(e)(s) de**:

Il nous a fallu rentrer tout de suite.
We had to return at once.

Elle sera obligée de démissionner.
She will have to resign.]

TRAIL → 54
page 231

→ TRAIL 59

We must first stress the important distinction between these two verbs. The problem arises with the English words *can* and *could*. Where a **skill** is involved, where something has had to be **learnt, savoir** is used:

Elle sait jouer du piano.
She can (knows how to) play the piano.

Ils savaient nager.
They could (knew how to) swim.

If we were to use **pouvoir** with these two examples, the sense would alter:

Elle peut jouer du piano.
She can (is free to) play the piano.

Ils pouvaient nager.
They could (were allowed to) swim.

◆

We will now take a look at the various meanings of **pouvoir**:

• present tense

Puis-je entrer ?
May (Can) I come in?

Elle peut rester à l'hôtel.
She can (may) stay at the hotel.

Il peut lever 150 kilos.
He can lift 150 kilos.

• perfect tense

Elle a pu le faire.
She was able to do it (on one occasion, in the end).
She has been able to do it.

Ils ont pu réussir.
They may have succeeded.
They were able to succeed.

• imperfect tense

Il pouvait voir que sa mère était gravement malade.
He could (was able to) see that his mother was seriously ill.

• conditional tense

Si on avait de l'argent, on pourrait vous aider.
If we had money, we could (would be able to) help you / we might help you.

NB When translating the word *could*, we must always consider whether it means *was/were able to* – **imperfect**, or *would be able to* – **conditional**.

- conditional perfect tense

Il aurait pu envoyer une lettre.
*He **could (might) have** sent a letter. (He **would have been able to** send a letter.)*

Si j'avais su, j'aurais pu vous faire un chèque.
*If I had known, I **could (might) have** written you a cheque. (I **would have been able to** write you a cheque.)*

◆

Verbs of perception (*to see, hear* etc) in the **present** and **imperfect** tenses do not require the verb **pouvoir**:

Je vois le problème.
*I **(can) see** the problem.*

Il entendait des bruits.
*He **heard (could hear)** noises.*

Le prisonnier sentait les roses mais il ne les voyait pas.
*The prisoner **could smell** the roses but **couldn't see** them.*

[It would, however, not be incorrect to say: **Je peux voir** ... / **Il pouvait entendre** ... / **le prisonnier pouvait sentir** ...]

TRAIL → 60
page 231

→ TRAIL 31

It would have been possible to include **il manque** with the impersonal verbs, but, because **manquer** has so many meanings and uses, we feel it best to devote a separate section to it.

1. Impersonal verb

il manque
there is a lack of, (something) is missing:

Il manque dix euros.
There are ten euros missing. / I'm (We're / You're) ten euros short.

Il manquait deux élèves à l'appel.
Two pupils were missing from registration.

Il ne manquait plus que ça !
That's all we needed! That's the last straw!

To indicate the person who is short of something, an indirect object, pronoun or noun is used:

Il lui manque un stylo.
He's (She's) short of (needs) a pen.

Il manque un pneu à cette voiture-là.
That car's missing a tyre.

2. **Manquer de** + infinitive

This construction translates *to nearly (do)* or *to fail to (do)* something:

Elle avait manqué de se noyer.
*She had **nearly** drowned.*

Sometimes **de** is omitted:

Ils ont manqué mourir.
*They **almost** died.*

Je n'ai pas manqué de leur écrire.
*I didn't **fail (omit)** to write to them.*

3. **Manquer de** + noun

Mes parents manquent de patience.
*My parents **have no (are short of)** patience.*

Vous ne manquez pas de toupet.
You are very cheeky. (You're not short of cheek.)

4. **Manquer à** + indirect object

Il a manqué à son devoir.
*He **failed** in his duty.*

Je n'y manquerai pas.
*I won't **fail** to do it.*

La voix lui manquait souvent.
*Words often **failed** him.*

Je n'ai jamais manqué à ma parole.
*I have always kept my word (never **failed** to keep my word).*

5. **Manquer** + direct object

Nous avons manqué le train.
*We **missed** the train.*

Ne manquez jamais l'occasion de gagner de l'argent.
*Never **miss** the opportunity to earn some money.*

6. **Manquer** – to miss

When we use the word *miss* in the sense of regretting a person's absence, the construction in French is not the same as in English:

Ma mère me manque.
*I **am missing** my mother.* (Literally: *My mother is lacking to me.*)

Je manque à ma mère.
*My mother **is missing** me.*

Here are some further examples of this point which often causes confusion:

Mon chien me manquait.
*I **was missing** my dog.*

Elle manquait à sa grand-mère.
*Her grandmother **was missing** her.*

Je te manquerai quand je ne serai plus là.
*You **will miss** me when I'm not here any more.*

Paris nous manque déjà.
*We **are** already **missing** Paris.*

7. **Manqué(e)** as an adjective

C'est un cuisinier manqué.
He should (could) have been a cook.

That is, he has all the talent to make him a cook, but he isn't one.
We use the term in English: a poet *manqué* – a *would-be* poet.

TRAIL → 32
page 232

→ TRAIL 33

You will already be aware of circumstances where English uses the verb *to be* but French does not use the verb **être**:

Comment vas-tu ? – Je vais bien, merci.
How are you? – I'm fine, thanks.

[NB **Comment est votre père ?**
What is your father like?
asks for a physical description or about his temperament.]

Quel âge avez-vous ? – J'ai dix-neuf ans.
How old are you? – I'm 19.

Qu'est ce qu'il y a dans le tiroir ? – Il y a des lettres.
What is there in the drawer? – There are (some) letters.

Quel temps fait-il ? – Il fait beau.
What's the weather like? – It's fine.

Here are some further points which in our experience are often forgotten:

1. Hot and cold – **être**, **avoir** or **faire**?

- **être** – for OBJECTS
  Le potage est froid !
  The soup is cold!
  La mer était bien chaude.
  The sea was very warm.

- **avoir** – for PEOPLE
  Elle a froid.
  She is cold.
  J'avais très chaud.
  I was hot.

- **faire** – for WEATHER
  Il fait froid.
  It is cold.
  Il faisait trop chaud.
  It was too hot.

2. Important constructions with **avoir**

- **avoir ... ans** *to be ... (years old)*
  Papa a quarante ans.
  Dad is forty.

- **avoir raison** – *to be right*
  Vous avez raison de payer vos impôts.
  You are right to pay your taxes.

- **avoir tort** – *to be wrong*
  Elle aura tort d'insister.
  She'll be wrong to insist. (It will be wrong of her to insist.)

- **avoir honte** – *to be ashamed*
  Nous avions honte de ne pas être là.
  We were ashamed not to be there.

- **avoir faim** – *to be hungry*
  Ils n'ont pas faim.
  They're not hungry.

  Les randonneurs avaient une faim de loup (*wolf*).
  The hikers were starving / ravenous.

- **avoir soif** – *to be thirsty*
  Avez-vous soif ?
  Are you thirsty?

  Vos parents ont-ils soif ?
  Are your parents thirsty?

- **avoir sommeil** – *to be sleepy*
  Le professeur a toujours sommeil l'après-midi.
  The teacher is always sleepy in the afternoon.

- **en avoir pour** + time – *to be a certain time (in doing)*
  Vous en avez pour longtemps ?
  Will you be long?

  J'en ai pour une heure.
  I'll be an hour.

  Nous n'en avons pas pour très longtemps.
  We'll not be very long.

3. Useful examples of **faire**
   Ça fait combien ?
   How much is that?

   Ça fait 20 euros.
   That is 20 euros.

   Il fait 25 degrés.
   It is 25 degrees.

   Il fait bon se reposer ici.
   It is lovely to rest here.

   Il fait bon vivre à la campagne.
   It is good to be living in the country. (Living in the country does / is doing me / us etc good.)

Il faisait jour.
It was (day)light.

Il fera bientôt nuit.
It will soon be dark (night).

Il se fait tard.
It is getting late.

Ça se fait. Ça ne se fait pas.
That is (not) OK. That is (not) the done thing.

4. Useful examples of **aller**

Ça va ?
How are things?

Ça va.
OK.

Ça va aller.
Things will be fine. (It will be OK.)

Cela va de soi.
That is obvious. (That goes without saying.) (We can make the same point with: **Cela va sans dire**.)

[**Ça** and **cela** mean the same; however, **ça** is only used informally.]

Il y va de votre santé.
Your health is at stake.

TRAIL → 34
page 233

→ TRAIL 73

CHOOSING A DICTIONARY

When you come to select a bilingual dictionary for your own use, either to purchase or to consult in a library, it is a good idea to check that it includes plenty of example sentences to illustrate words in context.

USING A DICTIONARY

A. Looking up verbs

Suppose we look up in the English–French section the verb *to return*. We may find in brackets the pronunciation of the word *return* according to the International Phonetic Alphabet (this will normally be explained at the beginning of the dictionary). The representation of the pronunciation will be of particular use to you when you consult the French–English section.

The next item of information we meet may be **vi**, standing for **intransitive verb**. This could also be expressed as **vb intr.** or **v. intr.** It is vital that you should know what this means. An intransitive verb cannot have a direct object. We are then offered some possible verbs which we could use to translate *return* as an intransitive verb – **revenir**, **retourner**, **rentrer**, for example. These three verbs, however, are not identical in meaning.

Imagine that we are translating the sentence *She has returned **to** the States*. Which verb, or verbs, can we use? Certainly not **revenir** which means *to return* in the sense of *to come back*. We can say either **Elle est retournée aux États-Unis** or **Elle est rentrée aux États-Unis**. Had the English been *She has returned **from** the States*, we could not have used **retourner**. We would have had to say **Elle est revenue / rentrée des États-Unis**.

A good dictionary will point out these differences in meaning and will offer example sentences. If you are still unsure, look up any verb you are thinking of using in the French–English section. Ultimately your best guide to correct usage will be a French–French (monolingual) dictionary.

Still considering the verb *to return*, we will find further down in the entry examples preceded by **vt**, or **vb tr.** standing for **transitive verb**. This means that the verbs suggested as possible translations for *return* in this section will take a direct object – il a rendu l'argent (*money*); il a retourné le livre (*book*); elle a renvoyé la balle (*ball*); le marchand a remboursé le client (*customer's money*).

The English verb *to return*, in common with many others, has such a wide variety of meanings that we have to be very careful in translating it.

We will now make some further important points regarding **transitive** and **intransitive** verbs, aiming in particular to show where the French usage differs somewhat from the English.

It may help to explain what these terms mean. They derive from the Latin *transire – to go across*. The action of the **transitive** verb passes across to a person or thing (its direct object), eg:

> **Il a saisi** le voleur.
> *He seized the thief.*
> **Il a pris** la décision.
> *He took the decision.*

Such verbs are defined in French as **transitifs directs** as there is no preposition linking them to their object.

Some verbs are defined as **transitifs indirects** as they are linked to their object by a preposition (often **à**):

> **Il a parlé** à sa fille.
> *He spoke to his daughter.*

where the daughter is referred to as the indirect object (**complément d'objet indirect**). English regards *to speak* in this sense as an intransitive verb.

An **intransitive** verb (**verbe intransitif**) cannot in French have any object, direct or indirect. This can seem confusing as many verbs can be used in a variety of ways. We will continue to use **parler** as an example:

a. With a direct object (**complément d'objet direct**)

> **Il parle** allemand.
> *He speaks German.*
> **Il parlait** politique **sans arrêt**.
> *He was always talking politics.*

b. With an indirect object (**complément d'objet indirect**):

> **Elle a parlé** aux enfants.
> *She spoke to the children.*
> **Il** lui **avait parlé comme à un chien.**
> *He had spoken to him as he would to a dog.*

c. With no object

> **Le bébé apprend à parler.**
> *The baby is learning to talk.*
> **Ne parle pas si bas !**
> *Don't speak so quietly!*

Many verbs are always directly transitive – **quitter**, **mettre**, **rencontrer** are examples – and they must have a direct object. Similarly, many verbs are intransitive and cannot have an object – **arriver**, **partir**, **mourir**. Some verbs can be used both transitively and intransitively. For example, **fermer** can be used with a direct object – **Le professeur ferme** le livre – and in a sense where it cannot take a direct object – **Le magasin ferme le dimanche** – *The shop is closed on Sundays* (a shop cannot close anything). A door, of course, can shut and this meaning requires the use of the pronominal form, **se fermer** – **La porte** se ferme.

The verb **ouvrir** is treated similarly. **Il ouvre** la porte; **le magasin ouvre demain** *(tomorrow)*; **la porte** s'ouvre **doucement** *(slowly, softly, quietly, gently)*.

Verbs such as **attendre, chercher, écouter, payer, regarder** will not cause you any problem if you remember that they are directly transitive verbs and any object they take will be **direct**. In English, their equivalents are linked to the noun by a preposition:

Elle attendait son copain.
*She waited **for** her boyfriend.*

Nous les avions cherchés partout.
*We had looked everywhere **for** them.*

J'écouterai la radio ce soir.
*I will listen **to** the radio this evening.*

C'est lui qui a payé la bouteille.
*He is the one who paid **for** the bottle.*

Le contrôleur regarda attentivement le billet.
*The inspector looked closely **at** the ticket.*

B. Finding the correct construction

As a speaker of English, you would have little hesitation in translating the verb **persister** as *to persist* or *to go on happening*. When you consult a good dictionary, you will find a variety of constructions:

Used impersonally:

Il persiste un doute.
There remains a doubt.

Used intransitively:

Les symptômes persistent.
The symptoms are still there.

Used with **dans**:

Elle persiste dans son attitude deplorable.
She persists in her deplorable attitude.

Used with **à**:

Elle persiste à croire que tout finira bien.
She persists in believing that everything will turn out fine.

A further dictionary abbreviation will be used here. **Persister dans qc (qch)** *to persist in something* (**quelque chose**). **Persister à faire qc (qch)** *to persist in doing something.*

Our aim is not to list every prepositional use, but to encourage you to consult a good dictionary. Here you will meet constructions which do not correspond exactly to English:

- **dépendre de qch**
  to depend on something

- **dépendre de qn (qqn)**
  to depend on someone (**quelqu'un**)

  Tout dépend de sa réaction ; tout dépend de lui.
  Everything depends on his reaction; everything depends on him.

- **déjeuner de qch**
  to lunch on something (to have something for lunch)

  Elle déjeune de fromage (*cheese*).

The verb **demander** can be particularly difficult:

- **demander qqn / qch**
  to ask for someone / something

  Le patron vous demande.
  The boss is asking for you.

  J'ai demandé un reçu.
  I asked for a receipt.

- **demander à faire qch**
  to ask to do something

  Elle demande à vous voir.
  She is asking to see you.

  Il demande à manger.
  He is asking for something to eat.

- **demander qch à qqn**
  to ask someone for something

  Il demande des renseignements à un passant.
  He asks a passer-by for information.

- **demander à qqn de faire qch**
  to ask someone to do something

  Il leur a demandé de faire la lessive.
  He asked them to do the washing.

NB **Demander** que will require a subjunctive:

Il demande que tout soit prêt avant dix heures.
He is asking for everything to be ready before ten o'clock.

C. Faux amis (false friends)

We should be aware of words which are spelt the same or nearly so in both languages but which have different meanings. If we have any doubt we should check in a dictionary.

actuellement *currently* (**en fait** *actually*)

curé *parish priest* (**vicaire** *curate*)

déception *disappointment* (**tromperie** *deception*)

large *wide* (**grand**, **gros** *large*)

librairie *book shop* (**bibliothèque** *library*)

raisin *grape* (**raisin sec** *raisin*)

sensible *sensitive* (**sensé** *sensible*)

surnom *nickname* (**nom de famille** *surname*)

TRAIL → 74
page 267

→ TRAIL 2

A. VERBS – VERBS IN THE PRESENT TENSE

1. Example:

Nous ..... heureux de vous voir. (être)

Nous sommes heureux de vous voir.

a) Ils ..... du vin à la table. (porter)

b) Elle ..... souvent le soir. (sortir)

c) Papa et maman ..... un cadeau pour mon frère. (choisir)

d) Je ..... tout de suite. (descendre)

e) Vous ..... des bêtises. (dire)

f) Ils ..... bien attention, ces enfants. (faire)

2. Example:

Elle ..... deux frères. (avoir)

Elle a deux frères.

a) Nous ..... à six heures. (manger)

b) Mes amis ..... de la chance. (avoir)

c) Ils ..... rentrer. (vouloir)

d) Vous ..... sûrs, n'est-ce pas ? (être)

e) Tes amis ..... rester. (pouvoir)

f) Le cinéma ..... à huit heures. (ouvrir)

TRAIL → 2 ANSWERS
page 234

→ TRAIL 6

PRESENT TENSE – QUESTION FORM

3. Example:

Ils arrivent ce soir.

Est-ce qu'ils arrivent ce soir ? Arrivent-ils ce soir ?

a) Nous devons rentrer.

b) Il lit un journal tous les jours.

c) Le chien est dans la cuisine.

d) Je peux vous téléphoner.

e) Les voisins font du bruit.

f) Je crois ce qu'il dit.

PRESENT TENSE – NEGATIVE FORM

4. Example:

Ils achètent le journal.

Ils n'achètent pas le journal.

a) Nous mangeons le gâteau.

b) Elle a peur du chien.

c) Ont-ils les passeports ?

d) Est-ce qu'il sait la vérité ?

e) Voyez-vous la solution ?

f) Les autorités comprennent bien.

PRESENT TENSE – COMMAND FORM

5. Example:

Vous donnez de l'argent à votre ami.

Donnez de l'argent à votre ami !

a) Nous restons ici.

b) Tu vas au bureau du directeur.

c) Vous ne renvoyez pas le paquet.

d) Tu ne parles pas en classe.

e) Vous répétez la question.

f) Nous n'achetons pas les journaux.

TRAIL → 6 ANSWERS
page 234

→ TRAIL 8

PRESENT TENSE – PRONOMINAL VERBS

6. Example:

Il se cache derrière l'arbre.

Il ne se cache pas derrière l'arbre.

a) Je m'intéresse à la politique.

b) Elle se promène en ville.

c) Levons-nous !

d) Se lave-t-il les dents ?

e) Cache-toi !

f) Asseyez-vous là !

TRAIL → 8 ANSWERS
page 235

→ TRAIL 10

PRESENT TENSE – DEPUIS AND VENIR DE

7. Translate into French:

a) I have just eaten some sandwiches.

b) They have been waiting for two hours.

c) My parents have just left.

d) How long has he been listening at the door?

e) Have you (*tu*) just got up?

f) I have been reading the newspaper for an hour.

g) She has just opened the present.

TRAIL → 10 ANSWERS
page 236

◆

→ TRAIL 12

VERBS AND TENSES

Our aim in drawing up the exercises in this section is to consolidate our explanation of how to form and use the tenses. Although some of our examples will make use of regular verbs, we will mainly draw on our list of irregular verbs so that with this practice you may remember them more easily.

EXERCISE I. PRESENT → PERFECT

1. Example:

Il donne beaucoup d'argent à sa femme.

Il a donné beaucoup d'argent à sa femme.

a) Elle boit du vin.

b) Nous ouvrons la fenêtre.

c) Ils prennent le petit déjeuner à huit heures.

d) Vous êtes contents de le voir.

e) J'appelle mon ami tous les soirs.

f) Tu finis tes devoirs avant ton frère.

2. Example:

Elle arrive de bonne heure.

Elle est arrivée de bonne heure.

a) Pierre et Marie rentrent mardi.

b) Maman descend à la plage.

c) « Ma tante et moi restons à l'hôtel », crie la jeune fille.

d) Papa va au pub.

e) Nos deux amis viennent chez nous aujourd'hui.

f) Je pars pour la France.

3. Example:

Il ne dit pas la vérité. (*which auxiliary verb?*)

Il n'a pas dit la vérité. (avoir - *this time.*)

a) Elle ne ment pas.

b) Nous n'allons pas au cinéma.

c) Il ne voit pas ses amis pendant la semaine.

d) Vous n'avez pas de chance !

e) Le médecin ne veut pas attendre.

f) Le professeur ne répète pas ses instructions.

4. Example:

Elle la voit.

Elle l'a vue. (*agreement with preceding direct object*)

a) Les livres ? Je les cherche en France.

b) Le Premier ministre ? Le Président le reçoit ce matin.

c) Je la rencontre devant le théâtre.

d) Tu le mènes en ville.

e) Je le suis jusqu'à l'église.

f) Elle le jette par la fenêtre.

5. Example:

Mangez-vous à midi ?

Avez-vous mangé à midi ?

a) Comprends-tu ?

b) Remplit-il le questionnaire ?

c) Est-ce qu'elle parle à son père ?

d) Écrivez-vous la lettre ?

e) Fait-il de son mieux ?

f) Pleut-il ?

6. Example:

Nous nous couchons à onze heures et demie.

Nous nous sommes couchés (couchées) à onze heures et demie.

a) Mes parents se promènent en ville.

b) Elle se lave les mains.

c) Ils se battent pour un rien.

d) Elles s'asseyent au premier rang.

e) Tu te lèves tard.

f) Nous nous cachons derrière le garage.

7. Now try these:

Again they are to be put in the perfect tense. They combine the points tested in the previous exercises.

a) Elle ne le mange pas.

b) Nous ne nous levons pas trop tôt.

c) Ne vient-elle pas ?

d) Le vois-tu ?

e) Je reçois les paquets de mon voisin.

f) Elle oublie de mettre la table.

EXERCISE II. PERFECT → PRESENT

1. Example:

Vous avez causé avec vos amis.

Vous causez avec vos amis.

a) Il a répondu à ma question.

b) Nous avons fini de laver la vaisselle.

c) Tu as oublié de me rendre l'argent.

d) J'ai ennuyé le professeur.

e) Ils ont employé des ciseaux pour couper le papier.

f) Vous êtes sortis de la maison à minuit.

2. Example:

Nos amis n'ont pas appelé le médecin.

Nos amis n'appellent pas le médecin.

a) Nous n'avons pas commencé à lire le roman.

b) Pierre et Jean n'ont pas payé le repas.

c) Je n'ai pas dormi toute la nuit.

d) Elles n'ont pas appris à parler espagnol.

e) Vous n'êtes pas parti de l'hôpital.

f) Tu n'as pas répété ton erreur.

3. Example:

As-tu ennuyé le patron ?

Ennuies-tu le patron ?

a) Ont-ils jeté des pierres dans la rivière ?

b) Avons-nous mangé ce soir à sept heures ?

c) Pierre est-il revenu à la maison ?

d) Avez-vous fini vos devoirs ?

e) As-tu dormi devant le feu ?

f) Est-elle sortie de chez elle ?

4. Example:

A-t-il pu manger tout le gâteau ?

Peut-il manger tout le gâteau ?

a) Nous avons dû traverser le pont.

b) Vous avez dit au revoir à votre chien.

c) Ils ont craint le pire.

d) Elle n'a pas eu beaucoup à faire.

e) As-tu bu de la bière ?

f) Je n'ai pas voulu perdre mes lunettes.

5. Example:

Elle s'est cachée dans l'armoire.

Elle se cache dans l'armoire.

a) Je me suis demandé pourquoi il est si bête.

b) Nous nous sommes endormis dans le train.

c) S'est-elle assise tout de suite ?

d) Vous êtes-vous couchés de bonne heure ?

e) Ils ne se sont pas battus.

f) Ne t'es-tu pas posé cette question ?

6. Example:

La règle ? Je l'ai rendue à ma sœur.

La règle ? Je la rends à ma sœur.

a) Les fléchettes ? Il les a jetées contre la cible.

b) Le thé ? Vous l'avez bu.

c) La porte ? Tu l'as ouverte à notre arrivée.

d) Les lettres ? Je ne les ai pas écrites.

e) La carte d'anniversaire ? Elles ne l'ont pas choisie.

f) Les touristes ? Les guides les ont-ils menés vers le château ?

TRAIL → 12 ANSWERS
page 237

→ TRAIL 14

EXERCISE III. USING THE IMPERFECT AND PLUPERFECT TENSES

Translate into French:

a) We used to leave the house at 9:30 a.m.

b) Mum was reading her new novel.

c) My sisters were often sad at the end of the holidays.

d) The sun was shining and the sea was blue.

e) She had rung her father earlier in the evening.

f) My brother had not heard the teacher.

g) His uncle and his daughter had not stood up.

TRAIL → 14 ANSWERS
page 240

→ TRAIL 18

EXERCISE IV. USING THE PRESENT AND FUTURE TENSES

Example:

S'il (pleuvoir), je (rester) chez moi.

S'il pleut, je resterai chez moi.

a) S'il (falloir) partir, nous (partir) demain.

b) Si vous (lire) la lettre, il (être) fâché.

c) Si elle (rire), nous (rire) aussi.

d) Si les enfants (mettre) la table, ils (avoir) de l'argent.

e) Si tu ne (vivre) pas sainement, tu ne (perdre) pas de poids.

f) Si elles (savoir) la vérité, elles vous la (dire).

EXERCISE V. USING THE IMPERFECT AND CONDITIONAL TENSES

Example:

Si elle (connaître) mes amis, elle ne (venir) pas !

Si elle connaissait mes amis, elle ne viendrait pas !

a) Si elles se (sentir) malades, leur mère (appeler) le médecin.

b) S'il (neiger), les trains ne (circuler) pas.

c) Si vous (courir) moins de risques, vos parents (être) contents.

d) Si je (gagner) au loto, ma copine (mourir) de joie.

e) Si tu lui (sourire) comme ça, il (vouloir) sûrement danser avec toi !

f) Si tu (se servir) du nouvel aspirateur, tu (avoir) une maison propre.

TRAIL → 18 ANSWERS
page 240

→ TRAIL 22

EXERCISE VI. USING THE PLUPERFECT AND CONDITIONAL PERFECT TENSES

Example:

Si je (savoir), je (venir).

Si j'avais su, je serais venu(e).

a) Si nous (savoir), nous (te téléphoner).

b) Si tu ne (parler) pas, il (être) déçu.

c) Si le chauffeur de taxi (rouler) moins vite, il (éviter) l'accident.

d) Si vos parents (l'inviter) à la boum, il (dire) oui.

e) Si je (être) malade, je ne (revenir) pas si tôt.

f) Si vous (y aller), vous (les voir).

In Exercises IV and V (Trail 18) and Exercise VI (above), we have concentrated on the tenses used after **si** which we know students find difficult.

You will have noticed that the sentences are divided into two parts (or clauses). [A clause, as you will remember, is simply a part of a sentence containing a verb and its subject.] There is an **if** clause and a **result** clause. The order of these may be changed, but the tenses will remain the same; this table may help you to remember:

SI CLAUSE	RESULT CLAUSE
present	future
imperfect	conditional
pluperfect	conditional perfect

We feel that translating from English into French is a good indicator of how well you have absorbed the information covered by Exercises IV, V and VI.

We offer, therefore, the following:

EXERCISE VII.

Translate into French:

a) If she opened the door, she would see him.

b) You (*vous*) would have been able to stay, if you had reserved a room.

c) My parents and I will go out tomorrow, if it is fine.

d) If he has any letters, the postman will arrive at ten o'clock.

e) The teacher would buy a new car, if he had enough money.

f) If you (*tu*) had stayed at home, we would have understood.

g) I would not have sent the parcel, if you (*vous*) had phoned me.

EXERCISE VIII. MORE ABOUT THE FUTURE TENSES IN FRENCH

First of all, consider the following sentence:

When I go into town, I buy (some) shoes.

This poses no problem in French:

Quand je vais en ville, j'achète des chaussures.

As you see, the tenses are the same as in English.

However, if we say in English *When I go into town, I **will buy** (some) shoes*, whilst the second clause is straightforward (**j'achèterai des chaussures**), the future tense will be required in the first clause too, as clearly it is a future action which is envisaged. The full sentence will read – **Quand j'irai en ville, j'achèterai des chaussures**.

This use of the future tense where future time is meant will be found after **quand** and **lorsque** (*when*), **aussitôt que** and **dès que** (*as soon as*) and **une fois que** (*once*):

Quand je le **verrai**,	
Lorsqu'il **sera** de retour,	
Dès que j'**aurai** de ses nouvelles,	je vous **préviendrai**.
Aussitôt que mon père **dira** oui,	
Une fois que le Président **prendra** sa décision,	

When I see him	
When he gets back	
As soon as I have news of him / her	*I will let you know.*
As soon as my father says yes	
Once the President makes his decision	

However, French does not use a future tense after **si** (*if*), which clearly implies a future action:

S'il fait mauvais, je resterai chez moi.
If the weather's bad, I'll stay at home.

The tenses here, you will note, are the same as in English.

You may, on the other hand, find a future tense after **si** when its meaning is *whether*:

Je ne sais pas si elle arrivera ce soir.
I don't know whether she'll arrive this evening.

For the sake of completeness, we will now point out two further problems concerning future tenses.

Let us consider this sentence:

Il dit qu'il descendra quand il aura fini son travail.
*He says that he will come down when he **has finished** his work.*

However as the verb after **quand** looks to a time in the future, the French literally means *When he **will have finished** ...* (future perfect).

Similarly, French would have:

Il a dit qu'il descendrait quand il aurait fini son travail.
*He said that he would come down when he **had finished** his work.*

Here again, French sees the finishing of the work as a future event and so uses the conditional perfect (*would have finished*).

This translation exercise will help:

a) As soon as she leaves, I will do the washing up.

b) If she is ill, her friend will do the washing (*faire la lessive*).

c) He says he will do the hoovering (*passer l'aspirateur*) when he has read the paper.

d) Tell me if (whether) you (*vous*) will be there.

e) Once we have the money, we will invite you out for a meal (*inviter au restaurant*).

f) His father said that he would buy the bicycle when he had earned enough money (*gagner assez d'argent*).

TRAIL → 22 ANSWERS
page 241

→ TRAIL 52

EXERCISE IX. USING THE PAST HISTORIC AND PAST ANTERIOR TENSES

Although you will seldom find these tenses in other than written form, we have still recorded the correct versions for you.

Change the verbs in these sentences to the past historic:

a) Elle est arrivée à sept heures.

b) Maman et papa sont revenus de bonne heure.

c) La famille a lu la lettre en silence.

d) Ils ont vu le cambrioleur devant la maison.

Translate these sentences into French putting the main verb in the past historic:

e) As soon as he had left the house, the firemen arrived.

f) Hardly had she arrived at the market square when the man spoke to her.

TRAIL → 52 ANSWERS
page 242

→ TRAIL 46

EXERCISE X. USING THE SUBJUNCTIVE

In the following sentences, give the correct form of the present subjunctive:

a) Elle regrette que nous ne (pouvoir) pas venir.

b) J'ai peur qu'ils ne (être) malades.

c) Ta mère est contente que tu (faire) tes devoirs.

d) Vous ne croyez pas qu'il (dire) la vérité.

e) Il se peut que vous (avoir) tort.

f) C'est le roman le plus intéressant que nous (avoir) jamais lu.

g) J'ai envoyé la lettre pour qu'elle (revenir) tout de suite.

EXERCISE XI. USING THE SUBJUNCTIVE OR THE INDICATIVE

In the following sentences, give the correct form of the present subjunctive or of the present indicative as required:

a) J'espère que vous (avoir) compris.

b) Il est possible qu'elle (avoir) raison.

c) Elle dit que ses parents ne (être) pas encore arrivés.

d) Elle attend que tu (finir) la lettre.

e) Il faut que je (s'en aller).

f) Il croit que nous (être) partis.

g) Nous doutons que ses enfants (savoir) la vérité.

EXERCISE XII. TRANSLATION

a) We (masc.) are surprised that you (*tu*) say that.

b) We fear (*craindre*) that she has decided to leave.

c) The teacher has ordered that you all stay in the classroom.

d) Is it possible that she has lost her passport?

e) She will stay on condition that he writes the article for her.

f) Long live the President!

g) They must leave before it is too late.

TRAIL → 46 ANSWERS
page 243

→ TRAIL 58

EXERCISE XIII. USING ACTIVE AND PASSIVE VOICES

Example:

Les journaux ont été livrés par Pierre. (*passive*)

Pierre a livré les journaux. (*active*)

a) Ma cousine est toujours suivie par le chien. (*present*)

b) Le jeune homme a été invité à la soirée par le maire. (*perfect*)

c) Le verdict sera prononcé par le jury. (*future*)

d) Les fleurs n'avaient pas été cueillies (picked) par les passants. (*pluperfect*)

e) Marat fut assassiné par Charlotte Corday. (*past historic*)

f) La nouvelle serait mal reçue par la population. (*conditional*)

EXERCISE XIV. USING ACTIVE AND PASSIVE VOICES

Example:

Le directeur a pris la décision. (*active*)

La décision a été prise par le directeur. (*passive*)

a) Le professeur corrigera les copies. (*future*)

b) Mes parents invitaient souvent les voisins à dîner chez nous. (*imperfect*)

c) Les voleurs ont agressé le vieillard. (*perfect*)

d) Le principal ne félicite pas les bons élèves. (*present*)

e) Les agents de police avaient arrêté les malfaiteurs. (*pluperfect*)

f) La nouvelle bouleversa mes parents. (*past historic*)

EXERCISE XV. USING ACTIVE AND PASSIVE VOICES

Example:

L'annonce a été faite. (*passive*)

On a fait l'annonce. (*active*)

a) Le but avait été marqué à la dernière minute.

b) La maison ne serait pas vendue.

c) Les lettres auraient été envoyées plus tôt.

d) Les photos seront volées.

e) Le corps fut trouvé dans un bois.

f) Les mots français sont souvent mal prononcés.

EXERCISE XVI. TRANSLATION

a) The boys have been told to stay.

b) The tickets have been lost.

c) My sister will not be asked to take the exam.

d) The injured had been taken to hospital.

e) Paul, bring your friend. She is invited.

f) The burglars would have been surprised by my neighbour.

g) Yesterday my brother was told the truth.

TRAIL → 58 ANSWERS
page 244

→ TRAIL 62

EXERCISE XVII. THE PRESENT PARTICIPLE

Translate into French:
a) Not wanting to make a noise, she took off her shoes.
b) Knowing the truth is always preferable.
c) On seeing the dead body, we let out a cry (*pousser un cri*) of horror.
d) She sat down, wondering if she had enough money.
e) It was an embarrassing situation.
f) By saying that, she made (*se faire*) many friends.
g) I have just received some surprising news.

TRAIL → 62 ANSWERS
page 245

→ TRAIL 24

B. NEGATIVES

1. In these sentences, put the negative words in their correct position to give the opposite meaning to the original. To help you, words in bold type will not appear in your answer.

Example:

Elle va **toujours** à l'école. (ne ... jamais)

Elle ne va jamais à l'école.

a) L'agent de police sait **tout**. (ne ... rien)

b) Je connais **tout le monde** ici. (ne ... personne)

c) Les étudiants sont **toujours** au réfectoire. (ne ... plus)

d) Elles sont allées **parfois** à la bibliothèque. (ne ... jamais)

e) Elle a rencontré **des amies** au café. (ne ... personne)

f) Lève-toi ! (ne ... pas)

2. In these sentences, put the negative words in their correct position to give the opposite meaning to the original. To help you, words in bold type will not appear in your answer.

a) Les élèves ont stylos **et** cahiers. (ne ... ni ... ni ...)

b) J'avais envie d'aller au spectacle. (ne ... aucune)

c) Nous aurions donné **beaucoup d'argent**. (ne ... que dix euros)

d) Nous avions décidé de nous lever **toujours** avant midi. (ne ... plus)

e) Vous auriez eu besoin de le faire. (ne ... aucun)

f) Achetez-les ! (ne ... jamais)

g) Papa a décidé de **tout** faire. (ne ... rien)

3. Translate into French:

a) She will not say anything any more.

b) They no longer saw anyone at the factory.

c) Nobody wants to help me.

d) Neither my brother nor my sister will come.

e) Nothing has happened.

f) She will only come and pick you (*vous*) up (*venir chercher*) at the airport if you telephone tomorrow evening.

g) My parents have never seen anyone at that house.

TRAIL → 24 ANSWERS
page 246

◆ ◆ ◆

C. NOUNS AND ARTICLES

→ TRAIL 4

EXERCISE I. THE DEFINITE ARTICLE

Give the definite article for each of these nouns:

a) ... printemps, ... grec, ... jaune, ... métallurgie, ... boucherie.

b) ... page, ... stage, ... couteau, ... peau, ... caquet.

c) ... filet, ... surréalisme, ... magnétophone, ... sucette, ... squelette.

d) ... communication, ... victime, ... couloir, ... bonté, ... couverture.

e) ... personne, ... soulagement, ... silence, ... diligence, ... vedette.

f) ... Mexique, ... Belgique, ... Canada, ... Provence, ... Québec.

g) ... Loire, ... Tamise ... Rhin, ... Jura, ... Caucase.

EXERCISE II. THE PLURALS OF NOUNS

Give the plurals of the following nouns:

a) la voix, le château, le pneu, le journal, l'animal.

b) le carnaval, le bijou, le travail, le chou-fleur, le tire-bouchon.

c) le porte-monnaie, l'œil, le monsieur, mademoiselle, le bras.

TRAIL → 4 ANSWERS
page 247

◆

→ TRAIL 16

EXERCISE III. USE OF THE DEFINITE ARTICLE

Translate into French:
a) I like eggs but I don't like tomatoes.
b) Children respect good teachers.
c) Germany is bigger than Belgium.
d) She works in Scotland. Her husband works in Japan.
e) Marie speaks French and she understands Chinese.
f) On Thursdays we go to the library.
g) He washed his hands and face.

EXERCISE IV. USE OF THE DEFINITE ARTICLE

Translate into French:
a) The car stopped at the traffic lights.
b) Are you (*vous*) going to market?
c) Do you (*tu*) go to church on Sundays?
d) In the morning I go to the swimming baths.
e) The garden gate was open.
f) We paid five euros a kilo.
g) The hero and the heroine got married (*se marier*).

EXERCISE V. USE OF THE INDEFINITE ARTICLE

Translate into French:
a) Her father is a doctor.
b) We have friends in Canada.
c) Here are some newspapers.
d) She received the news with indifference.
e) She received the news with extraordinary indifference.
f) He has made astonishing progress.
g) Did she buy sweets?

EXERCISE VI. USE OF THE PARTITIVE ARTICLE

Supply the partitive article (**du, de la, de l', des, de, d'**) in the following:
a) Maman a … eau mais elle n'a pas … ail.
b) … fromage et … crème, s'il vous plaît.
c) Je n'ai pas … vin blanc mais j'ai … vin rouge.
d) A-t-elle … argent ? Oui, elle a … euros et … livres.
e) Il lui a acheté … belles roses.

f) Allez me chercher … petits pois.

g) Donnez-moi un kilo … beurre, s'il vous plaît.

TRAIL → 16 ANSWERS
page 248

◆ ◆ ◆

→ TRAIL 28

D. PRONOUNS

1. In these sentences, replace the words given in italics by pronouns. We are testing the position of the pronouns here.

Example:

Elle envoie *le cadeau à sa tante*.

Elle le lui envoie.

a) Elle avait envoyé *le cadeau à sa tante*.

b) A-t-elle envoyé *le cadeau à sa tante* ?

c) Elle n'a pas envoyé *le cadeau à sa tante*.

d) N'aurait-elle pas envoyé *le cadeau à sa tante* ?

e) Veut-elle envoyer *le cadeau à sa tante* ?

f) Elle refusera d'envoyer *le cadeau à sa tante*.

2. Replace the words given in italics by pronouns:

a) *Les petits enfants* ont trouvé *les chiens*.

b) *Maman* n'a pas parlé *au directeur*.

c) *Mes amies* ont décidé d'acheter *le vin*.

d) Papa lui a acheté *le journal*.

e) Elle parlera demain *au directeur*.

f) Nous avions donné *l'argent à notre grand-mère*.

g) Elle veut montrer *la chemise à sa cousine*.

TRAIL → 28 ANSWERS
page 249

◆

→ TRAIL 36

3. Replace the words given in italics by pronouns:

a) Buvez *de la limonade* !

b) Donne-moi *du gâteau* !

c) Ne montrez pas *ces cartes à vos parents* !

d) Mettez *vos jouets dans le placard* !

e) Je ne m'intéresse pas *à la musique classique*.

f) Je pense souvent à *cette jolie rousse* (redhead).

g) Il t'a parlé *du match* ?

4. Translate the following sentences into French:

a) Let's not give him any!

b) Stand up, my friend.

c) Don't sit down, children.

d) I don't remember it. (*se souvenir de*)

e) We remember them.

f) What does he think of her?

g) I will go with him tomorrow.

5. Translate into French:

a) The cups? We've put them on the sideboard (*le buffet*).

b) Mum did not lend her any.

c) The flowers? Didn't she send them to him? (Use the inverted form of the question.)

d) We are going to show them (to) them.

e) He has spoken to us about it himself.

f) She can't get used to it (*s'habituer à*).

g) Let's not listen to them!

TRAIL → 36 ANSWERS
page 250

→ TRAIL 40

6. Complete the following sentences with the correct relative pronoun (**qui, que, qu',
dont**):

a) Dis bonjour à la dame ..... te parle.

b) Voilà le dictionnaire ..... vous avez besoin.

c) Les exercices ..... a donnés le professeur sont difficiles.

d) C'est le chien ..... elle a peur.

e) C'est le Président lui-même ..... a annoncé la nouvelle.

f) Je n'aime pas la manière ..... il s'exprime.

g) Voulez-vous voir la veste ..... ma femme m'a offerte ?

7. Complete the following sentences with the correct relative pronoun (**ce qui, ce que, ce
qu', ce dont**):

a) Je peux vous dire tout ..... est arrivé.

b) ..... vous me dites est vrai.

c) Nous ne savions pas ..... elle avait fait.

d) Comprenez-vous ..... il parle ?

e) ..... m'inquiète, c'est son attitude envers ses parents.

f) ..... elles ont envie, c'est de réussir aux examens.

g) Avez-vous déjà oublié tout ..... a dit le maire ?

8. Complete the following sentences with the correct relative pronoun (**lequel, laquelle**
etc):

a) Je vais vous montrer le bois dans ..... il a caché le butin (*loot*).

b) Elle vous expliquera les raisons pour ..... elle était partie.

c) C'était une histoire à ..... il pensait souvent.

d) Le commissaire a envoyé des agents aux magasins près ..... le corps a été trouvé.

e) Les chats ..... vous donnez à manger sont déjà très gros.

f) Voici le puits au fond ..... il s'est noyé.

g) Les collines vers ..... il se dirigeait étaient couvertes de brume.

TRAIL → 40 ANSWERS
page 251

→ TRAIL 44

9. Answer the following questions in the two ways indicated:

Example:

À qui est la cravate ? (*mine*)

C'est la mienne. Elle est à moi.

a) À qui est la voiture ? (*his*)

b) À qui sont ces chaussettes ? (*hers*)

c) À qui est ce vélo ? (*ours*)

d) À qui sont ces billets ? (*theirs, belonging to a group of men*)

e) À qui sont ces lunettes ? (*yours, speaking to a friend*)

f) À qui sont ces sacs à main ? (*theirs, belonging to a group of women*)

10. Translate into French the English reply in the following using the interrogative pronoun (**lequel**) or the demonstrative pronoun (**celui**).

a) J'ai perdu une photo. – Which one?

b) Je cherche un mouchoir. – The one your mum gave you?

c) Ce soir je vais mettre une cravate. – This one or that one?

d) Je cherche mes boucles d'oreille (*earrings*). – These?

e) Je ne sais pas lequel des tableaux je préfère. – This one, your sister's, perhaps?

f) J'ai invité des amis à la maison. – Which ones?

g) Odette a téléphoné à Jeanne. Elle a refusé son invitation. Qui ? – The latter or the former?

11. Translate into French using the interrogative pronoun (**qui**, **que**, **quoi** etc).

a) Who do you (*vous*) want to see?

b) Who spoke to them?

c) What would have happened?

d) What do you (*tu*) want to buy?

e) Who is she going out with?

f) What are you (*vous*) writing with?

g) Who is he doing this work for?

TRAIL → 44 ANSWERS
page 252

◆ ◆ ◆

→ TRAIL 20

E. THE ADJECTIVE

In these exercises, we will aim to reinforce your knowledge of agreement of adjectives and their position relative to the nouns they describe. We would like you to listen carefully to the answers for changes in the way the adjective is pronounced according to feminine and plural agreements. Of course where there is no change in sound, there will still be changes to written forms which are important.

EXERCISE I. THE POSSESSIVE ADJECTIVE

Example:

..... père n'aime pas ..... amis. (*my*)

Mon père n'aime pas mes amis.

a) ..... mère adore ..... amie. (*my*)

b) Tu vas voir ..... oncle, ... tante et ..... cousines. (*your*)

c) ..... enfant n'écoute jamais ..... conseils. (*her*)

d) ..... sœur veut mettre ..... pantalon. (*his*)

e) ..... professeur a noté ..... exercices. (*our*)

f) Je n'aime ni ..... chien ni ..... enfants ! (*their*)

EXERCISE II. THE DEMONSTRATIVE ADJECTIVE

Example:

..... garçon-ci ne comprend jamais rien. (*this*)

Ce garçon-ci ne comprend jamais rien.

a) Je vais acheter ..... veston et ..... chaussures-là. (*this, those*)

b) ..... arbre-là n'a jamais de feuilles en hiver. (*that*)

c) ..... élève-là est plus intelligent que ..... élèves-ci. (*that, these*)

d) Je viens de casser ..... assiette. (*this*)

e) Il m'a recommandé ..... hôtel-là. (*that*)

f) ..... histoire m'a fait rire. (*this*)

EXERCISE III. THE INTERROGATIVE ADJECTIVE

Example:

..... magazine a-t-il acheté ? (*which / what*)

Quel magazine a-t-il acheté ?

a) ..... ville ! ..... gosses ! (*What a town! What kids!*)

b) ..... femmes as-tu vues devant le cinéma ?

c) ..... horreur !

d) ..... articles lisez-vous ?

e) ..... erreurs !

f) ..... est pour vous un dimanche typique ?

EXERCISE IV. AGREEMENT IN GENERAL

1. In each case give the correct form of the adjective in brackets:

a) Il a donné des cadeaux à ses ..... filles. (petit)

b) Cette ..... serveuse te connaît ? (jeune)

c) « Je suis ..... », a dit ma mère. (fatigué)

d) Ce qu'elles sont ..... ! (bête)

e) Elle a acheté une robe ...... (vert clair)

f) Elle aime bien ces rubans ...... (rose)

2. In each case give the correct form of the adjective in brackets:

a) Hier nous avons acheté une auto ...... (neuf)

b) Les ..... semaines des vacances étaient fantastiques. (premier)

c) Elle était ...... (inquiet)

d) Il m'a raconté des histoires ...... (affreux)

e) Il est mort à la suite d'une ..... maladie. (cruel)

f) Une ..... intervention chirurgicale sera nécessaire. (pareil)

3. In each case give the correct form of the adjective in brackets:

a) Sa grand-mère est très ...... (gentil)

b) Il a passé une nuit ...... (blanc). (*sleepless*)

c) Le trottoir est couvert de feuilles ...... (sec)

d) Voilà la ..... solution. (meilleur)

e) Il n'aime pas les femmes ...... (flatteur)

f) C'était une tornade des plus ...... (destructeur)

4. In each case give the correct form of the adjective in brackets:

a) Il a payé une ..... somme d'argent. (gros)

b) Attention à la peinture ...... (frais)

c) Il travaille de ..... heures le soir. (long)

d) Il soufflait une brise ...... (doux)

e) Connaissez-vous cette ..... dame-là ? (vieux)

f) Elle habite une très ..... maison à la campagne. (beau)

5. In each case give the correct form of the adjective in brackets:

a) Ma sœur vient d'épouser un ..... homme riche. (beau)

b) Il a fait ses résolutions du ..... an. (nouveau)

c) Soudain un ..... homme s'est approché de moi. (vieux)

d) M. Martin est fier de ses ..... enfants. (beau)

e) J'aime bien regarder les ..... arbres au printemps. (vieux)

f) Les ..... élèves seront là à neuf heures. (nouveau)

6. In each case give the correct form of the adjective in brackets:

a) Je viens de recevoir deux ..... paquets. (gros)

b) Ils sont toujours ..... ces garçons-là. (heureux)

c) Je l'ai remercié pour ses bons et ..... services. (loyal)

d) Il avait reçu des coups ...... (fatal)

e) Le gouvernement ne peut pas résoudre tous les problèmes ...... (national)

f) J'aime passer les ..... jours d'été sur la plage. (beau)

7. In each case give the correct form of the word in brackets:

a) Dans la cour il y avait ..... étudiantes. (plusieurs)

b) ..... les professeurs sont en grève. (tout)

c) Je veux voir ..... la section à quatre heures. (tout)

d) Elles étaient ..... pénibles. (tout)

e) Elles seraient ..... anxieuses. (tout)

f) Les jeunes filles sont ..... joyeuses. (tout)

TRAIL → 20 ANSWERS
page 253

→ TRAIL 66

EXERCISE V. POSITION OF ADJECTIVE

1. In the following sentences, put the adjective into its correct position:
a) Elle vient d'acheter une jupe. (verte)
b) Mon père adore les voitures. (allemandes)
c) C'est un garçon ! (méchant)
d) On m'a dit que c'est une école. (excellente)
e) Je connais un restaurant près de la gare. (bon)
f) Y a-t-il de l'eau ? (chaude)

2. Translate into French:
a) He bought an expensive book.
b) This poor man has just lost his sister.
c) I have a clean handkerchief in my pocket.
d) He didn't recognise his own brother.
e) We want to help the poor countries of the world.
f) Last year she moved house. (*déménager*)

EXERCISE VI. COMPARATIVES AND SUPERLATIVES

1. Translate into French:
a) She is not as intelligent as her brother.
b) Here is a better solution.
c) The girls are taller than the boys.
d) He is the laziest boy in the class.
e) The youngest pupils can leave early.
f) She is the smallest pupil in the school.

2. Translate into French:

a) My best friends are richer than I.

b) It was the worst catastrophe.

c) The teachers are as happy as the pupils.

d) I know the best restaurants.

e) It was the coldest day of the year.

f) Your homework is worse than the previous one.

TRAIL → 66 ANSWERS
page 255

◆ ◆ ◆

→ TRAIL 72

F. PREPOSITIONS

1. Complete the following sentences by inserting the correct preposition where required. We have deliberately chosen some examples which are not in our lists. You may need to consult a good dictionary!

a) Vous avez tort ..... faire ça.

b) Il a failli ..... se noyer.

c) Elle a négligé ..... apporter son parapluie.

d) Papa perd son temps ..... regarder les feuilletons.

e) Le médecin a ordonné ..... l'infirmière ..... assister à la consultation.

f) Le directeur attend ..... vous voir.

g) Je me suis refusé ..... les défendre.

2. Do the same with the following:

a) Que comptez-vous ..... faire ?

b) Mes parents avaient consenti ..... les recevoir.

c) J'ai prié ..... les agents de police ..... téléphoner à mes parents.

d) Elle s'est apprêtée ...... partir.

e) Pourquoi a-t-il fallu ..... revenir si tôt ?

f) Petit à petit j'ai amené mes copains ..... comprendre.

g) Je ne sais pas pourquoi elle s'obstine ..... mentir.

3. Translate into French (here you need only manipulate example sentences from the grammar section):

a) My father had made up his mind not to smoke any more.

b) He would have been delighted to go out with her.

c) They will finish watching television at midnight.

d) I would have preferred to stay with her.

e) Is she ready to follow us? (use the inverted form of the question)

f) They had not succeeded in finding a good job.

g) We will tell her to come and see him.

TRAIL → 72 ANSWERS
page 256

◆ ◆ ◆

→ TRAIL 26

G. THE ADVERB

1. In the following sentences, insert the adverb (given in English in brackets).

Example:

Maman joue ..... du piano. (*well*)

Maman joue bien du piano.

a) Ma sœur joue ..... que mon frère. (*better*)

b) Il faut parler ..... aux voisins. (*politely*)

c) C'est elle qui écrit ..... en français. (*best*)

d) ..... je n'ai rien dit. (*fortunately, happily*)

e) Nous n'avons ..... pas envie d'y aller. (*really*)

f) Le premier ministre avait ..... refusé de les voir. (*constantly*)

2. Translate into French:

a) She will always tell the truth.

b) We had already seen them.

c) They played badly yesterday.

d) Let's speak louder!

e) She walked slowly to the check-out.

f) He speaks Russian fluently.

g) We recently read his article.

TRAIL → 26 ANSWERS
page 257

→ TRAIL 64

H. IL EST OR C'EST

1. In this exercise, insert **il est, elle est, ils sont, elles sont, c'est** or **ce sont** as appropriate:

a) Quelle heure est-il ? – ..... trois heures et demie.

b) Que fait ton père ? – ..... ingénieur.

c) Je viens de visiter la Corse (*Corsica*). – ..... magnifique.

d) Est-il possible de lire ce livre en deux heures ? – Oui, ... possible.

e) ..... difficile de supporter son avarice.

f) Qu'est-ce que c'est ? – ..... des stylos à bille. ..... verts.

g) Que fait votre oncle ? – ..... un journaliste réputé.

2. Again insert **il est, elle est, ils sont, elles sont, c'est** or **ce sont** as appropriate:

a) C'est qui à la porte ? – ..... eux.

b) A qui sont ces chapeaux ? – ..... à elles.

c) A qui est cette montre-là ? – ..... la sienne.

d) Vous aimez mon champagne ? – ..... magnifique.

e) Je n'aime pas la natation, ... fatigant.

f) Vous aimez manger les champignons ? – Oui, ... délicieux.

g) Qui est-ce ? – ..... mes neveux (*nephews*).

TRAIL → 64 ANSWERS
page 258

→ TRAIL 48

I. INVERSION

Translate into French:

a) We asked him, 'Do they know this lady?'

b) 'Do they know this lady?' we asked him.

c) 'You (*tu*) will stay at home,' my father shouted.

d) Perhaps she will come this evening. (Give three possible translations.)

e) Hardly had he closed the door when the phone rang (past historic).

f) In vain she had tried to convince him.

g) I would like to know what M. and Mme Dubois are doing.

TRAIL → 48 ANSWERS
page 259

→ TRAIL 50

J. DIRECT AND INDIRECT QUESTIONS

1. Complete the following sentences using **que, qu'est-ce que, qu'est-ce qui, de quoi, à quoi** as required:

a) ..... vous avez vu ?

b) ..... leur avez-vous dit ?

c) ..... il en pense ?

d) ..... a-t-elle peur ?

e) ..... pensaient-ils ?

f) ..... parlez-vous ?

g) ..... vous est arrivé ?

2. Complete the following sentences using **ce qui, ce que, ce dont** as required:

a) Je vais vous expliquer ..... m'est arrivé.

b) Il ignore ..... nous avons besoin.

c) ..... m'énerve, c'est son impatience.

d) Dites-moi ..... vous avez fait.

e) Elle se demande ..... vous intéresse.

f) Impossible de comprendre ..... disent les hommes politiques.

g) ..... nous avons envie, c'est de visiter Strasbourg.

TRAIL → 50 ANSWERS
page 260

◆ ◆ ◆

→ TRAIL 30

K. DEPUIS, POUR, PENDANT

Complete the sentence with the correct word:

a) Hier soir j'ai fait un mots-croisés ..... deux heures.

b) Je fais ce mots-croisés ..... deux heures.

c) Elle étudie le japonais ..... longtemps.

d) La semaine prochaine nous serons à Paris ..... deux jours.

e) L'année dernière nous avons loué un appartement ..... deux mois.

f) Ils habitaient ..... six semaines à Londres quand Pierre a perdu son poste.

g) Je serai là ..... deux heures.

TRAIL → 30 ANSWERS
page 261

→ TRAIL 70

L. OÙ

Translate into French:

a) Where does he come from?

b) Tell me where you're going. (to a friend)

c) Where she lives there aren't many shops.

d) I don't know the street in which his house is located.

e) It was raining the evening when he arrived.

f) It's the second time I've said no.

g) Wherever we go, we never see him.

TRAIL → 70 ANSWERS
page 261

→ TRAIL 68

M. PRICE, SPEED, MEASUREMENT

Translate into French:

a) She has paid ten euros a kilo.

b) Cauliflowers – two euros each.

c) He usually travels at fifty kilometres an hour.

d) How long is this field?

e) The yard was sixty metres (long) by twenty (metres wide).

f) The ocean is three hundred metres deep.

g) The tyre is fifteen centimetres wide.

TRAIL → 68 ANSWERS
page 262

◆ ◆ ◆

→ TRAIL 38

N. QUANTITIES

Translate into French:

a) My friends didn't have enough money.

b) How many letters did she write?

c) Most Norwegians (*Norvégiens*) like the snow.

d) We always have too much work!

e) They will have as much money as him.

f) So many passengers travel without a ticket.

g) Waiter, bring me some more water, please.

TRAIL → 38 ANSWERS
page 262

◆ ◆ ◆

→ TRAIL 56

O. IMPERSONAL VERBS

1. Translate into French using **il y a** in the form required:

a) Suddenly there was a noise.

b) There will be no wine.

c) There must be a problem.

d) There had been a misunderstanding (*un malentendu*).

e) Are there any peas?

f) There wouldn't have been any difficulty.

g) Were there any children in the yard?

2. Translate into French:

a) What is this article about?

b) We had only twenty euros left.

c) Do we have any water left?

d) There were often accidents at the corner of the street. (use *se produire*)

e) We had to return home at once. (use *falloir*)

f) A plaster (*un sparadrap*) is needed.

g) We would have had to refuse.

TRAIL → 56 ANSWERS
page 263

→ TRAIL 42

◆ ◆ ◆

P. THE FACTITIVE VERB

1. Insert **le, la, les, lui** or **leur** in the following sentences:

a) Mon professeur. Je ..... ferai voir que j'ai raison.

b) Ma mère. Ma sœur ..... fera chanter avec elle.

c) Nos voisins. Mon père ..... a fait fermer la télévision.

d) Mon copain. Nous ..... faisions souvent rester chez nous.

e) Les voleurs. On ..... a fait arrêter.

f) Ma grand-mère. Le médecin ..... faisait venir à la clinique tous les vendredis.

g) Ces hommes politiques. Je voudrais ..... faire comprendre que nous payons déjà trop d'impôts (*taxes*).

2. Translate into French:

a) We will have them leave tomorrow.

b) She made them write the letter. / She got them to write the letter.

c) Make him speak!

d) His teacher made him study the whole text. / ... had him study ...

e) I am going to have a cake made.

f) You (*tu*) often made me wash the car.

g) She got herself punished.

TRAIL → 42 ANSWERS
page 264

◆ ◆ ◆

→ TRAIL 54

Q. DEVOIR

Translate into French using **devoir**:

a) She owes us some money.

b) We have to leave now.

c) My parents must have gone out.

d) We often had to walk the dog.

e) I ought to go and see him.

f) They should have listened.

g) She ought to have stayed at home.

TRAIL → 54 ANSWERS
page 265

◆ ◆ ◆

→ TRAIL 60

R. POUVOIR AND SAVOIR

Translate into French:

a) Can her father play chess (*jouer aux échecs*)?

b) If dad says yes we can go out.

c) Suddenly she could understand her mistake.

d) If she had the address she could go and see him.

e) When he had a car he could go to the seaside.

f) She could hear the river in the wood.

g) He could have listened to us.

TRAIL → 60 ANSWERS
page 265

◆ ◆ ◆

→ TRAIL 32

S. MANQUER

Translate into French:

a) I was missing my sister.

b) My friends are missing me.

c) Does he miss her?

d) She had missed her bus.

e) The policemen never failed to catch the thieves.

f) Do your parents have no patience?

g) She will not fail in her duty.

TRAIL → 32 ANSWERS
page 266

◆ ◆ ◆

→ TRAIL 34

T. TO BE – ÊTRE ?

Complete the following sentences using the appropriate verb in the tense indicated:

a) Le fer ..... chaud. (*imperfect*)

b) Mes parents ..... froid. (*future*)

c) Il ..... beau ce jour-là. (*pluperfect*)

d) Ton grand-père ..... bien ? (*present*)

e) Je croyais qu'il ..... toujours malade. (*imperfect*)

f) Elle ..... honte de sortir sans payer l'addition. (*perfect*)

g) Ça lui ..... du bien de passer la nuit à la belle étoile. (*conditional perfect*)

TRAIL → 34 ANSWERS
page 267

A. VERBS IN THE PRESENT TENSE

→ TRAIL 2 ANSWERS

1.

a) Ils portent du vin à la table.

b) Elle sort souvent le soir.

c) Papa et maman choisissent un cadeau pour mon frère.

d) Je descends tout de suite.

e) Vous dites des bêtises.

f) Ils font bien attention, ces enfants.

2.

a) Nous mangeons à six heures.

b) Mes amis ont de la chance.

c) Ils veulent rentrer.

d) Vous êtes sûrs, n'est-ce pas ?

e) Tes amis peuvent rester.

f) Le cinéma ouvre à huit heures.

TRAIL → 3
page 85

◆

→ TRAIL 6 ANSWERS

PRESENT TENSE – QUESTION FORM

3.

a) Est-ce que nous devons rentrer ? Devons-nous rentrer ?

b) Est-ce qu'il lit un journal tous les jours ? Lit-il un journal tous les jours ?

c) Est-ce que le chien est dans la cuisine ? Le chien est-il dans la cuisine ?

d) Est-ce que je peux vous téléphoner ? Puis-je vous téléphoner ?
e) Est-ce que les voisins font du bruit ? Les voisins font-ils du bruit ?
f) Est-ce que je crois ce qu'il dit ?

PRESENT TENSE – NEGATIVE FORM

4.
a) Nous ne mangeons pas le gâteau.
b) Elle n'a pas peur du chien.
c) N'ont-ils pas les passeports ?
d) Est-ce qu'il ne sait pas la vérité ?
e) Ne voyez-vous pas la solution ?
f) Les autorités ne comprennent pas bien.

PRESENT TENSE – COMMAND FORM

5.
a) Restons ici !
b) Va au bureau du directeur !
c) Ne renvoyez pas le paquet !
d) Ne parle pas en classe !
e) Répétez la question !
f) N'achetons pas les journaux !

TRAIL → 7
page 18

→ TRAIL 8 ANSWERS

PRESENT TENSE – PRONOMINAL VERBS

6.

a) Je ne m'intéresse pas à la politique.

b) Elle ne se promène pas en ville.

c) Ne nous levons pas !

d) Ne se lave-t-il pas les dents ?

e) Ne te cache pas !

f) Ne vous asseyez pas là !

TRAIL → 9
page 22

→ TRAIL 10 ANSWERS

PRESENT TENSE – DEPUIS AND VENIR DE

7.

a) Je viens de manger des sandwich(e)s.

b) Ils attendent depuis deux heures.

c) Mes parents viennent de partir.

d) Depuis quand (combien de temps) écoute-t-il à la porte ? (est-ce qu'il écoute ...)

e) Est-ce que tu viens (Viens-tu) de te lever ?

f) Je lis le journal depuis une heure.

g) Elle vient d'ouvrir le cadeau.

TRAIL → 11
page 23

VERBS AND TENSES

EXERCISE I. PRESENT → PERFECT

1. **Avoir** verbs:

a) Elle a bu du vin.

b) Nous avons ouvert la fenêtre.

c) Ils ont pris le petit déjeuner à huit heures.

d) Vous avez été contents de le voir.

e) J'ai appelé mon ami tous les soirs.

f) Tu as fini tes devoirs avant ton frère.

2. **Être** verbs:

a) Pierre et Marie sont rentrés mardi.

b) Maman est descendue à la plage.

c) « Ma tante et moi sommes restées à l'hôtel », a crié la jeune fille.

d) Papa est allé au pub.

e) Nos deux amis sont venus chez nous aujourd'hui.

f) Je suis parti pour la France. (partie *for a female*)

3. Negatives:

a) Elle n'a pas menti.

b) Nous ne sommes pas allés au cinéma. (allées *if all are females*)

c) Il n'a pas vu ses amis pendant la semaine.

d) Vous n'avez pas eu de chance !

e) Le médecin n'a pas voulu attendre.

f) Le professeur n'a pas répété ses instructions.

4. With preceding direct objects:

a) Les livres ? Je les ai cherchés en France.

b) Le Premier ministre ? Le Président l'a reçu ce matin.

c) Je l'ai rencontrée devant le théâtre.

d) Tu l'as mené en ville.

e) Je l'ai suivi jusqu'à l'église.

f) Elle l'a jeté par la fenêtre.

5. Questions:

a) As-tu compris ?

b) A-t-il rempli le questionnaire ?

c) Est-ce qu'elle a parlé à son père ?

d) Avez-vous écrit la lettre ?

e) A-t-il fait de son mieux ?

f) A-t-il plu ?

6. Pronominal verbs:

a) Mes parents se sont promenés en ville.

b) Elle s'est lavé les mains. (*no agreement here*)

c) Ils se sont battus pour un rien.

d) Elles se sont assises au premier rang.

e) Tu t'es levé tard. (levée if **you** *refers to a female*)

f) Nous nous sommes cachés derrière le garage. (cachées if **we** *are all female*)

7. Varied examples:

a) Elle ne l'a pas mangé.

b) Nous ne nous sommes pas levés trop tôt. (levées if **we** *are all female*)

c) N'est-elle pas venue ?

d) L'as-tu vu ?

e) J'ai reçu les paquets de mon voisin.

f) Elle a oublié de mettre la table.

EXERCISE II. PERFECT → PRESENT

1. Regular verbs and variants:

a) Il répond à ma question.

b) Nous finissons de laver la vaisselle.

c) Tu oublies de me rendre l'argent.

d) J'ennuie le professeur.

e) Ils emploient des ciseaux pour couper le papier.

f) Vous sortez de la maison à minuit.

2. Regular verbs – negative:

a) Nous ne commençons pas à lire le roman.

b) Pierre et Jean ne payent (paient) pas le repas.

c) Je ne dors pas toute la nuit.

d) Elles n'apprennent pas à parler espagnol.

e) Vous ne partez pas de l'hôpital.

f) Tu ne répètes pas ton erreur.

3. Regular verbs – questions:

a) Jettent-ils des pierres dans la rivière ?

b) Mangeons-nous ce soir à sept heures ?

c) Pierre revient-il à la maison ?

d) Finissez-vous vos devoirs ?

e) Dors-tu devant le feu ?

f) Sort-elle de chez elle ?

4. Irregular verbs:

a) Nous devons traverser le pont.

b) Vous dites au revoir à votre chien.

c) Ils craignent le pire.

d) Elle n'a pas beaucoup à faire.

e) Bois-tu de la bière ?

f) Je ne veux pas perdre mes lunettes.

5. Pronominal verbs:

a) Je me demande pourquoi il est si bête.

b) Nous nous endormons dans le train.

c) S'assied-elle tout de suite ?

d) Vous couchez-vous de bonne heure ?

e) Ils ne se battent pas.

f) Ne te poses-tu pas cette question ?

6. Pronoun object positioning:

a) Les fléchettes ? Il les jette contre la cible.

b) Le thé ? Vous le buvez.

c) La porte ? Tu l'ouvres à notre arrivée.

d) Les lettres ? Je ne les écris pas.

e) La carte d'anniversaire ? Elles ne la choisissent pas.

f) Les touristes ? Les guides les mènent-ils vers le château ?

TRAIL → 13
page 34

→ TRAIL 14 ANSWERS

EXERCISE III. USING THE IMPERFECT AND PLUPERFECT TENSES

a) Nous quittions la maison à neuf heures et demie du matin.

b) Maman lisait son nouveau roman.

c) Mes sœurs étaient souvent tristes à la fin des vacances.

d) Il faisait du soleil (Le soleil brillait) et la mer était bleue.

e) Elle avait téléphoné à son père plus tôt dans la soirée.

f) Mon frère n'avait pas entendu le professeur.

g) Son oncle et sa fille ne s'étaient pas levés.

TRAIL → 15
page 90

◆

→ TRAIL 18 ANSWERS

EXERCISE IV. USING THE PRESENT AND FUTURE TENSES

a) S'il faut partir, nous partirons demain.

b) Si vous lisez la lettre, il sera fâché.

c) Si elle rit, nous rirons aussi.

d) Si les enfants mettent la table, ils auront de l'argent.

e) Si tu ne vis pas sainement, tu ne perdras pas de poids.

f) Si elles savent la vérité, elles vous la diront.

EXERCISE V. USING THE IMPERFECT AND CONDITIONAL TENSES

a) Si elles se sentaient malades, leur mère appellerait le médecin.
b) S'il neigeait, les trains ne circuleraient pas.
c) Si vous couriez moins de risques, vos parents seraient contents.
d) Si je gagnais au loto, ma copine mourrait de joie.
e) Si tu lui souriais comme ça, il voudrait sûrement danser avec toi !
f) Si tu te servais du nouvel aspirateur, tu aurais une maison propre.

TRAIL → 19
page 127

◆

→ TRAIL 22 ANSWERS

EXERCISE VI. USING THE PLUPERFECT AND CONDITIONAL PERFECT TENSES

a) Si nous avions su, nous t'aurions téléphoné.
b) Si tu n'avais pas parlé, il aurait été déçu.
c) Si le chauffeur de taxi avait roulé moins vite, il aurait évité l'accident.
d) Si vos parents l'avaient invité à la boum, il aurait dit oui.
e) Si j'avais été malade, je ne serais pas revenu(e) si tôt.
f) Si vous y étiez allé(e)(s), vous les auriez vu(e)s.

EXERCISE VII. TRANSLATION

a) Si elle ouvrait la porte, elle le verrait.
b) Vous auriez pu rester, si vous aviez réservé une chambre.
c) Mes parents et moi sortirons demain, s'il fait beau.
d) S'il a des lettres, le facteur arrivera à dix heures.
e) Le professeur achèterait une nouvelle auto, s'il avait assez d'argent.

f) Si tu étais resté(e) à la maison, nous aurions compris.

g) Je n'aurais pas envoyé le paquet, si vous m'aviez téléphoné.

EXERCISE VIII. MORE ABOUT THE FUTURE TENSES IN FRENCH

a) Aussitôt (Dès) qu'elle partira, je ferai la vaisselle.

b) Si elle est malade, son ami(e) fera la lessive.

c) Il dit qu'il passera l'aspirateur quand il aura lu le journal.

d) Dites-moi si vous serez là.

e) Une fois que nous aurons l'argent, nous vous inviterons au restaurant.

f) Son père a dit qu'il achèterait la bicyclette quand il aurait gagné assez d'argent.

TRAIL → 23
page 75

→ TRAIL 52 ANSWERS

EXERCISE IX. USING THE PAST HISTORIC AND PAST ANTERIOR TENSES

a) Elle arriva à sept heures.

b) Maman et papa revinrent de bonne heure.

c) La famille lut la lettre en silence.

d) Ils virent le cambrioleur devant la maison.

e) Dès (Aussitôt) qu'il eut quitté la maison, les pompiers arrivèrent.

f) À peine fut-elle arrivée à la place du marché que l'homme lui parla.

TRAIL → 53
page 182

◆

EXERCISE X. USING THE SUBJUNCTIVE

a) Elle regrette que nous ne puissions pas venir.

b) J'ai peur qu'ils ne soient malades.

c) Ta mère est contente que tu fasses tes devoirs.

d) Vous ne croyez pas qu'il dise la vérité.

e) Il se peut que vous ayez tort.

f) C'est le roman le plus intéressant que nous ayons jamais lu.

g) J'ai envoyé la lettre pour qu'elle revienne tout de suite.

EXERCISE XI. USING THE SUBJUNCTIVE OR THE INDICATIVE

a) J'espère que vous avez compris.

b) Il est possible qu'elle ait raison.

c) Elle dit que ses parents ne sont pas encore arrivés.

d) Elle attend que tu finisses la lettre.

e) Il faut que je m'en aille.

f) Il croit que nous sommes partis.

g) Nous doutons que ses enfants sachent la vérité.

EXERCISE XII. TRANSLATION

a) Nous sommes surpris (étonnés) que tu dises cela.

b) Nous craignons qu'elle (**n'**)ait décidé de partir.

c) Le professeur a ordonné que vous restiez tous dans la salle de classe.

d) Est-il possible qu'elle ait perdu son passeport ?

e) Elle restera à condition qu'il écrive l'article pour elle.

f) Vive le Président !

g) Ils doivent partir avant qu'il (**ne**) soit trop tard.

→ TRAIL 58 ANSWERS

EXERCISE XIII. USING ACTIVE AND PASSIVE VOICES

a) Le chien suit toujours ma cousine. (*present of* suivre)

b) Le maire a invité le jeune homme à la soirée. (*perfect of* inviter)

c) Le jury prononcera le verdict. (*future of* prononcer)

d) Les passants n'avaient pas cueilli les fleurs. (*pluperfect of* cueillir)

e) Charlotte Corday assassina Marat. (*past historic of* assassiner)

f) La population recevrait mal la nouvelle. (*conditional of* recevoir)

EXERCISE XIV. USING ACTIVE AND PASSIVE VOICES

a) Les copies seront corrigées par le professeur. (*future of* être)

b) Les voisins étaient souvent invités à dîner chez nous par mes parents. (*imperfect of* être)

c) Le vieillard a été agressé par les voleurs. (*perfect of* être)

d) Les bons élèves ne sont pas félicités par le principal. (*present of* être)

e) Les malfaiteurs avaient été arrêtés par les agents de police. (*pluperfect of* être)

f) Mes parents furent bouleversés par la nouvelle. (*past historic of* être)

EXERCISE XV. USING ACTIVE AND PASSIVE VOICES

a) On avait marqué le but à la dernière minute.

b) On ne vendrait pas la maison.

c) On aurait envoyé les lettres plus tôt.

d) On volera les photos.

e) On trouva le corps dans un bois.

f) On prononce souvent mal les mots français.

EXERCISE XVI. TRANSLATION

a) On a dit aux garçons de rester.

b) Les billets ont été perdus. On a perdu les billets.

c) On ne demandera pas à ma sœur de passer l'examen.

d) Les blessés avaient été emmenés à l'hôpital. On avait emmené les blessés à l'hôpital.

e) Paul, amène ton amie. Elle est invitée. / On l'invite.

f) Les cambrioleurs auraient été surpris par mon voisin. Mon voisin aurait surpris les cambrioleurs.

g) Hier on a dit la vérité à mon frère.

TRAIL → 59
page 184

→ TRAIL 62 ANSWERS

EXERCISE XVII. THE PRESENT PARTICIPLE

a) Ne voulant pas faire de bruit, elle a ôté (enlevé) ses chaussures.

b) Savoir la vérité est toujours préférable.

c) En voyant le cadavre (corps) nous avons poussé un cri d'horreur.

d) Elle s'est assise se demandant si elle avait assez d'argent.

e) C'était une situation embarrassante.

f) En disant cela, elle s'est fait beaucoup d'amis.

g) Je viens de recevoir des nouvelles surprenantes.

TRAIL → 63
page 157

◆ ◆ ◆

→ TRAIL 24 ANSWERS

B. NEGATIVES

1.

a) L'agent de police n'en sait rien.

b) Je ne connais personne ici.

c) Les étudiants ne sont plus au réfectoire.

d) Elles ne sont jamais allées à la bibliothèque.

e) Elle n'a rencontré personne au café.

f) Ne te lève pas !

2.

a) Les élèves n'ont ni stylos ni cahiers.

b) Je n'avais aucune envie d'aller au spectacle.

c) Nous n'aurions donné que dix euros.

d) Nous avions décidé de ne plus nous lever avant midi.

e) Vous n'auriez eu aucun besoin de le faire.

f) Ne les achetez jamais !

g) Papa a décidé de ne rien faire.

3.

a) Elle ne dira plus rien.

b) Ils n'ont plus vu personne à l'usine. (Ils ne voyaient plus personne à l'usine.)

c) Personne ne veut m'aider.

d) Ni mon frère ni ma sœur ne viendra / viendront.

e) Rien ne s'est passé. / Rien n'est arrivé. (Il ne s'est rien passé. / Il n'est rien arrivé.)

f) Elle ne viendra vous chercher à l'aéroport que si vous téléphonez demain soir.

g) Mes parents n'ont jamais vu personne à cette maison-là.

TRAIL → 25
page 152

→ TRAIL 4 ANSWERS

C. NOUNS AND ARTICLES

EXERCISE I. THE DEFINITE ARTICLE

a) le printemps, le grec, le jaune, la métallurgie, la boucherie.

b) la page, le stage, le couteau, la peau, le caquet.

c) le filet, le surréalisme, le magnétophone, la sucette, le squelette.

d) la communication, la victime, le couloir, la bonté, la couverture.

e) la personne, le soulagement, le silence, la diligence, la vedette.

f) le Mexique, la Belgique, le Canada, la Provence, le Québec.

g) la Loire, la Tamise, le Rhin, le Jura, le Caucase.

EXERCISE II. THE PLURALS OF NOUNS

a) les voix, les châteaux, les pneus, les journaux, les animaux.

b) les carnavals, les bijoux, les travaux, les choux-fleurs, les tire-bouchons.

c) les porte-monnaie, les yeux, les messieurs, mesdemoiselles, les bras.

TRAIL → 5
page 13

→ TRAIL 16 ANSWERS

EXERCISE III. USE OF THE DEFINITE ARTICLE

a) J'aime les œufs mais je n'aime pas les tomates.
b) Les enfants respectent les bons professeurs.
c) L'Allemagne est plus grande que la Belgique.
d) Elle travaille en Écosse. Son mari travaille au Japon.
e) Marie parle français et elle comprend le chinois.
f) Le jeudi nous allons à la bibliothèque.
g) Il s'est lavé les mains et le visage / la figure.

EXERCISE IV. USE OF THE DEFINITE ARTICLE

a) La voiture s'est arrêtée aux feux.
b) Allez-vous au marché ?
c) Vas-tu à l'église le dimanche ?
d) Le matin je vais à la piscine.
e) La porte du jardin était ouverte.
f) Nous avons payé cinq euros le kilo.
g) Le héros et l'héroïne se sont mariés.

EXERCISE V. USE OF THE INDEFINITE ARTICLE

a) Son père est médecin.
b) Nous avons des amis au Canada.
c) Voici des journaux.
d) Elle a reçu la nouvelle avec indifférence.
e) Elle a reçu la nouvelle avec une indifférence extraordinaire.

f) Il a fait des progrès étonnants / d'étonnants progrès.

g) A-t-elle acheté des bonbons ?

EXERCISE VI. USE OF THE PARTITIVE ARTICLE

a) Maman a de l'eau mais elle n'a pas d'ail.

b) Du fromage et de la crème, s'il vous plaît.

c) Je n'ai pas de vin blanc mais j'ai du vin rouge.

d) A-t-elle de l'argent ? Oui, elle a des euros et des livres.

e) Il lui a acheté de belles roses.

f) Allez me chercher des petits pois.

g) Donnez-moi un kilo de beurre, s'il vous plaît.

**TRAIL → 17
page 40**

→ **TRAIL 28 ANSWERS**

D. PRONOUNS

1.

a) Elle le lui avait envoyé.

b) Le lui a-t-elle envoyé ?

c) Elle ne le lui a pas envoyé.

d) Ne le lui aurait-elle pas envoyé ?

e) Veut-elle le lui envoyer ?

f) Elle refusera de le lui envoyer.

2.

a) Ils les ont trouvés.

b) Elle ne lui a pas parlé.

c) Elles ont décidé de l'acheter.

d) Papa le lui a acheté.

e) Elle lui parlera demain.

f) Nous le lui avions donné.

g) Elle veut la lui montrer.

TRAIL → 29
page 167

→ **TRAIL 36 ANSWERS**

3.

a) Buvez-en !

b) Donne-m'en !

c) Ne les leur montrez pas !

d) Mettez-les-y !

e) Je ne m'y intéresse pas.

f) Je pense souvent à elle.

g) Il t'en a parlé ?

4.

a) Ne lui en donnons pas !

b) Lève-toi, mon ami.

c) Ne vous asseyez pas, les (mes) enfants.

d) Je ne m'en souviens pas.

e) Nous nous souvenons d'eux / d'elles.

f) Que pense-t-il d'elle ? / Qu'est-ce qu'il pense d'elle ?

g) J'irai avec lui demain. / Je l'accompagnerai demain.

5.

a) Les tasses ? Nous les avons mises sur le buffet.

b) Maman ne lui en a pas prêté.

c) Les fleurs ? Ne les lui a-t-elle pas envoyées ?

d) Nous allons les leur montrer.

e) Il nous en a parlé lui-même.

f) Elle ne peut pas s'y habituer.

g) Ne les écoutons pas ! (écouter *takes a direct object*)

TRAIL → 37
page 172

◆

→ TRAIL 40 ANSWERS

6.

a) Dis bonjour à la dame qui te parle.

b) Voilà le dictionnaire dont vous avez besoin.

c) Les exercices qu'a donnés le professeur sont difficiles.

d) C'est le chien dont elle a peur.

e) C'est le Président lui-même qui a annoncé la nouvelle.

f) Je n'aime pas la manière dont il s'exprime.

g) Voulez-vous voir la veste que ma femme m'a offerte ?

7.

a) Je peux vous dire tout ce qui est arrivé.

b) Ce que vous me dites est vrai.

c) Nous ne savions pas ce qu'elle avait fait.

d) Comprenez-vous ce dont il parle ?

e) Ce qui m'inquiète, c'est son attitude envers ses parents.

f) Ce dont elles ont envie, c'est de réussir aux examens.

g) Avez-vous déjà oublié tout ce qu'a dit le maire ?

8.

a) Je vais vous montrer le bois dans lequel il a caché le butin.

b) Elle vous expliquera les raisons pour lesquelles elle était partie.

c) C'était une histoire à laquelle il pensait souvent.

d) Le commissaire a envoyé des agents aux magasins près desquels le corps a été trouvé.

e) Les chats auxquels vous donnez à manger sont déjà très gros.

f) Voici le puits au fond duquel il s'est noyé.

g) Les collines vers lesquelles il se dirigeait étaient couvertes de brume.

TRAIL → 41
page 179

→ TRAIL 44 ANSWERS

9.

a) C'est la sienne. Elle est à lui.

b) Ce sont les siennes. Elles sont à elle.

c) C'est le nôtre. Il est à nous.

d) Ce sont les leurs. Ils sont à eux.

e) Ce sont les tiennes. Elles sont à toi.

f) Ce sont les leurs. Ils sont à elles.

10.

a) J'ai perdu une photo. – Laquelle ?

b) Je cherche un mouchoir. – Celui que ta mère t'a donné ?

c) Ce soir je vais mettre une cravate. – Celle-ci ou celle-là ?

d) Je cherche mes boucles d'oreille. – Celles-ci ?

e) Je ne sais pas lequel des tableaux je préfère. – Celui-ci, celui de ta (votre) sœur, peut-être ?

f) J'ai invité des amis à la maison. – Lesquels ?

g) Odette a téléphoné à Jeanne. Elle a refusé son invitation. Qui ? – Celle-ci ou celle-là ?

11.

a) Qui voulez-vous voir ? / Qui est-ce que vous voulez voir ?

b) Qui leur a parlé ? / Qui est-ce qui leur a parlé ?

c) Qu'est-ce qui se serait passé ? / Qu'est-ce qui serait arrivé ?

d) Que veux-tu acheter ? / Qu'est-ce que tu veux acheter ?

e) Avec qui sort-elle ? / Avec qui est-ce qu'elle sort ? / Elle sort avec qui ?

f) Avec quoi écrivez-vous ? / Avec quoi est-ce que vous écrivez ? / Vous écrivez avec quoi ?

g) Pour qui fait-il ce travail ? / Pour qui est-ce qu'il fait ce travail ? / Il fait ce travail pour qui ?

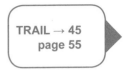
TRAIL → 45
page 55

◆ ◆ ◆

→ TRAIL 20 ANSWERS

E. THE ADJECTIVE

EXERCISE I. THE POSSESSIVE ADJECTIVE

a) Ma mère adore mon amie.

b) Tu vas voir ton oncle, ta tante et tes cousines.

c) Son enfant n'écoute jamais ses conseils.

d) Sa sœur veut mettre son pantalon.

e) Notre professeur a noté nos exercices.

f) Je n'aime ni leur chien ni leurs enfants !

EXERCISE II. THE DEMONSTRATIVE ADJECTIVE

a) Je vais acheter ce veston et ces chaussures-là.

b) Cet arbre-là n'a jamais de feuilles en hiver.

c) Cet élève-là est plus intelligent que ces élèves-ci.

d) Je viens de casser cette assiette.

e) Il m'a recommandé cet hôtel-là.

f) Cette histoire m'a fait rire.

EXERCISE III. THE INTERROGATIVE ADJECTIVE

a) Quelle ville ! Quels gosses !

b) Quelles femmes as-tu vues devant le cinéma ?

c) Quelle horreur !

d) Quels articles lisez-vous ?

e) Quelles erreurs !

f) Quel est pour vous un dimanche typique ?

EXERCISE IV. AGREEMENT IN GENERAL

1.

a) Il a donné des cadeaux à ses petites filles.

b) Cette jeune serveuse te connaît ?

c) « Je suis fatiguée », a dit ma mère.

d) Ce qu'elles sont bêtes !

e) Elle a acheté une robe vert clair.

f) Elle aime bien ces rubans roses.

2.

a) Hier nous avons acheté une auto neuve.

b) Les premières semaines des vacances étaient fantastiques.

c) Elle était inquiète.

d) Il m'a raconté des histoires affreuses.

e) Il est mort à la suite d'une cruelle maladie.

f) Une pareille intervention chirurgicale sera nécessaire.

3.

a) Sa grand-mère est très gentille.

b) Il a passé une nuit blanche.

c) Le trottoir est couvert de feuilles sèches.

d) Voilà la meilleure solution.

e) Il n'aime pas les femmes flatteuses.

f) C'était une tornade des plus destructrices.

4.

a) Il a payé une grosse somme d'argent.

b) Attention à la peinture fraîche.

c) Il travaille de longues heures le soir.

d) Il soufflait une brise douce.

e) Connaissez-vous cette vieille dame-là ?

f) Elle habite une très belle maison à la campagne.

5.

a) Ma sœur vient d'épouser un bel homme riche.

b) Il a fait ses résolutions du nouvel an.

c) Soudain un vieil homme s'est approché de moi.

d) M. Martin est fier de ses beaux enfants. (belles *if all his children are girls*)

e) J'aime bien regarder les vieux arbres au printemps.

f) Les nouveaux élèves seront là à neuf heures.

6.

a) Je viens de recevoir deux gros paquets.

b) Ils sont toujours heureux ces garçons-là.

c) Je l'ai remercié pour ses bons et loyaux services.

d) Il avait reçu des coups fatals.

e) Le gouvernement ne peut pas résoudre tous les problèmes nationaux.

f) J'aime passer les beaux jours d'été sur la plage.

7.

a) Dans la cour il y avait plusieurs étudiantes.

b) Tous les professeurs sont en grève.

c) Je veux voir toute la section à quatre heures.

d) Elles étaient toutes pénibles.

e) Elles seraient tout anxieuses.

f) Les jeunes filles sont toutes joyeuses.

TRAIL → 21
page 48

→ TRAIL 66 ANSWERS

EXERCISE V. POSITION OF ADJECTIVES

1.

a) Elle vient d'acheter une jupe verte.

b) Mon père adore les voitures allemandes.

c) C'est un méchant garçon !

d) On m'a dit que c'est une excellente école.

e) Je connais un bon restaurant près de la gare.

f) Y a-t-il de l'eau chaude ?

2.

a) Il a acheté un livre cher.

b) Ce pauvre homme vient de perdre sa sœur.

c) J'ai un mouchoir propre dans ma poche.

d) Il n'a pas reconnu son propre frère.

e) Nous voulons aider les pays pauvres du monde.

f) L'année dernière elle a déménagé. (L'an dernier ...)

EXERCISE VI. COMPARATIVES AND SUPERLATIVES

1.

a) Elle est moins intelligente que son frère. (Elle n'est pas si intelligente ...)

b) Voici une meilleure solution.

c) Les filles sont plus grandes que les garçons.

d) C'est le garçon le plus paresseux de la classe.

e) Les plus jeunes élèves peuvent partir de bonne heure. (Les élèves les plus jeunes ...)

f) C'est l'élève la plus petite de l'école. (la plus petite élève ...)

2.

a) Mes meilleurs amis sont plus riches que moi.

b) C'était la pire catastrophe.

c) Les professeurs sont aussi contents que les élèves.

d) Je connais les meilleurs restaurants.

e) C'était la journée la plus froide de l'année. (le jour le plus froid de l'an.)

f) Votre / Ton devoir est plus mauvais que le précédent.

TRAIL → 67
page 170

◆ ◆ ◆

→ TRAIL 72 ANSWERS

F. PREPOSITIONS

1.

a) Vous avez tort de faire ça.

b) Il a failli se noyer.

c) Elle a négligé d'apporter son parapluie.

d) Papa perd son temps à regarder les feuilletons.

e) Le médecin a ordonné à l'infirmière d'assister à la consultation.

f) Le directeur attend de vous voir.

g) Je me suis refusé à les défendre.

2.

a) Que comptez-vous faire ?

b) Mes parents avaient consenti à les recevoir.

c) J'ai prié les agents de police de téléphoner à mes parents.

d) Elle s'est apprêtée à partir.

e) Pourquoi a-t-il fallu revenir si tôt ?

f) Petit à petit j'ai amené mes copains à comprendre.

g) Je ne sais pas pourquoi elle s'obstine à mentir.

3.

a) Mon père s'était décidé à ne plus fumer.

b) Il aurait été ravi de sortir avec elle.

c) Ils finiront de regarder la télévision à minuit.

d) J'aurais préféré rester avec elle. / J'aurais mieux aimé rester avec elle.

e) Est-elle prête à nous suivre ?

f) Ils n'avaient pas réussi à trouver un bon poste.

g) Nous lui dirons de venir le voir.

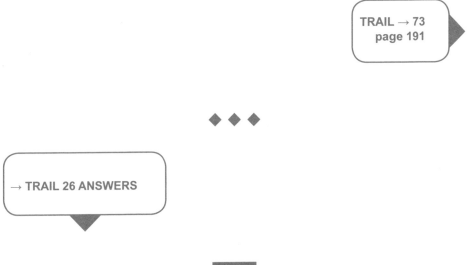

TRAIL → 73
page 191

◆ ◆ ◆

→ TRAIL 26 ANSWERS

G. THE ADVERB

1.

a) Ma sœur joue mieux que mon frère.

b) Il faut parler poliment aux voisins.

c) C'est elle qui écrit le mieux en français.

d) Heureusement je n'ai rien dit.

e) Nous n'avons vraiment pas envie d'y aller.

f) Le premier ministre avait constamment refusé de les voir.

2.

a) Elle dira toujours la vérité.

b) Nous les avions déjà vus.

c) Ils ont mal joué hier.

d) Parlons plus fort !

e) Elle s'est approchée lentement de la caisse. / Elle a marché lentement à (vers) la caisse.

f) Il parle couramment le russe.

g) Nous avons lu récemment son article. / Nous avons récemment lu son article.

TRAIL → 27
page 101

◆ ◆ ◆

→ TRAIL 64 ANSWERS

H. IL EST OR C'EST

1.

a) Quelle heure est-il ? – Il est trois heures et demie.

b) Que fait ton père ? – Il est ingénieur.

c) Je viens de visiter la Corse. – C'est magnifique.

d) Est-il possible de lire ce livre en deux heures ? – Oui, c'est possible.

e) Il est (C'est) difficile de supporter son avarice.

f) Qu'est-ce que c'est ? – Ce sont des stylos à bille. Ils sont verts.

g) Que fait votre oncle ? – C'est un journaliste réputé.

2.

a) C'est qui à la porte ? – Ce sont (C'est) eux.

b) À qui sont ces chapeaux ? – Ils sont à elles.

c) À qui est cette montre-là ? – C'est la sienne.

d) Vous aimez mon champagne ? – Il est magnifique.

e) Je n'aime pas la natation, c'est fatigant.

f) Vous aimez manger les champignons ? – Oui, c'est délicieux.

g) Qui est-ce ? – Ce sont mes neveux..

TRAIL → 65
page 135

◆ ◆ ◆

→ TRAIL 48 ANSWERS

I. INVERSION

a) Nous lui avons demandé, « Connaissent-ils cette dame ? »

b) « Connaissent-ils cette dame ? » lui avons-nous demandé.

c) « Tu resteras à la maison ! » a crié mon père.

d) Peut-être viendra-t-elle ce soir. / Elle viendra ce soir peut-être. / Peut-être qu'elle viendra ce soir.

e) À peine eut-il fermé la porte que le téléphone sonna.

f) En vain / Vainement avait-elle essayé de le convaincre.

g) Je voudrais savoir ce que font M. et Mme Dubois.

TRAIL → 49
page 165

◆ ◆ ◆

→ TRAIL 50 ANSWERS

J. DIRECT AND INDIRECT QUESTIONS

1.

a) Qu'est-ce que vous avez vu ?

b) Que leur avez-vous dit ?

c) Qu'est-ce qu'il en pense ?

d) De quoi a-t-elle peur ?

e) À quoi pensaient-ils ?

f) De quoi parlez-vous ?

g) Qu'est-ce qui vous est arrivé ?

2.

a) Je vais vous expliquer ce qui m'est arrivé.

b) Il ignore ce dont nous avons besoin.

c) Ce qui m'énerve, c'est son impatience.

d) Dites-moi ce que vous avez fait.

e) Elle se demande ce qui vous intéresse.

f) Impossible de comprendre ce que disent les hommes politiques.

g) Ce dont nous avons envie, c'est de visiter Strasbourg.

TRAIL → 51
page 50

◆ ◆ ◆

→ **TRAIL 30 ANSWERS**

K. DEPUIS, POUR, PENDANT

a) Hier soir j'ai fait un mots-croisés pendant deux heures.

b) Je fais ce mots-croisés depuis deux heures.

c) Elle étudie le japonais depuis longtemps.

d) La semaine prochaine nous serons à Paris pour deux jours.

e) L'année dernière nous avons loué un appartement pendant deux mois.

f) Ils habitaient depuis six semaines à Londres quand Pierre a perdu son poste.

g) Je serai là pour deux heures.

TRAIL → 31
page 186

→ **TRAIL 70 ANSWERS**

L. OÙ

a) D'où vient-il ? / D'où est-ce qu'il vient ?

b) Dis-moi où tu vas.

c) Là où elle habite il n'y a pas beaucoup de magasins.

d) Je ne connais pas la rue où se trouve sa maison.

e) Il pleuvait le soir où il est arrivé.

261

f) C'est la deuxième fois que j'ai dit non.

g) Où que nous allions, nous ne le voyons jamais.

TRAIL → 71
page 140

→ TRAIL 68 ANSWERS

M. PRICE, SPEED, MEASUREMENT

a) Elle a payé dix euros le kilo.

b) Choux-fleurs – deux euros la pièce.

c) Il roule d'habitude à cinquante kilomètres à l'heure.

d) Quelle est la longueur de ce champ ?

e) La cour faisait soixante mètres de long sur vingt mètres de large.

f) L'océan fait trois cents mètres de profondeur.

g) Le pneu fait quinze centimètres de large.

TRAIL → 69
page 168

→ TRAIL 38 ANSWERS

N. QUANTITIES

a) Mes amis n'avaient pas assez d'argent.

b) Combien de lettres a-t-elle écrites ?

c) La plupart des Norvégiens aiment la neige.

d) Nous avons toujours trop de travail !

e) Ils auront autant d'argent que lui.

f) Tant de passagers voyagent sans billet.

g) Monsieur, apportez-moi encore de l'eau, s'il vous plaît.

TRAIL → 39
page 114

→ TRAIL 56 ANSWERS

O. IMPERSONAL VERBS

1.

a) Soudain il y a eu (il y eut) un bruit.

b) Il n'y aura pas de vin.

c) Il doit y avoir un problème.

d) Il y avait eu un malentendu.

e) Y a-t-il des petits pois ? / Est-ce qu'il y a des petits pois ?

f) Il n'y aurait pas eu de difficulté.

g) Y avait-il des enfants dans la cour ? / Est-ce qu'il y avait des enfants dans la cour ?

2.

a) De quoi s'agit-il dans cet article ? / Cet article, de quoi s'agit-il ?

b) Il ne nous restait que vingt euros. / Il nous restait seulement ...

c) Nous reste-t-il de l'eau ? / Est-ce qu'il nous reste ... ?

d) Il se produisait souvent des accidents au coin de la rue.

e) Il (nous) a fallu rentrer tout de suite.

f) Il faut un sparadrap.

g) Il (nous) aurait fallu refuser.

TRAIL → 57
page 65

◆ ◆ ◆

→ TRAIL 42 ANSWERS

P. THE FACTITIVE VERB

1.

a) Mon professeur. Je lui ferai voir que j'ai raison.

b) Ma mère. Ma sœur la fera chanter avec elle.

c) Nos voisins. Mon père leur a fait fermer la télévision.

d) Mon copain. Nous le faisions souvent rester chez nous.

e) Les voleurs. On les a fait arrêter.

f) Ma grand-mère. Le médecin la faisait venir à la clinique tous les vendredis.

g) Ces hommes politiques. Je voudrais leur faire comprendre que nous payons déjà trop d'impôts.

2.

a) Nous les ferons partir demain.

b) Elle leur a fait écrire la lettre.

c) Fais-le parler ! / Faites-le parler !

d) Son professeur lui a fait étudier le texte entier (tout le texte).

e) Je vais faire faire un gâteau.

f) Tu me faisais souvent laver la voiture.

g) Elle s'est fait punir.

TRAIL → 43
page 119

◆ ◆ ◆

→ TRAIL 54 ANSWERS

Q. DEVOIR

a) Elle nous doit de l'argent.
b) Nous devons partir maintenant.
c) Mes parents ont dû sortir.
d) Nous devions souvent promener le chien.
e) Je devrais aller le voir.
f) Ils auraient dû écouter.
g) Elle aurait dû rester à la maison (chez elle).

TRAIL → 55
page 174

◆ ◆ ◆

→ TRAIL 60 ANSWERS

R. POUVOIR AND SAVOIR

a) Son père sait-il jouer aux échecs ?

b) Si papa dit oui nous pouvons sortir.

c) Soudain elle a pu comprendre son erreur (sa faute).

d) Si elle avait l'adresse elle pourrait aller le voir.

e) Quand il avait une voiture il pouvait aller au bord de la mer.

f) Elle entendait (pouvait entendre) la rivière dans le bois.

g) Il aurait pu nous écouter.

TRAIL → 61
page 71

→ **TRAIL 32 ANSWERS**

S. MANQUER

a) Ma sœur me manquait.

b) Je manque à mes amis.

c) Lui manque-t-elle ? / Est-ce qu'elle lui manque ?

d) Elle avait manqué son autobus.

e) Les agents de police ne manquaient jamais d'attraper les voleurs.

f) Vos parents manquent-ils de patience ? / Est-ce que vos parents manquent de patience ?

g) Elle ne manquera pas à son devoir.

TRAIL → 33
page 188

ANSWERS TO EXERCISES

◆ ◆ ◆

→ TRAIL 34 ANSWERS

T. TO BE – ÊTRE ?

a) Le fer était chaud.
b) Mes parents auront froid.
c) Il avait fait beau ce jour-là.
d) Ton grand-père va bien ?
e) Je croyais qu'il était toujours malade.
f) Elle a eu honte de sortir sans payer l'addition.
g) Ça lui aurait fait du bien de passer la nuit à la belle étoile.

TRAIL → 35
page 108

◆ ◆ ◆

→ TRAIL 74

Bravo !

You have reached the end of our Trail.

If you have worked carefully through all the exercises, you should have given yourself a firm grasp of the essentials of French grammar.

Listening to and repeating the example sentences will have given you a feel for the rhythm of the language and improved your accent.

We, the authors, hope you have enjoyed the journey and that you will continue to consult our book as your studies progress.

D.F.; B.S.

ENGLISH INDEX

INDEX FRANÇAIS